French Planning in Theory and Practice

Saul Estrin *and* Peter Holmes

London
GEORGE ALLEN & UNWIN
Boston   Sydney

George Allen & Unwin (Publishers) Ltd,
40 Museum Street, London WC1A 1LU, UK

George Allen & Unwin (Publishers) Ltd,
Park Lane, Hemel Hempstead, Herts HP2 4TE, UK

Allen & Unwin Inc.,
9 Winchester Terrace, Winchester, Mass 01890, USA

George Allen & Unwin Australia Pty Ltd,
8 Napier Street, North Sydney, NSW 2060, Australia

First published in 1983

British Library Cataloguing in Publication Data

Estrin, Saul
　French planning in theory and practice.
1. France—Economic policy—20th century
I. Title　　　II. Holmes, Peter.
330.944′081　　　HC276

ISBN 0-04-339028-5

Library of Congress Cataloging in Publication Data

Estrin, Saul.
　French planning in theory and practice.
Bibliography: p.
Includes index.
1. France—Economic policy—1945- . 2. Administra-
tive agencies—France—Planning. 3. Planning—France.
I. Holmes, Peter.　　　II. Title.
HC276.2.E8 1983　　　338.944　　　82-13853
ISBN 0-04-339028-5

Set in 10 on 11 point Times Roman by Preface Limited, Salisbury, Wilts.
and printed in Great Britain by Billing and Sons Ltd, London and Worcester

Contents

iii

List of Tables

List of Abbreviations

I. French

BIPE	Bureau d'Information et de Prévision Economiques
BNP	Banque Nationale de Paris
CEPII	Centre d'Etudes Prospectives et d'Informations Internationales
CEPREMAP	Centre d'Etudes Prospectives d'Economie Mathématique Appliquées à la Planification
CERC	Centre d'Etudes des Revenus et des Coûts
CFDT	Confédération Française Démocratique du Travail
CFTC	Confédération Française du Travail Chrétienne
CGP	Commissariat Général du Plan
CGT	Confédération Général du Travail
CIASI	Comité Interministeriel sur l'Aménagement des Structures Industrielles
CODER	Commission de Développement Economique Régionale
CORDES	Comité d'Organisation des Recherches Appliquées sur le Développement Economique et Social
CREDOC	Centre de Recherche et de Documentation sur la Consommation
DATAR	Délégation de l'Aménagement du Territoire et à l'Action Régionale
DF	Documentation Française
DMS	(Modèle) Dynamique Multi-Sectoriel
DP	Direction de la Prévision
ENA	Ecole Nationale d'Administration
FDES	Fonds de Développement Economique et Social
FIFI	(Modèle) Physico-Financier
FO	Force Ouvrière
GAMA	Groupe d'Analyses Macro-Economiques Appliquées
IDI	Institut de Développement Industriel
IFCE	Institut Français des Conjonctures Economiques
INSEE	Institut National de la Statistique et des Etudes Economiques
PAP	Programme d'Action Prioritaire
PAPIR	Programme d'Action Prioritaire à l'Initiative Régionale
PDG	Projections Détaillées Glissantes

PEON	(Commission) Consultative pour Production d'Electricité d'Origine Nucléaire
la PIB	La Production Intérieure Brute
le PIB	Le Produit Intérieur Brut
PRDE	Programmes Régionaux de Développement et d'Equipement
RATP	Régie Autonome des Transports Parisiens
RCB	Rationalization des Choix Budgétaires
SNCF	Société Nationale des Chemins de Fer

II. Other

BIS	Bank for International Settlements
DRI	Data Resources Incorporated
EEC	European Economic Community
FRB	Federal Reserve Bank
GDP	Gross Domestic Product
GFCF	Gross Fixed Capital Formation
GNP	Gross National Product
IMF	International Monetary Fund
IRC	Industrial Reconstruction Corporation
NIESR	National Institute of Economic and Social Research
OECD	Organization for Economic Cooperation and Development
OPEC	Organization of Petroleum Exporting Countries

Preface

The material for this book was gathered in the course of a series of visits to Paris between 1975 and 1981. We were inspired to write it by our dissatisfaction with most of the work in English about planning in a market economy, with respect to both theory and French practice. In our view, the models point to an unsatisfactory notion of indicative planning while the literature on the French experience, published largely in the 1960s, gives a misleading view of the planners' status and role. In fact, the French planning exercise lost virtually all practical relevance after 1965, and we wished to discover why this came about, and what it could tell us about the potential for planning. Our theoretical chapters suggest that the French planners were attempting an impossible task, given the complexities and uncertainties of the 1970s, but they also pinpoint a number of possible valuable functions. These are combined with the detailed lessons of the French experience in our applied chapters to define a role for planning in a market economy. Apart from the general conclusions, we have tried to use this information to evaluate the prospects for the kind of exercise to which the new Socialist régime in France is committed.

The bulk of our material about France was gathered from various documents, published and unpublished, and our interpretation was clarified by widespread informal discussions and interviews with French civil servants, politicians, and academics. We met with planners from the CGP, INSEE, the DP, and CEPII as well as officials from other parts of the administration. We were also fortunate in having discussions with members of the incoming Socialist government, including the Finance Minister and Planning Commissaire, as a result of the contacts of our colleague David Bell and at a conference at Sussex University in 1976 whose proceedings have been published in Holland (1978). In general, we found the people whom we saw extremely frank and cooperative, and although it would be impossible to name them all, we must express our thanks to a few in particular: C. Sautter, J. Vignon, P. Roux-Vaillard, D. Vallet, R. Guesnerie, C. Henry, R. Courbis, J. Delors, H. Prévot, R. Cessieux, M. Bidegain, and B. Brunhes. We offer our special thanks to David Bell for his help and for his stimulating company on some of our trips. If we still remain ignorant about the French Socialist Party, it must be because we have not had the opportunity to read his forthcoming book on the subject (Bell and Criddle, 1982).

We are also indebted to colleagues in the UK, especially Geoff

Heal who provided the impetus to start this work, and who also commented on Part One. We have had many helpful discussions at the Universities of Southampton, Sussex, British Columbia, and Cornell, and particular thanks for comments are due John Aldrich, Lesley Cook, John Helliwell, Anne Stevens, and participants in Sussex European Research Centre's Project on Industrial Adjustment. Financial support has come from Southampton and Sussex Universities throughout, and the SSRC provided funds for one of the visits to Paris and for the invaluable research assistance Charlotte Keenan provided for Chapter 3. We also wish to thank Helen Berry for comments from the reader's viewpoint, and Nick Brealey of George Allen and Unwin who has been a stimulating taskmaster. Last, but by no means least, we thank the secretaries in England and America who have typed and re-typed an illegible script – Yvette Stone, Sheila Wahnsiedler, Audrey Holmes, Linda Majeroni, and Diana Horgan. Their valiant efforts, good humour, and patience were beyond anything we could have reasonably expected.

Despite this long list of mentors, the authors are solely responsible for the content of this book and any remaining errors. We have both worked on virtually the entire text, and the complications arising from sharing the relevant responsibilities and reaching consensus on various issues have brought home to us the awesome efforts involved in even the most modest co-ordination and planning operation.

Saul Estrin
Peter Holmes

Introduction

Economic planning embraces all activities which co-ordinate economic decision in a way that would not occur spontaneously. In a market system, co-ordination is decentralized and choices are left to independent decision makers; on the other hand, an agency directs the economy to its chosen outcome under central planning. This book is concerned with indicative planning, or planning in a market economy. It explores the scope for an agency to co-ordinate and disseminate economic information without attempting to direct private choices, considered from the perspective of economic theory and in the light of the French planning experience.

The election of the French Socialist Party to power in the spring of 1980 offers another way of expounding our theme. The new administration was committed to some form of economic planning, but severely criticized the practice of past governments. It claimed that French planning, which had been so highly regarded at home and abroad in the 1950s and 1960s, had faded almost out of existence in recent years. One of our tasks will be to establish this point (which contradicts the conventional wisdom on the subject) in detail. Moreover, although this book was substantially conceived before the election, it is addressed to the same problem that faces the new French government: in the light of theory and French experience, how can one successfully translate a predisposition in favour of planning into practice. One needs a conceptual rationale for the exercise in which the provision of information improves resource allocation. One must also know in detail what went wrong in France and why, to draw the lessons for actual planning in Western economies. In particular, one must judge whether French planning declined because of insuperable 'objective circumstances', or whether the problems were in principle capable of solution. Our theoretical work points out weaknesses in the existing models, which suggest how the traditional planning process could have been rendered inoperable by increasing complexity, openness, and uncertainty in the French economy after the late 1960s. It also indicates that there remains considerable scope for a less ambitious process, and the French planners seem to have been thinking on similar lines in recent years, developing interesting new techniques and methods. However, they have been prevented from adapting to the changing circumstances by institutional and political factors. Hence, we pay considerable attention to political, as well as economic, developments in the second part of the book.

Our study vindicates at a conceptual and practical level a particular form of indicative planning, rather more limited in scope than generally advocated but potentially significant in an uncertain world. It warns against the dangers of an excessively ambitious planning exercise whose costly detailed coverage may disguise practical irrelevance. It also stresses the obstacles to successful planning, including the desire for policy-making flexibility, the irrelevance of consultation or advice to pre-committed governments, the use of technocratic forecasts for political purposes, and administrative rivalries. Thus, we delineate the useful scope of indicative planning and the factors that will influence its practicability. This provides criteria from which we can judge the likely outcome of the French Socialists' experimentation.

Part One of the book considers indicative planning from the perspective of economic theory. The first chapter surveys the existing models and approaches, in particular the ideas of Meade (1970). The various models, and the case for planning implicit in each, differ primarily in their characterization of the economy itself: micro-economic, aggregate, disequilibrium, and expectational. In all cases, the planners provide information about an uncertain future not thrown up spontaneously by the relevant market mechanism. A general flaw in these cases for planning, related to their limitations in an informationally imperfect world, leads one to suspect the practical prospects for such plans and, insofar as the models formalize the French planners' activities, indicates the source of the problems which began to emerge in the late 1960s. We respond to these difficulties in the second chapter, which attempts to construct a case for planning based on imperfect information. The essence of the planning exercise rests in an attempt to provide co-ordination that would otherwise be prevented by informational blockages, with consultation and communication being supplemented wherever it is weakest. We have deliberately tried to deal with the complex analytic issues in an informal and non-technical way, so the numerous implications of the theoretical literature can be made accessible to readers primarily interested in France. However, non-economists wary of such material are directed to the summary of our ideas at the beginning of Chapter 2.

Part Two of the book is concerned with French planning. Two popular misconceptions must be dispelled at the outset: that French planning was important or significant in recent years, and that the French government policies were relatively well co-ordinated, whether by the planners or another administrative agency. Through the five substantive chapters we also trace the causes of the decline, and outline the considerable technical and consultative innovation by the planners during the era of operational insignificance. These ideas are interesting in their own right, and as an indication of the agency's own response to changing circumstances. The main themes are surveyed in more detail at the beginning of Part Two.

The third chapter provides the most important historical and quantitative material about French planning since its inception, and is intended to act as a point of reference for the rest of the study. It also evaluates the planners' forecasting record, noting that declining prestige was paralleled by worsening performance. Chapter 4 is central in every respect, giving an overview of the economic, institutional, and political context of French planning and introducing the following chapters which detail events in the three main spheres of planning activity: macro-economic, public sector, and industrial policies. In each area, the sad story of decline is told and explained, the planners' ideas on what could usefully be done are outlined, and the prospects for the Socialist government's proposals considered. Chapter 8 presents the overall conclusions from the study.

Part One

Planning Theory

1 Models of Indicative Planning

The Case for Indicative Planning

Indicative planning is based on the notion that, in an uncertain world, the allocation of resources can be improved by providing individuals and firms with information about everyone else's behaviour. Although it seems plausible to suppose that economic decisions will be, in some sense, improved for having been based on more information rather than less, and that this could be provided by a state-run mechanism to pool individual knowledge, the remainder of the chapter shows that this is a difficult general point to establish theoretically. We shall first outline intuitively the notion of indicative planning and consider the issues that the early contributors to the subject considered important. The two main approaches to the topic, based on a general equilibrium model (see Meade, 1970) and aggregate growth theory (see Harrod, 1973), are critically outlined in the following two sections. Certain weaknesses in these ideas led to our proposals for a more realistic theoretical and actual form of planning in Chapter 2, and help to explain what may have gone wrong in France in recent years. The chapter concludes with a brief discussion of potential developments in the literature – disequilibrium models and rational expectations. All these models are concerned with the provision of information in a market system, and differ primarily in their characterization of the economy itself. Indicative planning is meant to offer information that is not provided automatically in the market place, and one of our concerns throughout this chapter will be whether the factors preventing markets from operating in this way also pose obstacles to the function being carried out by an alternative institution.

The idea of indicative planning is hardly new, having been mentioned by Meade as early as 1936,[1] and widely discussed by economists since the French began planning in 1946. The earliest reference to the idea that we can find is from Keynes's 'The End of Laissez-Faire', published in *Essays in Persuasion*. This is worth quoting at length since it highlights several of the ideas in the following chapters (Keynes, 1931):

> Many of the greatest economic evils of our time are the fruits of risk, uncertainty and ignorance. It is because particular indi-

7

viduals, fortunate in situations or abilities, are able to take advantage of uncertainty and ignorance, and also because for the same reason big business is often a lottery, that great inequalities of wealth came about; and these same factors are also the cause of the unemployment of labour, or the disappointment of reasonable business expectations, and of the impairment of efficiency and production. Yet the cure lies outside the operation of the individuals; it may even be to the interest of individuals to aggravate the disease. I believe that the cure for these things is partly to be sought in the deliberate control of the currency and of credit by a central institution, and partly in the collection and dissemination on a great scale of data relating to the business situation, including the full publicity, by law if necessary, of all business facts which it is useful to know. These measures would involve society in exercising directive intelligence through some appropriate organ of action over many of the intricacies of private business, yet it would leave private initiative and enterprise unhindered. Even if these measures prove insufficient, nevertheless they will furnish us with better knowledge than we have now for taking the next step. (p. 317)

Of course, Keynes's agency to provide business with information is what we would now term an indicative planning board. The allocative improvement derives from a reduction in the waste which arises, ex post, if private decisions concerning the future fail to mesh with each other. There may also be a greater willingness to invest in productive assets if the perceived risk, and therefore the real cost of investment, is reduced. However, there can be no guarantee that the provision of information would improve the actual allocation of resources on every occasion because the forecasts may be incorrect and agents remain free to use the information in any way that they choose.

Massé (1962, 1965) provides the first sketch of a theory of indicative planning, in part as a rationale for the activities undertaken by the French in the late 1950s and early 1960s. He argues that people might make incorrect investment decisions because market prices are not currently quoted for goods and services to be supplied in the future. Therefore the state should engage in 'generalised market research' to bring about a common view of the future, whose consistent and coherent character should lead to its spontaneous adoption by all firms. The authorities should be ready to use their full range of policy instruments to ensure the attainment of this coherence, however, lest it not come about naturally. Since the plan figures have exhortative and informational as well as coercive elements, he denies that the French plans should be assessed on their forecasting accuracy. Massé's ideas have been severely criticized by Lutz (1969) and Richardson (1971). Lutz points out that diversity of entrepreneurial views is vital to the operation of a competitive market, the essence of which involves the rewarding of those with the best foresight. Moreover, a common view of the future risks putting all one's eggs in one basket, whereas variance of expectations provides a certain balance to the national portfolio of investments. Both Lutz and Richardson argue that Massé's formulation gives rise to insuperable problems in determining enterprise market shares, even if the industrial totals have been forecast correctly.

The arguments relating to the danger of a single potentially incorrect view of the future stand independently from the Austrian view of the market process. The former has been directly treated by James Meade (1970, 1971); we return to the latter in the next chapter. However, before proceeding to Meade's work, it is worth noting that Johansen (1978) provides the most general formal description of an indicative planning procedure, in which the authorities' forecasts are used as policy instruments to influence the future path of the economy by replacing private expectations. His formulation outlines the conditions for the existence of a unique solution to the choice of accurate plan forecasts.

The General Equilibrium Approach

Meade (1970) offers the first model of indicative planning to be explicitly based on a theoretical description of a market economy – the Arrow–Debreu model.[2] He establishes that an indicative plan is formally equivalent to the list of equilibrium prices that would emerge from the operation of a full system of forward conditional markets. He notes that market economies do not generally have such a system, so private decisions cannot be presumed to mesh efficiently over time. Hence, indicative planning actually offers an opportunity for allocative improvements. After outlining his arguments in some detail for later reference, we examine the consequences of relaxing the strong assumption of zero trans-actions costs in information, which is shown to undermine the apparently clear-cut case for procedure. Since positive transactions costs are an important reason for the absence of future markets, this raises the possibility that Meade's planners will not always be able to improve the allocation of resources.

The Model

Meade begins by analysing the role of the market mechanism as described in the Arrow–Debreu model, which is, for the most part, a general equilibrium formalization of text book supply and demand theory. Individuals and firms maximize utility and profits subject to given budget or technology constraints, with the system being solved for an equilibrium price vector which clears all markets simultaneously. All necessary markets exist and are perfectly competitive and there are no entrepreneurs although individuals own shares in firms. The world is of finite duration, with everyone assumed to make all the buying and selling contracts they will ever want at some initial date and never wanting to change them; they merely go through time activating pre-existing contracts.

The simplest version of the model assumes certainty. Individuals will not know the supplies and demands of anyone else until the market comes into play, but this 'market' uncertainty is strictly endogenous to the system. Once everyone meets in the market place and reveals his intentions to the anonymous 'auctioneer', the full set of contracts is made to be carried out over time. No one holds any money because what each has arranged to sell or borrow in every period·exactly finances what each has committed himself to buy or lend. Adding a time dimension to the market mechanism in this way preserves all the Pareto efficiency properties provided there is a 'complete set of markets', but mutually beneficial trades may be frustrated if any such market is absent.

This approach to time can be extended to allow for the fact that there is always exogenous uncertainty about the external environment as well. Meade exemplifies this in terms of the weather, but technical progress or the actions of foreigners are equally 'environmental'. It would be considered irrational to make firm contracts in advance if the 'weather' is unpredictable, but the model deals with the problem by adding a further dimension to the market mechanism – a full set of 'forward conditional markets'. These permit the formation of *conditional* contracts which stipulate in advance the commodity to be traded and the date of exchange for each possible environmental outcome, or 'state of the world'. All private decisions are still made in advance and there is no breaking of contracts, but agents do not know which conditional contract they will have to honour until the event. Even so, there is no need to hold reserves of cash because the conditional contracts ensure that commitments exactly match resources in every eventuality.

The model requires everyone to know what they would do in each and every possible situation, but not which of the environmental outcomes will actually occur. Such an arrangement removes all the 'market' risk, but leaves individuals exposed in the sense that the state of the world as it actually exists can make them better or worse off. Firms do not bear risk at all since they contract in advance to sell whatever they can produce and, in fact, zero pure profits are always received. However, the individual owners of factors of production, such as labour, land, or specialized machinery, run the risk of variations in the marginal product of what they process, and hence of their incomes. The risk about what environmental path will actually occur can be reduced by the inclusion within the set of conditional markets of a full set of insurance markets. Social risk cannot be eliminated in this way, but it can be pooled or shifted to non-risk-averse people. An insurance system can ensure average losses for everyone in the case of small random events whose overall incidence is predictable but whose specific location is not. On the other hand, those willing to gamble can undertake to compensate others less willing, in the event of a general misfortune, in exchange for the right to reap the full benefits of general good luck. People wishing to reduce risk in this way would have to take out a separate insurance policy for every economically distinct eventuality that might befall them. Arrow has written widely on why such conditional forward markets, and in particular insurance markets, might not function fully or effectively (Arrow, 1970). The main problem is 'moral hazard', the incentive that exists to avoid preventing an insured-against outcome once one has become indemnified against it; to claim that such an outcome has actually occurred when it has not; or to understate the true risks when taking out a contract with an insurer who cannot check up on each client individually. For these and other reasons, Meade considers the implications of the non-existence or malfunctioning of these markets, and whether an indicative plan could carry out their functions.

Meade shows that indicative planning could be a perfect substitute for a full set of forward conditional markets. Perhaps because there is no 'auctioneer' to reveal the full equilibrium price vector, he hypothesizes a world similar to the one above except that no one has yet signed any contracts. Consider first the case with no environmental uncertainty. Meade would gather everyone together 'in the Albert Hall' to announce how much they would be willing to buy or sell at various prices in each period in the future. The planners play the role of auctioneer, announcing prices to see if supplies everywhere equalled demands over time and, if not, changing them by the Walrasian method until they did. A set of prices would emerge such that, if they did rule, all markets at every date would clear. Meade's central point is that the mere announcement of these prices would eliminate the need to sign any contracts in advance. If people know what the equilibrium price will be, they will refuse to buy above it or sell below it in a competitive world. A full set of such price predictions would constitute a complete indicative plan, and would produce a resource allocation with all the properties of a market equilibrium, including efficiency. Everyone would voluntarily choose to comply with the plan because, on the basis of the information provided, people would realize that they could thereby achieve a superior outcome.

The existence of environmental uncertainty merely adds another dimension to the exercise, which must cover each and every environmental path. The planners cannot know which path will be taken, but once the full set of conditional prices has been determined, buyers and sellers will always choose to trade at the ones appropriate to the outcome that has materialized. The planning process would also facilitate the provision of insurance markets if we view them as just being one service like any other, which can be profitably provided once the number of takers is known. The plan will not reduce anyone's risk-aversion, so risk-shifting will not be brought about if no one is willing to gamble, but by removing market uncertainty it may induce moderately risk-inclined people to take on insurance gambles.

Meade's plan incorporates all responses to price information so that if it rained the price of umbrellas would reflect that this meant umbrella production would be more profitable and more firms would move in. Using his example, the value of non-adaptable umbrella-making machinery on Thursday depends on whether it will rain on Friday, which is not known with certainty, so the price will reflect the balance of opinion within the community. Meade assumes that we will have reached a *given* state of public opinion by Thursday; there is already a price system for every state of the world. This is illustrated in Figure 1.1, in which the environment can only take two values, rain or not rain (R or NR). By Thursday, we can have arrived at R or NR by any one of eight paths. It is assumed that knowledge of R vs NR, and how we got there, is sufficient to uniquely determine the demand for all goods and services on Thursday, even though we can have only narrowed Friday's outcome down to a choice of two of the sixteen possible paths leading thence from Monday. If the sequence of NRs and Rs, which need not be serially independent, is not sufficient to determine all supplies and demands at that point, we would have to distinguish more paths at each node, as in Figure 1.2. Meade assumes that each agent can work out fully on Monday what his expectations would be about Friday on Thursday, once it becomes known which intermediate point he is at in Figure 1.1. Once we actually reached Thursday and in fact landed at point 3, say, expectations would have to be what people thought they were going to be. Prices would be different, and the plan would not work, if a given set of past external events and realized outcomes

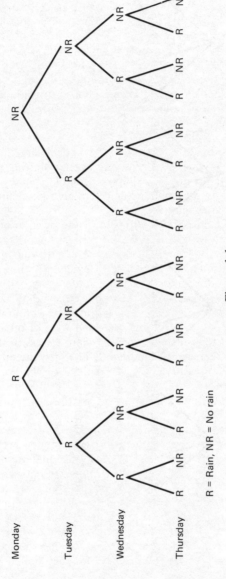

Monday

Tuesday

Wednesday

Thursday

R = Rain, NR = No rain

Figure 1.1

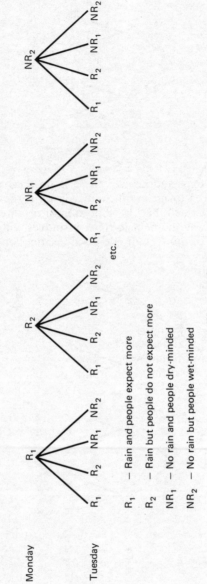

Monday

Tuesday

R_1 R_1 R_2 NR_1 NR_2

R_2 R_1 R_2 NR_1 NR_2

NR_1 R_1 R_2 NR_1 NR_2

NR_2 R_1 R_2 NR_1 NR_2

etc.

R_1 — Rain and people expect more

R_2 — Rain but people do not expect more

NR_1 — No rain and people dry-minded

NR_2 — No rain but people wet-minded

Figure 1.2

could lead people to non-unique expectations and hence actions. The sort of utility maximization assumed for the Arrow–Debreu model explicitly assumes that everyone can calculate in advance what they would do or think in any set of circumstances. They would not wish to revise anything if those exact circumstances actually prevailed. The logic of the model requires anything that causes expectations or actions to be different to be recognized as a separate case. We shall go on to argue in Chapter 2 that this is one of the main weaknesses of the Meade/Arrow–Debreu approach.

To summarize, Meade hypothesizes that actual economies have no adequate mechanism to transmit information between agents about future demand and supply conditions in different circumstances. In the absence of market prices, individuals must base their decisions on expectations and there is no reason for these decentralized choices to mesh efficiently. Even if the full set of current markets exists, so that the allocation of resources appears Pareto efficient at any moment in time, resources will be wasted over time because of the lack of adequate information. To quote Meade (1970): 'forward markets and indicative planning are in fact information systems which reduce uncertainty by passing to producers the knowledge which consumers have about future demand conditions, and passing to consumers the knowledge which producers have about future supply conditions' (p. 3). However, although either mechanism can make it easier to deal with environmental uncertainty by transmitting information about what agents would do in different circumstances, no one can transmit certain knowledge about future environmental uncertainties.

Some Criticisms

Meade's approach will be criticized in Chapter 2 for neglecting people's computational limitations, particularly when there is environmental uncertainty, but first we consider a basic logical problem of the model.[3] There is actually no reason for the absence of future conditional markets in the world initially specified by Meade, so that this must be assumed. His argument for the automatic implementation of indicative plans, as well as for their improving resource allocation through time, rests on the idea that the information provided would be privately beneficial, increasing profits or satisfaction. But this suggests the prospect of unexploited profits for private individuals who set up the procedure. Since this does not occur, whatever prevents the existence of future conditional markets must necessarily inhibit the effective functioning of an indicative plan.

The usual argument is that future conditional contracts are not widespread in actual economies because there are significant transactions costs associated with the gathering, co-ordination, and provision of such information, as well as the problem of 'moral hazard'. Following Coase (1960), many writers have argued that such markets do not exist because the costs of organizing them exceed the benefits, and the same would apply to alternative institutional arrangements. Taking Meade's assumptions, it would only be socially beneficial to introduce indicative planning if the benefits exceeded the costs, in which case a set of forward conditional markets would already be operating. His justification for the procedure relies on the assumption that indicative planning could function under conditions when a full market system could not, which is not convincing as it stands. In the following chapter we try to go further by showing that indicative planning can capture economies of scale in informational transactions costs in such a way that it could substitute for the absent markets at relatively lower cost than private initiatives. Yet even this leaves the prospect that private firms could profitably supply plans monopolistically, so state provision must be justified by locating public good properties for the procedure. The point to note at this stage is that Meade only justifies indicative planning by assumption.

Moreover, Meade's plans lose much of their effectiveness in a world with positive transaction costs. As he notes at length, transaction costs mean that the plans must be restricted in the number of agents, commodities, time periods, and environmental paths covered. The socially efficient degree of planning in these circumstances is determined by the rule that the marginal benefit of making the plan more detailed in some dimension must equal the marginal cost of acquiring the additional information. This leads us to refine Meade's concept of 'market' and 'environmental' uncertainty. 'Endogenous uncertainty' can be used to describe ignorance about events for which the private benefits of obtaining certain information concerning the outcome outweighs the costs. 'Exogenous uncertainty' will describe ignorance concerning events about which the costs of gathering and processing the information exceeds the benefits, so that agents would never choose to obtain information that could eliminate this uncertainty. Socially efficient indicative planning could eliminate endogenous uncertainty, which will not, however, necessarily be the same as Meade's market uncertainty if transaction costs are positive. But it could only reduce exogenous uncertainty by making everyone's knowledge equal to that of the least badly informed via pooling. The distinction between exogenous and endogenous uncertainty is therefore economic.

This leads to problems for Meade's planning exercise, in part because much of 'market' uncertainty is in an important sense exogenous. The original formulation invited all the firms in the economy to the 'Albert Hall', and of course a country that trades should also invite every foreign supplier and customer as well. Transactions costs would lead to the exclusion of numerous, individually insignificant or distant, firms whose behaviour can be predicted more cheaply by econometric means. This opens up the possibility of providing incorrect information if the econometricians do not have the right equations. More serious problems will emerge if cost considerations lead to a restriction in the number of commodity groups and scenarios examined. Socially efficient planning would not supply information to everyone, only directly influence agents in the relevant sectors, although it might have an impact on firms whose markets were correlated with those predicted. If costs lead the planners to consider only one (or a few) variant(s), the effectiveness of the procedure will depend on how the true environmental path is related to the chosen variant, and the extent to which enterprise expectations are influenced by the forecasts. Meade's conclusion about the allocative impact of planning will only hold if the planners have predicted the future state of the world correctly; agents' prior expectations were incorrect; and individual decisions were influenced by the plan forecasts. Otherwise, the restricted indicative planning exercise, contrary to what Meade implies, will not improve the allocation of resources. Take the example of a single variant plan. This could actually cause a Pareto-inferior outcome to the market if the forecasts led agents to alter their prior expectations incorrectly. The plan would not influence the allocation of resources at all if people chose to ignore the forecasts, whether or not the environmental path had been guessed correctly. This is to be expected because a single variant plan, or even one with a small number of variants, does not offer the comprehensive insurance implied by a future conditional contract, merely one or a few contingent outcomes for circumstances that the planners consider 'most likely'. Firms whose own decision-making is also limited by transactions costs will not use the information if they regard the planners' environmental path as unlikely.

These are similar problems to the ones raised by Lutz against Massé's 'common view of the future'. Meade's unrestricted model is immune to such criticisms because he distinguishes as many plan variants as environmental paths, so the procedure can only serve to increase information and improve resource allocation. But his conclusion does not carry over to a situation where transactions costs are significant or a high proportion of uncertainty is exogen-

ous. In general, for a given level of transactions costs, the more the
sources of unpredictability in the economy are exogenous, the less
useful Meade's exercise will be. We risk what Lutz feared – a con-
vergence of views on the wrong outcome rather than the right one,
hence worsening resource allocation. For example, surveying
everyone's private plans might show a majority believing that the
price of oil will remain at its current real level indefinitely, converting those who expected a rise or fall to this view and preventing a full 'portfolio' of investments from being made. Such an
outcome is not inevitable, but it is possible if only a few variants
can be considered, and it should be noted that the most elaborate
multivariant exercise in France only allowed three parameters to
take on three different values in three different states of the world
(see Chapter 5). However, we believe in practice that it is more
likely for the plan to be ignored than have perverse effects; a
socially efficient plan will be too narrow in scope, have insufficient
detail, and will be unable to convince people to trust its central
scenario.

This is probably what has happened in France in recent years.
The French economy was relatively simple when indicative
planning was introduced in 1946, so the planners could expect to
have a large impact on the system as a whole by focusing attention
on easily identifiable 'important' sectors. Moreover, the environmental path of the economy was relatively stable and predictable
between 1952 and 1973, at least compared with the route it has
taken more recently, and the planners appear to have forecast
reasonably accurately (see Chapter 3). As a consequence, the
procedure had a real impact on the economy – directly on agents
in the 'important' sectors and indirectly on the entire system –
which went hand in hand with the increasing faith that agents
placed in the forecasts. The 1950s and early 1960s were the
periods of highest prestige for the French planners, which we
associate with the way in which their influence on expectations
affected private profitability. The number of potential environmental paths had vastly multiplied by the end of the 1960s, with a
growth in foreign trade, the state and service sectors, and the
general sophistication of the economy. Moreover, the system was
sufficiently complex to lack obvious 'important' or leading sectors.
Chapter 3 suggests that planners judged the environmental paths
and 'important' sectors incorrectly in all plans after 1965, which
meant that there were serious errors in their predictions. The high
prestige which the plans had gradually built up could have led
people to incorrectly shift their expectations if they had believed
the planners, and thereby suffer losses relative to what would have
occurred in the absence of planning. But the actual long-term

effect was that agents completely lost faith in the plan forecasts. Hence, paradoxically, the institution designed to 'reduce uncertainty' lost its impact in a period of rising uncertainty.

Demand Expectations Models

A second strand of the literature views indicative planning as primarily a macro-economic policy tool acting to raise and stabilize the aggregate rate of growth by influencing businessmen's expectations of future demand (see Beckerman, 1965; Harrod, 1973; Collins and Turner, 1977). The model is Keynesian, with the growth rate determined by investment which depends on business expectations. In the absence of planning, these must be based on guesswork and intuition. The procedure provides quantitative forecasts about future demand conditions which firms take as proxies for their own prospects. Decisions based on the aggregate forecasts will prove to be justified in practice because the projections are constructed to be internally consistent. This characterization adopts the exhortative effect noted in the French literature (e.g. Shonfield, 1965; Carré *et al.*, 1975), with the planners augmenting expectations through their optimistic forecasts to the limit set by supply potential.[4] Planning can both ensure that the economy develops at its rate of supply potential and influence the underlying rate by reducing subjective risk, and therefore raising perceived profitability, investment, and the rate of technical advance. This type of procedure will henceforth be described as aggregate indicative planning, to distinguish it from Meade's process.

The demand expectations approach has not been based on an explicit growth model, but has made reference to Keynesian one-sector growth notions. We hope to clarify the impact of such plans by basing our description on the Harrod growth model (Harrod, 1939; see also Hahn and Matthews, 1964; Sen, 1970; Jones, 1975), and we also consider Harrod's own contribution to the subject (Harrod, 1973). Harrod (1939) distinguishes between the actual rate of growth, which depends solely on investment, and the maximum feasible growth of supply potential, termed the natural rate of growth. In his fixed coefficient economy, investment depends on private expectations which are exogenous to the system. The rate of growth resulting from a level of investment that would ensure that private expectations are justified by the outcome is called the warranted rate. From this simple and highly restrictive framework, Harrod deduces two fundamental problems for economic growth. There is no mechanism to ensure that the economy actually grows at its maximum feasible rate, even if, by some chance, private expectations were always justified ex post. Moreover, the actual rate of growth will be dynamically unstable in that private expectations will be adjusted further away from the warranted rate; there is no mechanism to ensure that the privately expected and warranted rates of growth are equalized.

The publication of aggregate indicative plan forecasts in this context should lead businessmen to substitute planners' expectations about future demand for their own. If the planners get their sums right, this would reduce the instability of growth by ensuring equality between the expected and warranted rates, and increase the actual growth rate by lowering risks and thereby raising the return to savers while reducing the required returns for investors. The plan could also be a framework for policies to influence the warranted and natural rates of growth if these were unequal; if the government can raise the rate of productivity growth or foresee an exogenous increase, 'expectational planning' can ensure that demand keeps pace. One should distinguish between the expectational impact of planning, which can be expected to primarily stabilize growth and will only increase it through influencing the aggregate savings and investment ratios, and the eventual effects of policies designed to influence the growth of supply potential.

Harrod himself essentially views indicative planning as a tool to balance actual growth and supply potential, though he notes that lowering risks could raise the pace of development. He envisages the plan forecasts as a supplement to, or even a substitute for, monetary and fiscal policies; potentially 'a weapon of superior sophistication to demand management policies' because they might avoid inflationary pressures (Harrod, 1973, p. 121). His characterization of the procedure also proposes some disaggregation of the forecasts. The planners would construct a balanced aggregate growth target for the next five years and disseminate the associated, and possibly varying, sectoral projections to industry representatives. The industry chiefs would comment on the feasibility of the proposals, upon which basis the planners would undertake further iterations until an agreed maximum rate emerges. Entrepreneurs would be expected to act on the forecasts because they would have been involved in their construction, and because they are internally consistent, and the projections would be relatively more optimistic than businessmen would have expected in the absence of planning. The expectations-augmenting impact would be increased by relatively high long-term forecasts of public sector demand. This description, which has distinct echoes of Massé's work, is probably closer to what the French actually did than Meade's, although the provision of information to influence private expectations about the future is central to all three authors. Harrod was sufficiently enamoured with indicative planning to declare: 'This idea has had a vogue for some time, but recently less has been heard about it. In my judgement, this has gone along with a decline in the quality of economic thinking in recent years' (Harrod, 1973, p. 119).

Beckerman (1965) has put forward a better known, if less convincing, model of aggregate indicative planning. He assumes economies of scale in production, making the pace of technical progress dependent on the rate of growth of output so the growth of supply potential becomes endogenous. He also sees the planners as producing optimistic and self-implementing forecasts of future demand to increase investment, but in this context the augmentation of expectations leads to a balanced increase in both supply potential and the actual rate of growth because of the economies of scale. Compared with Harrod's model, the weaknesses are that the informational and real impacts of the procedure are not distinguished, and it is a pure 'bootstrap' theory; the expectations-augmenting impact of the plan is never restricted by the growth of supply potential. Thus, according to Beckerman the economy will grow at the fastest balanced pace that people can be induced to believe.

More generally, there are a number of problems with the entire demand expectations approach which, as in the Meade model, help us to see what went wrong with indicative planning in practice. For the reasons outlined above, a single variant aggregate indicative plan would only have positive effects and be credible if there were no environmental uncertainty. As soon as one admits the possibility of uncertainty about events that are independent of agents' decisions, aggregate indicative planning could be considered to induce a misallocation of resources, for example, through the over-prediction of productivity growth, and the impact of the procedure would depend on the trust that business is willing to place on its projections. Practical experience in Britain and France suggests that firms do not, in general, believe growth forecasts which are either over-optimistic or over-pessimistic. As a consequence, the biggest weakness of aggregate indicative planning in practice has been its ineffectiveness, rather than its ability to distort the allocation of resources.

There are two additional problems with the demand expectations approach – the absence of any micro-economic basis and the inability to handle international trade and the balance of payments. Since aggregate plans contain no (or very little) micro-economic information, there is no mechanism to ensure that the supply for individual commodities will match the demand, even if the aggregates are balanced in value terms. This will lead to the type of problem which Meade-type planning was designed to solve – a waste of resources over time. The prices of goods which are in short supply during the planning period will have to rise while sectors with excess capacity, ex post, might find that market prices fall below average costs. Even though the plans appear to be self-justifying in an aggregate sense, expectations would be unrealized in particular sectors, leading to excessive profits for certain producers and losses for others. The fact that, in some sense, expectations in the aggregate will be realized cannot be generalized to the expectations of particular producers about their specific markets.

In a closed economy, the mismatch of resources at the micro-economic level could lead to structural unemployment, and possibly also inflation. The problems become more complex in an open economy, since an accurate forecast of domestic variables no longer necessarily implies that the proportions of the economy as a whole will be in balance. Moreover, the imbalance between demand and supply at the micro-economic level and differences between ruling domestic and world prices could lead to the purchase of certain goods abroad, so that the structural problems will be manifested in a balance of payments disequilibrium. This is another aspect of the argument that, if world markets are exogenous to the domestic economy, aggregate indicative planning may have no impact or worsen the allocation of resources when there is environmental uncertainty.

There is a further problem with this literature, which is related to the theoretical work on the dynamics of multi-sectoral growth (see Hahn, 1966; Shell and Stiglitz, 1967; Sen, 1970). Suppose an aggregate plan correctly predicts a substantial growth of consumer demand over a period, but incorrectly forecasts the patterns of demand. There may be an initial period when demand equals supply in every market while firms are investing, leading agents to believe that the economy is in full equilibrium. This could possibly accelerate further development along the same lines, a process which can be likened to the 'tulip-bulb' phenomenon (see Hahn, 1966). However, substantial disequilibria may arise unexpectedly after the consumer goods factories come on stream. Surplus items can always be exported in a fully open economy with flexible prices, but not necessarily at prices that cover full costs. Thus, even a multi-sectoral indicative plan must be careful not to lead the economy down a blind alley.

Aggregate indicative planning was a very popular policy proposal in the 1960s, and the demand expectations literature provided the main justification for the British experiment with planning in 1965 (for further details, see Beckerman, 1972; Blackaby, 1978). Experience with such plans has been unsatisfactory for reasons which are evident in the shortcomings of the theory. Although aggregate indicative plans could generate macro-economic expectations to balance demand and supply in total for a closed economy, the absence of micro-economic information meant that they could neither ensure balance in the various goods' markets, nor that micro-expectations about particular sectors would be realized. Even aggregate balance would not ensure balance of payments equilibrium in an open economy, where not all domestically produced output is sold at home, nor all domestic demand satisfied by production within the economy. Badly executed plans, which incorrectly project the future environmental path, will lose credibility as their macro and sectoral forecasts prove inaccurate, and may fail to influence the rate of growth. The British National Economic Plan of 1966–70 appears to have suffered from all these problems simultaneously. The demand expectations literature can provide only a limited general justification for indicative planning, but it may be of value in special circumstances.

New Approaches to the Theory of Indicative Planning

We have seen that the two best-known models do not convincingly justify the use of indicative planning, although they highlight what is likely to go wrong in practice. In this section we consider briefly two further approaches which may ultimately prove relevant: temporary equilibrium models and the notion of rational expectations. There has been virtually no explicit consideration of indicative planning in either context as yet, but they are worth considering since they offer the possibility of fruitful future research.

Planning for Markets in Disequilibrium

Meade's indicative plans provide price information while Harrod's predict the total quantities to be bought and sold. Actual planning exercises have primarily provided quantitative information, though not necessarily for Harrod's reasons; one can derive a role for quantitative forecasts from a general equilibrium model if markets are in disequilibrium. Meade assumes that agents will be able to buy and sell as much as they wish if markets are perfectly competitive and prices are flexible, but prices may not automatically adjust to prevent excess capacity from materializing, perhaps because firms do not know how much to adjust them

(Phelps, 1971) or because they consciously prefer quantity variation to price flexibility.[5] One consequence is that not all workers will invariably be able to find jobs in the labour market when wages do not move in such a way as to ensure permanent full employment. Without considering further the justification for assuming wage and price inflexibility, we shall proceed to consider heuristically the role of indicative planning in one such model, inspired by the recent work of Malinvaud (1977, 1980).

We suppose that everyone is familiar with a set of prices, including wage rates, for trading in the current period, but these are not necessarily assumed to clear markets. If they prove not to be equilibrium prices, agents will discover too late that they are unable to carry out all the sales and purchases that they planned, by which time they will have accumulated unsold goods, be unemployed, or have queued for goods but gone home empty-handed for the rest of the period. Prices can only alter at the start of the next period, although not necessarily so as to eliminate market disequilibria. Agents may continuously find themselves 'rationed' in their attempts to buy and sell, and firms which have produced more than they can sell at the going price are assumed to end up with unsold goods rather than cut prices, and may endure losses. Thus, the economy lurches back and forth with only the most limited foresight and hindsight, and firms have no guarantee that they will be able to sell anything at positive prices. The model assumes that firms are always demand constrained, presumably because prices are never cut below the cost of what is sold, which suggests that part of the reason for price inflexibility could be a degree of monopoly power that never gets competed away.

Clearly, in such a world firms would appreciate information on the minimum quantities that could be sold with certainty, since they would never need to produce less. Workers' savings and spending plans would also be aided if they knew the minimum quantities of labour that they could sell. An indicative plan could provide quantitative information on the bounds of the possible, thereby preventing losses due to frustrated expectations. Reducing uncertainty in this way could relax the constraints on possible transactions: for example, leading to a greater willingness to produce and plan demand for investment goods, thereby easing the constraints on people who sell them and therefore workers. The plan forecasts would attempt to predict the quantity constraints that firms would face, on the assumption that prices would at least cover average costs if there is a market at all, with firms guaranteed minimum sales at these prices though they may be able to sell more. In practice, plan forecasts are not usually cast in the form of minimum sales, but as likely estimates of actual sales, so firms might suppose the minimum sure value was somewhat below, and the maximum somewhat above, this figure. However, the repeated tendency of the French economy to exceed plan targets in the years before 1970 (see Chapter 3) is consistent with the interpretation that the forecasts represent minimum sure sales. Firms were guaranteed no losses if they expanded production at the forecast rate, and doing so acted to loosen the demand constraints throughout the economy with everyone able to sell more than the minimum. If this were the case, the planners' undue optimism in recent years (see Chapter 3) could explain the declining credibility of the exercise.

Unlike Meade-type planning, this version of the procedure does not require the prediction of the entire demand schedule in each market, now and in the future, to isolate equilibrium prices. The planners only need to know a segment of the demand schedules facing firms, and not necessarily the part relevant to market equilibrium. Although it may still not be easy, it is asking a lot less to determine some quantity that can be sold at a price which covers costs. But even this approach dodges the issue of why firms cannot predict sales properly for themselves in the first place. The case for planning continues to rest on some factor which influences the sort of calculation made in the market place, but not that made by planners. One such possible factor is economy of scale in information processing, especially where there are general equilibrium or macro-economic interdependences which can best be observed by planners who have a little information about each market and an understanding of how they all fit together, rather than a lot of detailed information about one or a few markets. If the market breaks down because of price rigidity due to firms' ignorance of factors that are in principle knowable, but are not necessarily known, we have an explanation of both the failure of markets to clear and why indicative planning may help.

Rational Expectations and Indicative Planning

Indicative planning rests on the notion that markets do not automatically provide sufficient information for the decentralised co-ordination of decisions. The 'rational expectations' school takes a diametrically opposed view; that markets always provide sufficient information to co-ordinate private decision-making efficiently. Their representation of the expectations formation process implies either perfect foresight or at least the employment of all the potentially available information to the best extent humanly possible. Learning from mistakes prevents agents from making systematic expectational errors over time. Laidler (1981) notes that rational expectations do not imply that agents have complete and correct econometric models of the economy in their heads, but simply that 'expectations will not be wrong systematically over time, and to that extent will resemble those generated by a "true" model in being unbiased and serially uncorrelated. An agent who forms expectations in a manner that leads to systematic error will find himself persistently making the wrong choice; hence in the very course of market activities, he will be provided *gratis* with the information necessary to eliminate that systematic error' (p. 11).

This idea provides a strong critique of indicative planning that will be relevant throughout our text. The case for planning is based on the inadequacy of information for private expectation formation in the absence of future markets. Rational expectations theorists point out that information provided may not be inadequate in a dynamic world where people can learn from their mistakes. One should not assume that the available information will necessarily be insufficient for decentralized co-ordination in the absence of future markets; if the endogenous variables in the system are determined by general rules which can be approximated by a model, agents should gradually be able to learn its structure from previous errors. If this view is correct, the best that planners could do would be to tell firms, at considerable cost, what they already know about the economy. Moreover, the exercise could not continually influence the real allocation of resources, for example, in the way suggested by Harrod, unless it operated on the economy through completely unpredictable shocks, or its impact would disappear by being assimilated into private expectations. The pragmatic exponent of rational expectations also has an answer for critics who point to repeated and systematic errors in actual enterprise forecasting. He will point out that there is no reason to expect planners to do any better; firms may not be omniscient but they will do as well as possible under the circumstances. But however rational they are, enterprises will not be provided with the information to make efficient decisions for free because experimentation is costly. A role for planning re-emerges if something enables the planners to reduce the variance of expectational errors, making private expectations more reliable though no more unbiased, at lower cost than enterprises could do for themselves.

One may wish to accept the general notion of rationality in expectation formation, yet believe costs constrain agents to act on less than full information. As Phelps (1971) stated in his volume on adaptive expectations: 'The actors of each model have to cope, ignorant of the future or even much of the present.

Isolated and apprehensive, these Pinteresque figures construct expectations of the state of the economy – over space and time – and maximise relative to that imagined world' (p. 22). Rational expectations theory was developed from this earlier view, which saw agents as only able to learn slowly, and not necessarily perfectly, from their mistakes. As Laidler (1981) points out, there is no reason to agree with Barro (1979) that: 'to postulate an infinite speed of price adjustment in the face of excess demand or supply is to conform to sound micro-economic principles and to postulate anything slower is to propose an "ad-hoc" non-theory' (Laidler, 1981, p. 13). With transactions costs in information dissemination, economies of scale provide a case for centralized forecasting, even if agents are fully rational, subject to what they know. In the following chapter we shall argue that this case is particularly strong when we also take into account the concept of bounded rationality. In the meantime, let us conclude with a further quotation from Phelps (1971): 'Obviously the soil of non-Walrasian product markets is one where any competent ad-man would flourish' (p. 23). Indicative planners too, perhaps.

Notes

1 We are indebted to John Wise for pointing this fact out to us.
2 This general equilibrium model was formulated in Arrow (1953) and Debreu (1959). Meade (1971) considers it fully and a recent comprehensive account is contained in Dasgupta and Heal (1979). Meade's work provides the best known justification for the procedure and has been a basis for further research (e.g. Albin (1971), Miller (1979)).
3 Meade (1970) actually covers numerous potential problems for indicative planning, but does not cover this point.
4 The procedure could also be used to reduce the rate of growth in economies with chronic inflationary tendencies by forecasting future demand conditions pessimistically to restrict the growth of demand relative to supply potential. This appears to have been the case for the Vth Plan (see Chapter 3).
5 Meade considers the effects of a further limitation on the amount that can be sold at a going price; monopoly power.

2 An Alternative Justification for Indicative Planning

In this chapter, we will attempt to outline discursively a convincing case for the centralized provision of economic information and suggest how the exercise might be carried out and what it might achieve. The ideas also throw some light onto the sources of the problems which have bedevilled French planning in recent years. Indicative planning will be useful when there are economies of scale, especially of information costs, and the case is strengthened if rationality is 'bounded'; there are limits to computations of the various possibilities in private decision-making. There is also a classic welfare case for the state rather than private agencies to provide the information because of the monopolistic properties of information systems and the public good character of plans. These issues are considered in the following sections, and lead to a discussion of 'strategic planning' as outlined by Lindblom (1977). Before proceeding, we summarize the whole argument to make it easier for readers to chart a course through the complex material that follows.

The Case

The argument is based on the premise that markets cannot be expected to handle problems of uncertainty in a way that will with hindsight appear optimal when people cannot make decisions using the full information set. The weakness of the Arrow–Debreu characterization of the economy is that uncertainty is treated as applying to an exogenously given set of potential events. However, as recent research in the theory of information has suggested, it is not entirely sensible to regard the structure of information as fixed in advance and immutable (see especially Radner, 1968). If people use information about each other's behaviour as well as what they discover for themselves about the environment, market activities automatically generate externalities, because each person's behaviour affects the information that he and others possess. Centralized co-ordination of information can improve on the decentralized market co-ordination in these circumstances if there are economies of scale in information processing.

The case for indicative planning is strengthened by the existence of 'bounded rationality' in individual decision-making. This idea was developed by Simon (1957), who explained it in the following terms: 'The capacity of the human mind for formulating and solving complex problems is very small compared with the size of the problems whose solution is required for objectively rational behaviour in the real world – or even for a reasonable approximation to such objective rationality' (p. 198). Agents must act on the basis of a simplified model of reality, and their behaviour will not necessarily be optimal with respect to the 'true' real world or even their perception of it if only a limited number of alternative strategies can be analysed. Bounded rationality obstructs the definition, let alone the attainment, of private or social optimality in the allocation of resources. In addition, private agents do not have the knowledge about their *own* plans required for Meade-type planning. As Radner (1968) concludes, 'The Arrow–Debreu world is strained to the limit by the problems of choice of information. It breaks down completely in the face of limits on the ability of agents to compute optimal strategies'.

There is an a-priori case for indicative planning if transactions costs force agents to make choices about information collection, and if economies of scale result in co-ordination costs that are lower for collective than private provision. This is considerably strengthened if one accepts the notion of widespread bounded rationality. It would be impossible for the plan to provide *full* information in these circumstances, so one could not be aiming for Pareto efficiency, exante. This implies a rather different role for the procedure to that envisaged by Meade, in which the attention of decision makers is drawn to information and opportunities that they had not previously considered. One could justify this approach if transactions costs leave agents with a choice of information, or there are limits to agents' 'computational' abilities, but it is particularly relevant if one makes both assumptions simultaneously. The planners could undertake a limited search through the implications of alternative scenarios in the hope of broadening the opportunity sets of decision makers, especially important ones.

These points do not necessitate government involvement, rather than that of private entrepreneurs, for profit (e.g. business consultants). The argument for state intervention depends on conventional 'market failures' in information, particularly monopoly and externality problems. Information must necessarily be exchanged on markets that are imperfectly competitive when only the seller knows the characteristic of the 'good' until after it has changed hands. There will also be efficiency problems in allocation through markets if there are economies of scale in the provision of information, especially if these apply to transactions costs. These conditions imply positive externalities for the provision of information which means that the quantity supplied by private agents will be insufficient from a social perspective. As a result, one should locate the indicative planning process in the hands of the collectivity. The most useful information that the authorities could supply in the circumstances would concern a limited number of variables which are closely correlated in a known way with those influencing private decisions. We will argue that in practice these will be largely macro-economic or concern specific issues.

Once we have established that the government must supply the plans, we see how positive transactions costs and bounded rationality would affect state decision-making. Lindblom (1975, 1977) believes that they will prevent public policy from being 'rational' in any conventional sense, and he proposes a loose form of 'strategic planning' for the public sector. The planning process should provide a mechanism for communication and discussion of general scenarios and like problems, rather than comprehensive information for optimal or rational private and public choices. The plan cannot hope to give the complete list of contingent solutions for every possible outcome, but it could provide an initial basis for decisions by presenting the broad outlines of a few likely environmental paths. 'Strategic planning' by the state would be similar to the type of corporate planning actually carried out in the private sector.

The Potential for Indicative Planning

This section examines the problems posed for individual decision-making and market allocation by transactions costs in information, bounded rationality, and both simultaneously. We begin with the implications for individual choice, supporting the discussion with empirical evidence, before proceeding to the market level. The inadequacies of decentralized co-ordination in these circumstances clearly delineates a potential role for planning. However, in itself this does not establish a case for the exercise because the costs may exceed the benefits. We conclude by showing that there are economies of scale in information, so that planners could operate more cheaply to provide information than private agents acting alone.

Models of Individual Decision-Making
Real transactions costs in collecting and processing information lead us away from the conclusions of classical economic theory, in

which agents are assumed to optimize over known alternatives. Firms and individuals will not necessarily know what they would do in the future because it will be prohibitively expensive or psychologically impossible to calculate optimal plans for every contingency. Instead, they will keep their options open, without knowing in advance exactly what those options are, so they simply will not have the information that would be pooled in a Meade-type plan. Firms may fail even to collect valuable data if that information is costly and they do not know its value in advance. In such a world, private decisions will necessarily be arbitrary to some degree.

The problem that arises is the sheer volume of information that agents would have to gather and process in order to make optimal decisions under uncertainty. In the Arrow–Debreu model, agents must define their intentions regarding every choice variable for every period of the future and every significantly different contingency. The contingencies that are equivalent from one's own point of view will be grouped together, so different decisions are only required for the remaining possibilities, but not all agents will 'partition' contingencies in the same way (see Radner, 1968). The relevant number of 'states of the world' will still be very large for each individual, and would lead to a myriad of possible environmental paths once the time dimension has been taken into account.

If this problem is acute for an individual, it would be all the more so for any process involving interactions of individuals. Any conditional contract between two parties in the Arrow–Debreu world would have to separately recognize changes in circumstances that were noticeable by either party. Suppose for example every firm in the economy has electric heating in its offices, which is always switched fully on or fully off, depending on whether the outside temperature is above or below a certain figure, which differs from firm to firm. Each of these firms would recognize only two states of the world and would have conditional contracts to purchase zero or a fixed amount of electricity in the two cases, but the power utility would face as many possible states of the world as it had customers, and its contract with the coal or oil supplier would have to be vastly more complex than those with each of its customers. Any Meade-type indicative plan would have to recognize each case separately.

Of course, such complicated procedures are not possible in practice. As noted above, transactions costs in information prevent individual optimization over every eventuality. Even if firms are able to act optimally with respect to the information they possess, this information is itself the endogenous product of past actions which will be further revised over time. But the choice of information to be used in private decision-making cannot be made by solving an optimization problem because there is no good guide, even in probabilistic terms, to the content of information not yet known. The gathering and processing of information necessarily involves an initial element of arbitrariness; experience will lead to useful rules of thumb but may be misleading for entirely novel situations (see Winter, 1964).

Moreover, the capacity of the human mind to absorb and process even the information directly available or implicit in past experience is severely bounded. This has similar and important implications about the desirability of planning and how it should be carried out. Because private decisions will not necessarily be efficient, even in an ex-ante sense, a slight re-casting of the decision maker's information or a second look at his situation from the outside may highlight an element that had been overlooked. In this way, the planners may be able to improve on what firms could do alone. The bounded rationality concept is in no way necessary to support the remaining arguments on the externality and public good aspects of information, although combined with positive transactions costs it offers a stronger case against the efficiency of perfectly decentralized co-ordination. In exploring the implications of bounded rationality for planning, we are following the advice of Radner (1975):

> It may be that an exclusive reliance on a framework of optimal decisions will not be fruitful for planning theory. On the one hand, a concern for economic planning seems to imply, almost by definition, a concern for a rational approach to the organisation of economic activity. On the other hand, the optimal solution of economic decision problems on a national scale, taking account of uncertainty, seems totally beyond our capacities, now and in the indefinite future. A promising approach to the solution of this dilemma is suggested by Simon's concept of 'bounded rationality'. (p. 95)

Simon's work is as much in psychology as economics and takes human cognitive limitations as its starting point. Economists traditionally assume that each decision maker exhaustively compares the outcomes of *all* the possible decisions he might make in every possible exogenous state of the world, and then chooses the decision that is the best in some probabilistic sense. But under uncertainty, it is not merely impossible for objective circumstances to dictate a unique profit-maximizing decision independent of the agents' attitude to risk; firms can no longer select among all possible choices. Simon (1978, p. 497) offers the interesting analogy of the relatively small number of possible moves actually examined by great chess masters in comparison to the thousands that had to be exhaustively evaluated by a chess-playing computer. The human player does not look many moves ahead, but usually wins. Simon stresses that for many practical problems the *best* modern computer algorithms are not those set up to guarantee exhaustive inspection of all possibilities, but are 'heuristic' programmes that simplify the problem by trying to imitate the human brain's capacity for recognizing solutions through certain simple features of a desirable decision rather than a full calculation. An example he gives is the difference between trying to locate the sharpest of an unknown number of needles in a haystack and simply finding one sharp enough to sew with. For most purposes it is the latter problem that it is wise to solve, even though the sharpest needle would be useful if you did happen to hit on it.

'Procedural rationality' cannot be expected to guarantee ex-post optimal decisions in most cases, in part because not every problem is tractable. Winter (1964) points out that there is 'infinite regress' in the search for optimal selection procedures for devices to revise search procedures. Agents have to continually collect additional information in order to decide whether to collect additional information. This may explain why they are forced to adopt 'rules of thumb'. Radner (1975) observes that mathematicians have not yet solved a great many operational research problems of an apparently simple nature for an uncertain environment, so it is unreasonable to assume that managers could do so in their everyday decision-making. This type of problem is right at the heart of statistical decision theory, for example, the decision as to whether a price variation indicates random disturbances or a change in the mean. Minimizing the risk of concluding that nothing has altered when it actually has raises the risk of concluding that a change has occurred when it has not. The statistician asks the individual to specify his own loss function as between these two types of error, which begs the crucial question. Even if rules of thumb provide an operational response to these problems, as Simon (1978, p. 503) points out, 'the accumulation of experience may allow people to behave in ways that are very nearly optimal in situations to which their experience is pertinent, but will be of very little help when genuinely novel situations are present'. A person's choices may be an unbiased, though not perfectly accurate, estimate of the optimum in a relatively stable environment, but systematic biases will creep in when the situation is altering. This gives us another clue as to the potential role of planners. When they have general environmental information about the way things are moving, for example, macro trends or new technologies, they can suggest to firms possibilities that should be, but are not necessarily being, investigated.

By denying the possibility of objectively rational behaviour, we lay ourselves open to the standard criticism that we are assuming agents to be irrational. This is inaccurate since no one knowingly opts for inconsistent or inferior choices in an informationally imperfect world. When costs make agents' information inadequate or arbitrary and there are limits to their capacity to compute different possibilities, it simply becomes impossible for them to judge whether their decisions are actually inconsistent or inferior. Information from another source may aid their judgements.

Empirical Evidence

A number of examples show how imperfectly firms actually master their own environment and how hard it would be to resolve their uncertainties by pooling their corporate plans and expectations in a mechanical way. But planners could still improve on what firms actually do in this informationally imperfect world.

Holmes (1978) examines the problems faced by business decision makers in searching for the right export price. It can be costly to test demand elasticities by varying prices because of accidental moves away from, rather than toward, an optimum and possible loss of goodwill. The investigation suggests that almost no major firms had contingency plans prepared in advance of the UK devaluation of 1967. Firms had learned some lessons from the earlier experience by the time the pound fell again in 1972–73, but each firm had learned somewhat differently according to its own policies and resulting experiences. The general conclusions of the study illustrate one of the main problems of bounded rationality: appropriate behavioural rules for periods when the pound is falling steadily in value are not necessarily the ones that will generate good results when the pound is rising.

J. K. Galbraith (1967) argues that large corporations do have firm detailed corporate plans extending over five-year periods which are capable of being implemented in practice. Stuart Holland (1975) takes this argument a step further, calling for planning agreements in which these 'plans' are integrated into a single consistent National Plan. However, as we shall see below, the evidence runs against this view of corporate planning and therefore against a national planning system founded on this basis. In fact, when corporate plans are of any use at all, they are tentative explorations of a limited number of scenarios.

An interesting study of Canadian firms in the 1960s by Helliwell (1965, 1968) shows that corporate plans are not used as the basis for objectively rational decision-making, nor do they precisely value the consequences of different strategies in various circumstances. His study of how investment decisions are made draws a picture of sketchy corporate 'plans' and more concrete short-term capital budgets, with a striking absence of precise quantification behind major investment projects. Businessmen emphatically argue that they do not base their operational plans on the medium-term projections of their corporate planning departments, or at least not on the precise numbers in them, except where very long gestation periods require current decisions to be based on estimates of future demand. One typical manager quoted by Helliwell (1965) 'prefers to have no formalised plan of activities, since in his industry there are apparently too many unknowns for forecasts beyond a year to be worth anything' (p. 84). Helliwell comments that 'five and ten year estimates of growth and capital expenditures are always treated with scorn by senior management officials for whom they are prepared' (p. 85), except in very special cases. When he does discover plans that stretch far into the future, they are generally on overall policy for growth rather than specific expenditure plans.

Another source of information on the nature of internal enterprise planning is contained in the Report of the UK House of Commons Select Committee on Nationalised Industries (1973). The hearings were designed to elucidate what lessons could be learned for nationalized industries from private sector corporate planning, so, while there might have been a political incentive to overstate competitive and environmental vulnerability, there would have been countervailing pressure to stress competence. All the firms giving evidence told the same story, in which corporations have two distinct sets of 'plans'. First, there are long- or medium-term 'corporate plans' which are sketchy and contain a number of alternative scenarios, not necessarily worked out in detail, to cover a period of five years or more. Any figures, including those for capital expenditure, are illustrative only. In addition, there are 'operating plans' which cover a period of eighteen months or two years, and contain the firm's intended financial outlay, including the best approximation to the capital budget, although this could be revised. For example, Shell is quite explicit about the distinction between short-term 'programming' over a two-year period and the long-range 'strategic planning period' which 'is essentially the whole future', although comprehensive studies only extend ten or fifteen years ahead. As they stated it in their evidence:

The strategic planning activity . . . is concerned with that period into the future for which options remain open; strategic decisions involve the exercise of these options by choosing to commit resources in a particular way. A strategic decision, when made, will cause immediate programming action for its implementation, but the strategy of which it is a part will consist of a pattern of subsequent decisions which do not have to be taken yet, and which are conditional on events which are at present uncertain. (Select Committee on Nationalised Industries, Sub-Committee B (1973), p. 195)

In fact, there are very substantial revisions to these plans during their operating period. Several studies have been undertaken on UK data to see whether it is better to predict private investment over the business cycle on the basis of stated intentions at an earlier point in the cycle, or by direct inference from the most recent macro-economic data (see Smyth and Briscoe, 1969; Lund *et al.*, 1980). The conclusion is that stated intentions are a worse predictor, which suggests that disaggregated investment forecasts always respond sharply to short-term macro-economic changes. The predictions were improved further by forecasting directly from current macro-economic variables, specifically capital-utilization estimates, and by asking firms to state their assumptions about inflation so that forecasters could consider the alternative values of exogenous variables.

Thus firms do not have the sort of information that would be pooled in a Meade-type plan. Their response to informational imperfections is to keep their long-term options open and their current stance flexible. They will consider in an imprecise way their strategies for a few contingencies, presumably the ones that they consider most likely, but not search through the various possibilities exhaustively. One cannot plan on the basis of explicit pre-commitments in such a world, but the pooling of the semi-operational corporate strategies does offer a real prospect for improving decisions by broadening the opportunity set. Firms are also clearly sensitive to macro-economic factors which suggests a role for aggregate plan forecasts.

Models of Markets with Transactions Costs and Bounded Rationality

Markets begin to lose some of their efficiency properties when agents' knowledge comes from their own experience rather than omniscient analysis.[1] The best decisions will not necessarily be taken because the right information is not available or decision makers fail to grasp its significance. We consider the problems for decentralized co-ordination, and therefore the potential for planning, in these circumstances from three related perspectives – informationally imperfect markets, biased expectations, and the 'Austrian' view. Even so, the case for planning actually rests on economies of scale in information, discussed at the end of this section.

We cannot hope to do justice to the large literature on informationally imperfect markets (see, for example, Radner, 1968; Grossman and Stiglitz, 1976, 1980; Hirshleifer and Riley, 1979; Dasgupta and Heal, 1979, contains a survey), but we will try to bring out a few relevant points for our discussion. Rothschild (1973) shows that learning behaviour in these circumstances will not invariably lead to optimal behaviour by individuals or markets, and Hart (1975) suggests that the resulting equilibria will not necessarily be unique or efficient. Numerous authors point out that when information is a choice variable, private decisions become interdependent because people necessarily receive information about each other's behaviour as well as prices (see Radner, 1968; Grossman and Stiglitz, 1976; Hirshleifer and Riley, 1979). An individual's actions in the market place, buying what he thinks is cheap and refusing what is dear, generate informational externalities that are felt by everyone whether or not they participate. Hirshleifer and Riley (1979) conclude that 'there is a market externality brought about in this way that tends to break down any equilibrium in which information is only available at a cost'. Grossman and Stiglitz (1976) draw attention to the parallels between the externalities generated by observation of another's market search and the public good aspect of a plan. Additional information which could benefit everyone but depends on the (costly) actions of one individual may well not be transmitted. All these points indicate a possibility of improving on the outcome of purely decentralized co-ordination. Associated problems for expectations in such a world also allow us to extend our consideration of rational expectations.

If expectations are rational, agents must rapidly adjust their models to ensure that any remaining errors are random over time. Bounded rationality also leads to the use of simplified models, but these are not restricted to be 'true', nor even approximate the truth in the rational expectations sense of eliminating serial correlation. Thus, we could observe systematic errors over time because agents were unable to calculate how to prevent them, or even because they had not yet perceived them. Lund *et al.* (1980) indicate that firms do not appear to form price expectation in a 'rational' manner. There is evidence of both a tendency to under-predict the degree of acceleration of inflation by UK enterprises between 1972 and 1975 (although there was an appreciation of

the deceleration after that date) and to underestimate the rate
of price increases. Although the degree of bias is quite small, it is
enough to suggest inadequacies in the rational expectations
approach. A study carried out at the Federal Reserve Bank of St.
Louis found that inflationary expectations from a widely used
survey 'do not conform to the criteria of rationality' (Hafer and
Resler, 1980, p. 11). Thus, private expectations may actually be
systematically biased as well as less than perfectly accurate
because of transactions costs and bounded rationality. Of course
the notion of bias is a slippery one. We would have to prove that
private expectations display systematic biases in an ex-ante sense,
evidence for which is bound to be a-priori rather than empirical.
Nevertheless there is a possibility of improvement over the initial
situation when private forecasts, even if unbiased, do not also
display zero variance around the final outcomes.

A third approach to the role of planning can be illustrated by
considering the views of a school of thought conveniently labelled
as 'Austrian'. These writers have always stressed the central role of
uncertainty, but also claim that the state cannot eradicate the
ensuing problems. Lutz (1969) and Richardson (1971) have
written critically of planning from this perspective, while Kirzner
(1979) has explored the issue of entrepreneurship and information
processing in depth. Writers in the Austrian tradition have always
been dissatisfied with static equilibria and the treatment of uncertainty as a special case of certainty through the use of certainty
equivalents. They focus on the consistent uncertainty and disappointment of agents who are driven to make entrepreneurial
profits by outguessing each other in the market place. The essence
of their system is an unsystematic search for unexploited gains so
there will be relatively more profit for agents with the best guesses,
even if everyone guesses incorrectly. This excludes an equilibrium
notion in which all expectations are realized, and no one would
engage in the massive pre-commitments implied by future conditional contracts. Such a description is similar to the one envisaged above, but many followers of this 'Austrian' approach
would further deny that private decisions could be improved by
the provision of information. Imperfect though market co-
ordination may be, it represents the 'best' that could be achieved
in an uncertain environment. However, although there is no
obvious way to evaluate the allocation that will arise from
decentralized co-ordination, our previous discussion suggests that
every profitable opportunity will not necessarily be exploited to
the full. Where transactions costs are positive and rationality
bounded, the essentially arbitrary nature of decision-making may
lead to overlooked opportunities or a failure to fully exploit

potential gains in order to keep options open.[2] There may be information in the hands of agents, including the state, which though necessarily imprecise could be pooled to generate gains for the community. The Austrian approach assumes that each firm knows its own market best; but an outsider may be able to make useful suggestions in an informationally imperfect world, in our view.

Yet even if the market outcome is less than the Panglossian ideal, planning may not be able to improve on it. Planners might merely generate a limited information structure of their own which could lead firms away to choices they will regret with hindsight, not to gains. If information gathering and processing is the result of arbitrary choices, why should the planners be expected to make better choices than private individuals? Moreover, if a centralized co-ordinating body could 'improve' private decisions in this way, surely it would be privately profitable to supply the indicative plans because agents would be willing to pay for the product. One might conclude that indicative plans cannot fulfil the task proposed above because they are not privately supplied in actual economies. Even though the market system does not pool sufficient information to guarantee an efficient allocation, the same factors which prevent markets from supplying the information will prevent indicative plans from doing the job.

This argument is weakened if there are economies of scale in the gathering and processing of information, in which case a centralized agency could pool information across a broader range of possibilities than any individual. There are strong reasons to suppose that such economies of scale do, in fact, exist.[3] There will generally be major fixed costs to setting up any mechanism to gather or process information and this 'lumpiness' is a major source of economies of scale. Casual introspection reveals that our capacity to absorb information rapidly increases with the familiarity of the material, as does our ability to usefully employ it. Moreover, there are economies of scale in the physical and human capital currently used to process data, which has led to a rapid centralization of data provision services in all Western economies. This centralized data gathering and processing normally concerns current or past information, not necessarily of an economic type, and does not always involve the provision of co-ordinated forecasts in the style of an indicative plan. But one must presume that information of this type would have the same properties.

There is evidence that supports this view from the limited forecasting activities currently undertaken. Whereas small firms do not generally maintain their own forecasting divisions, the larger corporations almost invariably do. Numerous private companies are profitably engaged in the activity of selling forecasts to those smaller or medium sized firms, who presumably buy the product rather than produce their own because economies of scale make this a relatively cheaper course of action. However, these private forecasts are limited in scope, and pool information across a restricted group of agents. If economies of scale are unlimited across the range of socially efficient plans, there is scope for the centralized provision of significantly more useful information through an indicative planning procedure. The extent of economies of scale in this area is illustrated by the relative dominance of a small number of organizations, notably DRI in the US and the St James's Group in the UK, itself a cooperative of a number of users of macro forecasts. We shall discuss below some of the unusual aspects of the use of the market mechanism to generate forecasts.

Bounded rationality and positive transactions costs undermine the logic of orthodox welfare economics. We cannot rely on the market to produce an efficient outcome. Planners may be able to generate, at a lower cost than each individual acting alone, information about interdependences and potential disequilibria at a micro or macro level that firms would not have thought of exploring for themselves. Being specialists in checking economic data, their comparative advantage can lead them to draw significant information to the attention of firms; the set of choices may be widened and unperceived profitable opportunities opened up. Because people only investigate a few of the consequences of some of these contingencies that they face, even the most important avenues may not be explored by the free market unaided.

The Plan and the State

This section explains why the state rather than private individuals must undertake indicative planning. There is a classic welfare economics case for government intervention in the supply of information because of the externality, public good, and monopolistic properties of the commodity. Moreover, the incentives for people to cheat in the planning exercise raises incentive compatibility problems which can best be dealt with by the state.

We have seen that there will be positive externalities in the provision of information in an informationally imperfect system. Market search or decisions by one person act as a guide for others, with the result that the private allocation of information will be socially inadequate. Information also has a public good aspect which is closely associated with the externalities, as well as the economies of scale discussed above. A full pool of privately available information cannot be constructed without involving every decision maker, after which it would be difficult to exclude anyone from the results. More seriously, particular agents may have information which they regard as insignificant yet others could value, and there is no private mechanism to transmit this demand. Miller (1979, 1980) has discussed problems caused by the public good aspect of plans. It would be difficult and expensive for interrelated firms to conduct private negotiations among themselves to internalize these externalities, although economies of scale mean that one or a few might undertake such a task. But this lends a strong monopolistic bias to the private market, a problem amplified by the fact that buyers will have to evaluate a 'pig in a poke', since the contents of any information sold cannot be revealed before purchase. These various market factors, separately and together, make a strong case for public involvement in the provision of information.

An example can illustrate these points. It has always puzzled the present authors how the UK stock market manages to generate a very substantial amount of research and forecasting data, much of which is circulated free of charge to business and academic readers.[4] The cost of this must be substantial but it is paid for by individual broking firms who have little direct incentive to set up a research department, often to forecast *macro*-economic developments which have distinct social value but little direct return to the broking firm. The fact that some firms also sell more specialized versions of their research output to companies as a form of consultancy service does not adequately explain what is going on. There is an externality of the information system that appears to be being internalized in some very mysterious manner. One might suspect that side-payments are being made. It turns out that there is an explanation along these lines, which shows that the government is not the only agency that can internalize externalities, but at the same time displays the weakness of purely market solutions to these problems. A management official of the London Stock Exchange informed us that the research was in effect being paid for by the UK's large institutional investors, that is, insurance companies and pension funds, who would direct and redirect the commissions from handling their business to firms that carry out interesting research. This cannot be profit maximizing behaviour on the part of the institutions, who, if they are paying for the information, would make more profits for their investors if they insisted it be kept for their use only. But non-profit maximizing behaviour is much easier for large investment funds, whose managers have hundreds of millions of pounds of other people's money at their disposal, than for relatively small firms or brokers. The cost of providing this information is socialized on to the insurance policy holders and pensioners.

This arrangement works at the moment, but is not socially optimal and may not generate appropriate incentives. The informational externality is being internalized by a lucky combination of institutional factors permitting the costs to be passed on, which may not last. The insurance companies have chosen to act this way rather than, for example, carry out in-house research in part from the laudable motive of stimulating multiple sources of information. But this does not imply that the market will *always* generate multiple sources; in this case it is merely because of the somewhat arbitrary decisions of investment managers. The only justification for the state of affairs we have outlined to be a substitute for publicly sponsored economic forecasting would be a belief that under all circumstances state officials, given the task of promoting the public good, would do it less effectively than employees of private firms for whom such an activity is an incidental by-product of their main responsibilities. Adequate information is not spontaneously emitted by the ordinary activities of markets, and to the extent it is offered, it is either monopolistically or via externalities. Such phenomena justify collective involvement.

In addition, there are serious 'incentive compatibility' problems with the provision of information about future behaviour, which will be reduced (though not eliminated) by state involvement. The problem arises because agents have a clear incentive to cheat, which disrupts the co-ordinating role of the information for themselves and all the other participants. For example, in a Meade-type plan, every agent could privately benefit from distorting the information that he supplied, provided everyone else told the truth. Everyone would gain by overstating both his demands and supplies, if no one else cheated, since this would help to create slackness in his input markets and shortages for his products. This problem is especially severe for information provided by firms who would have a monopoly in various circumstances. Consider the case of suppliers who know that they will run out of a particular good under a particular set of circumstances. It will be in their interest to promise a lower price than they know will be charged to firms who will still have stocks of the good, in order to keep up their demand for contingencies when supplies will be available. Examples of this type of distortion are common in practice, which explains the familiar unreliable promise: 'you can get spares for this model anywhere'. One would not expect this problem to seriously affect a competitive system, in which each firm supplies a minute proportion of future sales. However, it becomes magnified when markets are informationally imperfect because agents can realistically expect their demand to be sustained by promises to supply more than they can deliver. The supplier knows full well that this type of behaviour is not likely to rebound on him because it is very difficult for anyone to distinguish between genuine mistakes and dissimulation. However, he can profitably exploit the situation if he proves to have stocks ex post. These incentive compatibility problems are likely to deter many private agents from attempting to supply indicative plans.

Interestingly, the British employers' confederation, the CBI, operates privately what at first sight appears to be a Meade-type indicative plan. Member firms are sent a questionnaire to which they give yes or no answers. We discussed the activity with CBI research department officials, who felt that they could neither increase the number of questions on the form concerning expectations about people's own businesses, nor include any requiring numerical answers, with very rare exceptions such as the 1967 devaluation. This was because member firms would not consider the right to receive detailed summaries of all the other firms' answers adequate compensation for the effort of providing the information themselves, which implies that the costs of calculating or revealing information are perceived as very high, or firms hold their own micro-expectations with such a low degree of confidence that the average of other peoples' is not highly valued.

The isolation paradox is only partially dispelled in this example. As a collective body, the CBI can ensure that, if firms agree to accept more detailed questionnaires, each knows that this will go to every other participant and the findings will be commonly available. But the possibility remains that each member would wish to organize an exchange of information on a greater scale but is deterred by the lack of the right incentives. The CBI is not the state, and has no way of coercing its members to actually answer the questions, let alone tell the truth. The main incentive not to cheat in such a situation is that you will not be believed next time if you tell the truth. This is especially important if there is some other party who will identify your dissimulation and is in a position to penalize you by withholding information about his intents. In general, this has got to be the state.

The literature on incentive mechanisms in planning (e.g. Weitzman, 1976; Bonin, 1976) shows that one can devise systems to reduce deliberate misrepresentation, but these must be administered through the legal system by a central authority. The government takes a systematic overview of the economy which may help it to more easily identify cases of dissimulation. Even if this is not possible, in the spirit of the previous section it could point out to both receivers and providers of information the inconsistencies which could imply either dissimulation or genuine error. Most importantly, the collectivity is better placed than private individuals to enforce norms of conduct in this field. It could choose to use an informational approach, by creating an atmosphere of mutually agreed rules through the provision of as much information as possible about its expectations and the likely future decisions of the public sector. This could have a greater chance of success than one would initially expect because agents could perceive the indicative planning mechanism as permanent, and therefore seek to avoid the penalties of being discovered to have misrepresented their expectations by an agency with a significant potential for counter-attack. However, one can never be sure that agents will follow a code of conduct that runs against their own perceived best interests, so the coercive approach must also be considered. The government is the only agency capable of introducing and enforcing a suitable incentive scheme for honest revelation. The authorities could also choose to treat the incentive and public goods problem jointly, using a revelation mechanism on the lines proposed by Groves and Loeb (1975), and developed by Miller (1980) for the indicative planning context.

To conclude, information as a commodity displays economies of scale in production, monopoly power in exchange, positive external effects, and public goods properties in its supply, with incentives for traders to cheat. One cannot assume that a free market for such a commodity would lead to socially desirable allocations, so there is a strong case for public intervention. There is no reason to suppose that the authorities will get the supply absolutely right, but one can expect an improvement on purely decentralized co-ordination. Doubtless a free market protagonist would respond that this gives the government an absolute monopoly over the provision of information, which it will abuse in its own interests. Our own study provides examples of such behaviour by the French authorities, but such an outcome is not inevitable. While there is always some risk of abuse, its consequences are unlikely to outweigh the gains from providing information that would otherwise not be available.

Many of the issues in the previous sections were brought together in a discussion[5] between one of the authors and a leading monetarist economist who had just given a talk on lines not far from those of the Austrian school, assuming there was no Walrasian auctioneer to make prices adjust perfectly but also that the state knew nothing that could enable it to improve the situation. The free market protagonist insists that, although agents may make decisions on the basis of 'incorrect' information, there will be no systematic bias to their errors, and therefore no scope for the state to provide information to 'improve' private decisions. Firms would only be influenced by variables in their own market and movements in the aggregate price level which are best predicted by the money stock. We accept that the government cannot normally provide useful information about particular markets, but deny that this eliminates any role for planning. The government may have 'better information' about certain variables because it is a prime agent in their determination and has knowledge of the interactions in the economy as a whole. It is also well placed to pool the imprecise information from corporate plans to search for major inconsistencies. In this way it could indicate to firms which routes could lead to errors under certain circumstances, and where unexploited profits might still be available. The monetarist agrees this is logically possible but remains highly suspicious of the potential costs of such operations. Moreover, although it might not be prohibitively expensive to centrally co-ordinate in this way, the monetarist opposes the idea because he profoundly mistrusts government intervention of any type. He does not believe that the political system can be relied upon to administer economic information in an impartial and indicative manner. For example, he points out that pooling information on wage demands would probably lead to a rigid incomes policy in practice, that would distort the market. Similarly, the planners' discovery that a major firm would experience a significant loss of sales in the near future would lead to it being propped up at the expense of the rest of the economy. In other words, he regards a logical economic case for indicative planning as insufficient grounds in practice for public intervention because he would expect the authorities to act to win votes or pay off old scores. At this point, the argument turns on attitudes to government interventions, whatever their economic justification. We do not accept the completely cynical view.

The Role of Planning

At this point, we can establish more precisely what government sponsored indicative planning would look like in an informationally imperfect system – both the contents and consequences of the exercise. We can develop our previous discussion of this issue by considering the characteristics of actual forward and speculative markets. We examine the problems in using speculative profit as a reward to specialists who predict market movements for numerous non-speculative traders, and the kind of information for which these markets suggest the greatest need. From these deductions, we go on to outline what the plans might contain and the problems they might be most adept at solving. We conclude with some examples of the role that planning could play in contemporary problems.

Samuelson (1957) produced an interesting analysis of the speculative markets which anticipates Grossman and Stiglitz in suggesting that speculators will not provide a service in arbitrating and predicting prices in a socially efficient manner, because so much of their reward will be monopolistic. He notes that speculative profits are made by using monopolistic access to information to buy items whose price is soon expected to rise. The act of carrying out the purchase brings the price movement forward, if only by days or hours, and the social benefit takes the form of giving people information about the value of assets that they might have otherwise misused in the period before the price rise occurs. (People will be prevented from converting wheat stocks irrevocably into inedible corn doylies if they see speculative action push prices up.) The speculator's reward for this depends on his liquidity and on the number of people who do not correctly interpret his actions and willingly sell to him at a low price. Samuelson observes that enormous profits may be made by anticipating correctly and hence bringing forward a price increase by a matter of hours, an activity of little social benefit. A major part of the speculator's reward is strictly zero-sum, but he can only confer such social benefits as he does if he is motivated to predict prices by the prospect of monopolistic gain. There is an inherent contradiction between the efficient functioning of the commodity market and the information market; if the speculator is forced to give his information away free to other market participants the commodity market will be efficient, but there would be no incentive for the speculator to invest in research. On the other hand, if having carried out his research the speculator reveals it only to those who watch him or who pay him as a consultant, his incentives are to dissimulate in the market or to charge a monopolistically high price to users of his information service.

There are certain types of speculative markets whose main function involves the forecasting of future price movements to reduce the risk for non-speculating individuals. These are the commodity and currency forward markets, where speculators undertake to pay a fixed sum of money in advance for commodities or funds receivable several months hence. There is of course a public goods problem here, in that farmers who choose not to trade in the wheat futures market nevertheless benefit from knowledge of the quoted forward prices for wheat. The speculators who make predictions of future demand and supply make their profits from those traders who do choose to do business in the forward market. The non-appropriability problem is one of the reasons why there are still relatively few forward markets.

A fascinating analytical and empirical study of these markets was carried out by Houthakker (1959). His conclusions, though exclusively concerned with the micro-economics of the markets, provide interesting ideas for guidelines that might influence a government wishing to set up an indicative plan. Houthakker discovered that at the time he was writing there were only about 60 or 70 futures markets operating in the whole world, including dormant ones, with not more than 40 or 50 commodities traded on them. He outlines arguments on the lines of the previous chapter to suggest that 'futures trading would seem to be one of those marvels that ought to be invented if they did not already exist'. The criteria determining the feasibility of future trading are that the correlation of future and eventual spot prices should make hedging worthwhile, and that the volume of future trades is sufficient to reduce transactions costs below those in the spot market. These criteria dramatically oppose each other; a very narrowly defined contract, for example, for a particular grade of wheat in a specific location, would have a very low trading volume, so transactions costs would be at least as high as in the money market, while a broadly defined contract, which could generate high volume, might provide little information about the particular spot prices in which agents were interested. However, they are just as suitable for determining part of the contents of a useful indicative plan, which must also avoid the twin dangers of providing detailed information at excessive cost and general information which cannot be used by agents in their private decisions. Thus, the plans must seek to provide information that has the properties of being relatively general, and therefore cheap to gather and process, yet be correlated in a manner known by the relevant agents to important factors in their private decision-making

The exact nature of this information depends in part on the structure of the economy. Suppose that the economy can be described by an input–output matrix which is 'triangulated' so there is a hierarchy of industries with the higher supplying the lower but not vice versa. The plan can focus on forecasting demand for the higher order sector, in the knowledge that the lower ones can deduce their own derived demand from this information. However, if the economy is much more complex, it seems unlikely that there will be many micro-economic indicators which satisfy the criteria for inclusion in the plan. Austrian writers suggest that enterprise decisions are largely based on factors concerning their own markets, which are defined very specifically. Thus, there are thousands of varieties of even a single item like 'steel' or 'restaurant meals', and there are no single markets for general goods. Houthakker did consider the circumstances when one could avoid the prohibitive costs of such detailed forecasts, namely when one particular variable is closely correlated with all the others in a specific group of products – for example, forecasting one single future wheat price to give all agents in the various markets useful information because the prices of various grades of wheat all move together. This does appear to be one way out of our problem. The planners should forecast variables that agents have a limited capacity to project for themselves, that are closely correlated in a known way with factors influencing private decisions, and for which economies of scale in data processing and information can be achieved. However, at first sight it may appear that actual economies have very few variables of this type, either because the structure excludes such 'short cuts' or because of the costs of discovering, let alone forecasting, these variables. The scarcity of actual future markets, despite the clear advantages that they could provide, is evidence for this view. We would strongly disagree with this conclusion, and argue that macro-economic forecasts could satisfy all the criteria discussed above.

In practice many of the variables that will influence private decisions are correlated, in an approximately known way, with elements of aggregate demand. The street corner shop, as well as the large corporation, knows that its sales, the tightness or slackness of its input markets, and the availability of credit are loosely associated with the general market conditions prevailing in the economy. It is often argued that firms are primarily concerned with factors in their own industrial markets, but large corporations generally use the fact that their sales are correlated to GNP in a known way in their own forecasting, although there is necessarily significant leeway for price and marketing strategies to influence market shares. We have seen that corporations maintain flexible long-term strategies and associated short-term expenditure programmes which are subject to revision in the light of circumstances. The evidence suggests that the major cause of such revisions is fluctuation in the business cycle. Therefore both investment and production programmes will be influenced by forecasts of overall GNP or its components. Similarly, firms will find it useful to know what kind of wage increase other firms are likely to be able to pay, and the general level at which agreements are likely to settle. Even if relative prices might vary more in the short term than overall prices, the average can still be of use because it gives an idea of orders of magnitude and there may be known correlations with particular prices of interests. Thus, certain information, less detailed than their own market forecasts, could be of value to firms. Our prime candidates in this category are macro-economic or sectoral forecasts, from which firms can proceed to calculate the general conditions likely to prevail in their own markets. The information may be almost as useful as detailed micro-economic projections because agents actually operate simultaneously over a wide range of products and markets.

However, we also need to show that private agents have a limited capacity to accurately forecast these variables for themselves, despite the fact that there exist major economies of scale in gathering and processing such information. In fact, private agents are generally very poorly placed to develop projections about all the key interdependences in the economy and the likely future economic climate, partly because firms are not primarily interested in such issues, and the complexity of the problems implies that it could be very difficult and expensive to construct the appropriate econometric models based on large data sets and expensive processing equipment. However, the main reason is that firms will not, in general, have access to suitable information about the economy as a whole, because their major source of information is their own markets, and they cannot have access to the required prior information about government policy objectives. The government is the largest single agent in the economy, affecting every market as well as possibly constraining or directing private choices and is therefore well situated for macro-forecasting. Whether or not it intends to determine the level of aggregate demand, it must still make decisions that will affect the general economic climate. Since the authorities do not generally act as optimizing agents on particular markets, they are in a sufficiently 'disinterested' position to gather and collate individual plans for a picture of the economic totality. Indeed, they need to collect much of this information for other purposes (such as to provide a basis for their interventionist policies). In short, they must have developed a 'strategic plan' for the state, however flexible and imprecise that may be, and this is a crucial input for any forecasts of key economic interdependences; only they can project the aggregate outcomes once their own policy decisions have been taken into account. Moreover, the economies of scale in collecting and processing data are particularly marked for information of this type. One has only to consider the strength of the few private forecasting agencies, who specialize in macro-economic forecasting, against the continued scarcity of detailed micro-economic projections. The economies of scale arise because the major costs of this activity result from the building of a robust model and setting up the data, after which additional projections on the basis of alternative assumptions are relatively cheap. Thus, forecasting key interdependences and the general economic climate could be difficult for private agents, but feasible for the government who could then reap the economies of scale.

An interesting analogy is provided by the role of the OECD in forecasting world macro-economic trends. OECD forecasters claim that by using modelling techniques that take into account the interdependences between the major economies of the world they can produce superior results to what are achieved by simply aggregating the results of separate one-country models, even though these may be vastly more complex. Llewellyn and Samuelson (1981) remark that this cannot be tested by the accuracy of the predictions, because one of the purposes of the approach is to highlight disequilibria and identify situations where the simultaneous development of existing trends everywhere would lead to an inconsistency such as incipient signs of every country moving into balance of payments deficit. They report that the OECD forecasters use an iterative procedure to eliminate some, but not all, of the most obvious inconsistencies. They do not always try to produce a set of balance of payments forecasts that add up to zero for the whole world if the situation is such as to imply that 'something has to give' without it being obvious what. The OECD see their forecasts in part as an indication of actions that may be needed by governments to avoid the situation being projected in the forecasts.

The use of pooling forecasts to identify what is *not* going to happen rather than what is going to happen suggests a way of using the rather vague corporate plans discussed above. The evidence does not support the view of Holland (1975) that such plans are firm enough to be integrated into a coherent realizable framework. However, when, as Holland points out, a very high percentage of output is produced by a very few firms, comparison and summation of tentative projections could possibly highlight potential inconsistencies, for example, between forecasts of financial flow and firms' investment expectations. John Helliwell observed to one of the authors that 'a firm may know where it is in relation to the next whirlpool but not which way the current is flowing'. Helliwell's own work forecasting Canadian energy demand also illustrates the great potential for the reassessment by outsiders of forecasts made by corporate bodies where these are large enough to affect the macro-economy and even government agencies. His individual efforts to forecast the Canadian energy market proved consistently better than those of the National Energy Board (*Canadian Business*, 1980). Apart from political motivations, Helliwell attributed this to the way forecasters within an organization may build up a single-minded corporate view (which all their colleagues will be supporting) and fail to examine alternative scenarios that an outsider with less detailed information might pick up.

To carry out this activity properly, the planning agency should be independent from the rest of the state sector as well as from individual firms. From this position, it could bring firms and the state together to discuss mutually beneficial contractual arrangements that might be otherwise overlooked. There is also scope for a limited amount of individualized bargaining between firms and the state where macro variables or government policies impinge in a particular way on certain firms. We suggest in Chapter 5 that the notion of planning agreements with some large firms does have a considerable rationale where the cost of long-term capital outlays reduces the value of the freedom of manoeuvre that we have stressed as essential to decision-making in most contexts.

Sensible indicative planning should not try to impose a unique view on decision makers but rather to collect information on expectations and intentions that in an ideal world would be pooled quite spontaneously but in practice is not. Energy policy provides an example. Common sense would suggest that it would be natural for the government to get together with the corporate planning divisions of the coal, gas, and electricity industries, all state-owned in the UK, in order to compare views on macro-economic developments, energy prices, and market shares. In France this takes place through the National Plan (but probably also elsewhere). In the UK, however, the various energy industries appear to have resisted attempts to coordinate their plans. Each corporation was quite good at estimating total energy demand but each consistently overestimated its own market share. Eventually the Science Policy Research Unit at Sussex University found itself bringing the relevant bodies together in the course of its research work. The information provided by pooling the flexible 'strategic plans', although imprecise, would be attuned to the real decision-making procedures in the economy. Even so, it is important to stress that agents should be free to do what they had otherwise intended despite the planners' activities.

The recent development in France of the 'projections detaillées glissantes' (see Chapter 5) whereby firms can place their own assumptions about the environmental paths into the planners' econometric models, represents a move toward this notion of indicative planning. Another example, relevant for the UK, is a voluntary incomes policy which explicitly excludes the imposition of wage norms or attempts to directly control firms' own wage settlements. Instead, employers and unions would exchange information about expected profitability and real wage expectations in a number of key sectors and firms, especially the public sector, to expose inconsistencies. It is hoped that this would better inform people than a money stock target by reducing the possibility of expectations which, while rational from the perspective of the model used by particular agents, are irrational from the viewpoint of the economy as a whole. Thus, if the government were operating a tight monetary policy, the planning procedure could be used to explain the implication for bargaining level units so that unions could learn the inconsistency of the expectations without the potentially high costs of strikes or successful pay claims, followed by bankruptcies or redundancies. There is reason to believe that the announcement of an incomes policy for the UK in July 1975 led to a sharp deceleration of price expectations after a lag of a month or two, whatever the long-term consequences (see Lund *et al.*, 1980). It is unlikely that this could have been achieved at this time by a series of independent changes of mind by agents, or the simple announcement of a change in the money stock target.

There are many problems with incomes policies, particularly of the short-term, distortional type generally used in practice. However, they are a prime candidate for inclusion in an indicative planning structure because inflationary expectations may be biased in the short term and can be 'improved' by the elimination of inconsistencies. This also highlights the limitations of the procedure that we are proposing, compared with say a Meade-type plan. There is no necessity for agents to alter their behaviour on the basis of the pooled information from the indicative plan, even if their expectations are self-evidently contradictory. The procedure should provide enough information for agents to avoid the most serious inconsistencies if they wish, but would contain no controls or imperatives. It may also not be obvious who has to change direction or how straight away. Although it should be in agents' interest to iron out contradictory expectations in the cheapest possible manner, this will not always be the case and the plans may therefore sometimes be ignored. The free market protagonist would argue that the government would always impose a wages policy in these circumstances, but this is not necessarily so. The authorities should also accept the limitations of indicative planning.

A further example of our proposed type of indicative planning would be the widespread circulation of information about new technology and the promotion of research and development. This is not to suggest that the government can identify which new technologies will prove to be more successful better than the private sector. However, firms may fail to examine all potentially profitable new ideas, and the government's information and experience may guide them to see possibilities that they might otherwise have overlooked. A government initiative to disseminate information about new technologies through an indicative planning framework could widen technological horizons. The state also has a comparative advantage in analysing the consequences for firms of new developments in world markets, especially those with whom firms do not yet do business. Such information naturally falls into the hands of the state, directly or indirectly, through such channels as the diplomatic service or representatives on international economic agencies. One small example was once reported in the *Sunday Times*.[6] Published trade statistics revealed to a firm that a particular product, for which it believed itself to be the world's lowest cost supplier, was being imported. It requested that the government reveal the name of the importer so it could offer a quotation to the buyer, but in vain. For all the weaknesses of French indicative planning, we suspect that the French bureaucracy would not withhold information of that sort! In fact, we shall see in Chapter 7 that projecting major international market developments became a key activity of French industrial policy and planning.

Dasgupta and Heal (1979, Ch. 14), point out that markets for depletable resources suffer acutely from these kinds of informational market failures. They suggest that the magnitude of the oil price increase in 1973 strongly indicates that prices were *either* too low before 1973 *or* too high afterwards but that one cannot know which; it is not possible to know the appropriate policy response. An Austrian would reply that no policy response is required, not even this limited proposal of more government action to collect and disseminate information. It is inevitable, in the Austrian view, that unexpected shocks will hit the world and face entrepreneurs with new challenges. The fact that government agencies did not form any better views about future energy prices before 1973 cautions against any attempt to foster collective judgements in this area. But the government may be in a position to gain access to and circulate multiple views of the future, other than the currently fashionable ones.[7] It is also well-placed to gather intelligence on international developments, and to examine alternative forecasts for consistency. There is a modest case for supposing that private firms cannot internalize all the benefits of information-gathering activities in natural resource related fields, which may be true generally in speculative markets, and hence publicly sponsored research is desirable. The planners will not always end up knowing better than anyone else, but they may be able to add to others' knowledge.

Finally, there is strong appeal in the current situation for the

notion of a government trying to 'pick winners' for future production. It is not obviously in the best position to do this; firms have
better knowledge about their own markets. However, from the
vast span of its domestic and international activities, it may have
different, if not additional, information which could be usefully
passed on to the private sector. An inconsistency discovered in a
search through firms' strategic plans could also point the way to
hitherto unexploited profitable opportunities. The planners should
not be coercive in this regard, but if there are really suitable prospects which have been overlooked, once they have been spotted
one can rely on private initiative to fill the gaps.

We therefore envisage a less ambitious type of planning than did
Massé or Meade. Plans would not supply detailed information
about every good in every conceivable circumstance, but concentrate on leading indicators. These would be largely macro-
economic variables, but governments' and firms' imprecise information about the future would also be pooled over particular markets to highlight expectational inconsistencies and broaden opportunity sets. Obvious places for such activities include energy markets, research and development, and wage determination, and the
reader can rapidly add to this list further examples of this type.
This may appear to be a limited response to the allocative problems arising from uncertainty, but it is likely to be the best that one
could hope to achieve; one can only pool information of a form
that is actually available. On the other hand, free market protagon-
ists are wrong to use the inevitability of some ignorance as an
excuse for not designing mechanisms to transmit as much information as can be actually generated.

Planning for the State Sector

We have seen how indicative planning could improve on the spontaneous interactions of private agents on markets. We conclude
our discussion by extending the argument to cover public sector
decision-making imperfections. Charles Lindblom (1977) has suggested that the political process is a communication mechanism
broadly akin to an informationally imperfect market system in
allocating non-marketed goods. From this perspective, the arguments of the previous sections suggest that planners' activities
should include public goods as well as private ones, and improve
the functioning of government as well as market. We lead into the
discussion by considering how the authorities should determine
the provision of public goods.

Public finance economists have long been concerned with how

to induce people to reveal their true preferences for public goods. Those who are asked for their evaluation have an incentive to understate it in order to pay a lower share of the costs, the 'free rider' problem, which leads to underprovision. More recent empirical critiques focus on the possibility of over-provision for political reasons (see Buchanan and Flowers, 1979) while theoretical work has devised ingenious incentive formulas to elicit true preferences (see Tideman and Tullock, 1976).[8] It is interesting to see whether indicative planning could make a contribution to this problem. The planners would certainly have nothing to offer in an Arrow–Debreu world. Complex referenda could be held on every social choice, with each voter honestly expressing his preferences through a revaluation mechanism along the lines of Tideman and Tullock (1976). But informational imperfections prevent such an outcome; it would be prohibitively expensive to canvass every opinion on all local or national projects and people could not calculate how much they should offer to pay. Apart from the incentives to cheat, there is no reason for the public to expend a major effort to calculate true valuations for a variety of contingencies if they do not expect their votes to end up being influential.

This generates a need for a political process. Widespread consultation has been canvassed as a way of determining the appropriate scale and form of public good provision, and, more generally, representative democracy has a certain degree of practical second best efficiency to it when public decisions involve complex uncertainties and interdependences. Citizens elect political leaders upon whom they endow considerable discretion, but they also join specialized pressure groups to represent their particular interests when these are at stake. The voter has a vague idea of the menu from which each party will choose its public goods, though not the actual choices; a vote reflects preferences about who they would want to make choices. The government has a wide range of choices it could make while continuing to satisfy its voters, so politicians can exercise considerable influence by choosing the actions they most want from the list of acceptable options. Shareholders elect company boards for the same reasons, and permit a similar degree of operational leeway (see King, 1977). Yet the government needs to know the bounds of the acceptable, and cannot consult each voter separately on each issue so it contacts 'pressure groups', representative of a particular set of voters with respect to certain of their interests, who concentrate full time on processing and reacting to information on that topic. Citizens may join numerous such groups, ranging from charities and social organizations to business lobbies and trade unions. It is economies of scale in information processing which permit this diversification and specialization of the political process, with electors choosing certain people to oversee their general interests but others to concentrate on specific topics such as the provision of certain types of public goods. Consultative democracy is the interface between the two.

Lindblom has written extensively on this subject, arguing that the democratic process should explicitly incorporate some form of consultative planning and that this occurs naturally. We agree with the first proposition but not the second; a specific planning body may be needed to facilitate contacts. Members of consultative groups, politicians, and others already act as part of a broadly conceived 'planning' system, exchanging information to co-ordinate public actions and citizens' wants, but the exchange may be inadequate.

Lindblom's first argument is based on the belief that it is impossible for governments to make 'rational' choices. The public sector is enormously complex internally so no one body can acquire a comprehensive understanding of any issue; not all alternatives can be compared and there are no adequate choice criteria. In consequence, he supports 'methods of policy-making different from those endorsed by those who believe policy-making can be conventionally rational' (Lindblom, 1975, p. 24). He has in mind an osmotic process of discussion and information exchange.

Lindblom's perception of public decision-making is similar to Simon's description of private choices. Informational imperfections argue against the adoption of detailed long-term plans, but in favour of a 'strategic' flexible exercise to consider a number of possible ways to react in the face of unforeseen circumstances. One notes a similarity to observed corporate behaviour here. Lindblom gives the example of a fire drill for a ship, when one should not assign everyone to an assembly point on the assumption that people will be in particular places when an emergency strikes, but rather that no one will be where he is expected to be. The plan should not comprise a series of advanced decisions that will subsequently be overturned but a procedure for reacting sensibly to the likely possibility that current forecasts are wrong.

From this perspective, all consultative procedures can be seen as a form of planning. The authorities will not be able to find good solutions without such interactions, which invite the relevant interest groups to highlight the simultaneous interdependences of policy areas. According to Lindblom's theory of 'disjointed incrementalism', errors will not be eliminated by intensive effort as we go along but by being identified by concerned bodies through reaction and adaption. A coherent outcome should emerge spontaneously.

Lindblom also suggests that a broad process of 'fair' consultation should replace any attempt to aggregate individual preferences in formulating the state's 'strategic' plans.[9] In the absence of a social welfare function, consultative planning has a legitimizing role. A government may be better able to secure acceptance for a programme that emerges from an independent planning agency which developed it as a result of attempts to form a consensus on policy options. Thus, Lindblom's communication mechanism leads to a trial and error process generating efficient solutions by testing them for their acceptability to all parties until commonly approved outcomes emerge.

Lindblom is surely right to stress the importance of such consultative interactions, but he greatly overstates the spontaneity of their occurrence. He himself acknowledges as a counter-example that the strength of the Maginot line across the German border of France did not automatically bring about matching fortifications along the Belgian frontier. Similarly, the identification of the 'Macmillan Gap' in 1931, a lack of financial institutions catering to small and medium-sized British businesses that wanted to grow quickly, did not lead to any full solution by the 1980s. The number of examples can be extended at will. Special institutions, such as a planning body, may be necessary. This should not surprise readers since Lindblom is in the tradition of pluralist writers, and his description of the political process determining public decisions is analogous to the market mechanism as a method of co-ordinating private choices in an informationally imperfect world. Thus we do not have to repeat the arguments; the case for planning as a co-ordination device, which has already been made as an answer to private market failure, can also be made for government failure.[10]

Indicative planning for the public sector should play an equivalent role to that previously envisaged for the private sector: a mechanism to organize communication and discussion which would have a high social payoff but would not necessarily take place spontaneously. It should identify those sections of the frontier along which the Maginot line is not being extended. Costs mean that the planners cannot facilitate an infinite number of such meetings, but must focus on those contacts which seem most important. An obvious example for the UK could be employers, unions, and government who at the moment only meet to discuss macro-policy and respective reactions at the NEDC. We will show in the following chapters that 'Le Plan' did provide to some extent the forum for such discussions in France. However, such an activity would not improve decisions in the non-market sector if the government thinks it knows what it wants with certainty, and would take the same decisions regardless of the view of organizations not directly represented in the administration. Both Britain and France did have governments of this sort in the late 1970s and early 1980s, which must be a factor in the demise of the consultative element of French planning in recent years. Certain disadvantages of the resulting policies lend support to the case for our form of indicative planning.

Notes

1   This may explain why firms pay management consultants to provide an outside perspective on their businesses. However, they still have no way of knowing in advance which consultant will be of the most value to them.
2   Dasgupta and Heal (1979) discuss the problems raised by these issues for the efficient working of exhaustible resource markets. They point out the danger of assuming that the market can deal adequately with 'unthought of' possibilities, such as sudden technological or environmental changes.
3   See, for example, Wilson (1975) on the issue of informational economies of scale. One reason why the Austrians reject the potential for planning is that they deny the possibility of increasing returns to information processing.
4   For example, the monthly bulletins of Phillips and Drew, and Greenwells, both stockbroking firms.
5   In February 1980 in Vancouver.
6   Date unknown.
7   Dr Lesley Cook has pointed out to us that, in the 1960s, the UK government was being advised of the impending scarcity of oil by the Coal Board's economic adviser, the late E. F. Schumacher, but it chose to ignore him.
8   Miller (1980) investigates whether such procedures could be used to support an indicative plan.
9   Heal (1973) discusses the problems of aggregating individual preferences in the planning context.
10 In correspondence Professor Lindblom has stressed that, for him, the most important part of strategic planning is the adaptation of the type of analysis that takes place to the requirements of the interaction process.

Part Two

The Practice of French Planning

Introduction

The rest of the book is devoted to the French experience with
indicative planning. We will focus on developments since 1970,
and particularly since 1975, because there already exists a large
literature on the planners' activities prior to that time, though it
will sometimes be necessary to refer to or reinterpret the earlier
period. We commence with a historical and quantitative history of
the procedure since its inception, which sets the stage for the
remainder of the study and introduces some measure of the problems. Chapter 4 is our introduction to contemporary planning,
surveying in detail the institutional setting and the numerous facets
of the planners' activities. The following chapters each focus on
developments in one of the three most important elements of the
exercise: macro-economics, the public sector, and industrial policy. The final chapter outlines the conclusions of the study.

We do not merely wish to describe what happened to French
planning, a dismal chronicle of declining relevance and scope, but
also to explain why it occurred in order to draw lessons for the
practice of planning in developed Western economies. Our first
task is to show the nature of the decline, and establish that no
other central body actually assumed the planners' role. The latter
point is important since, if another apparatus simply undertook
central co-ordination, the events of the 1970s merely reflect a
reorganization within the state sector, and leave the potential for
planning untarnished. In fact, recent experience brings into question the very practicability of the whole exercise, a question of
current relevance given the intentions of the Socialist administration in France. Thus, in the following chapters we must discover
whether French planning declined because the procedure itself is
valueless, because the French were doing it badly, or because the
government chose not to avail itself of the information provided.
The following pages suggest that the latter two factors, and in
recent years particularly the last, predominated. Overall, the
French experience does not offer a practical counter-example to
the form of planning proposed in Chapter 2.

3 French Planning: A Quantitative History and Evaluation

Introduction

This chapter traces the history of French planning from its inception in 1946 up to 1981, and attempts to assess numerically the usefulness of the whole exercise.[1] It describes the orientation of each plan and the major circumstances and events which the planners have had to face,[2] and offers a quantitative history and evaluation of the procedure.

The numerical complement to the historical material is introduced in the third section with a discussion of the methodological issues, and in part merely reviews the record of plan implementation at the aggregate level. However, theory suggests that it is the plan forecasts that will affect resource allocation, so the numbers should also indicate how well the planners were doing their job. But even perfectly accurate plan forecasts would have no economic impact if everyone knew precisely what was going to happen, which leads us to undertake a series of further assessment exercises.[3] We search for systematic tendencies in the aggregate forecasting errors over time, and compare plan forecasts and outcomes to see whether the planners actually spotted important changes. Finally, we compare plan forecasts and outcomes against various estimates of what people might reasonably have expected at that time, to calculate the *additional* information embodied in the plans. To this end, we construct a series of figures which we call 'Alternative Forecasts' to represent the way a firm might have projected variables forward in the medium term if it had been equipped with past data but no model of the interdependences in the economy such as the planners tried to devise (albeit informally in the early years). In the final section we test the hypothesis from the demand expectations literature that French planning would have increased and stabilized the French rate of growth. The simple implementation ratios do not indicate a major change in the planners' performance over time, but the more sophisticated exercises suggest that little or no useful information was transmitted to private agents after 1965. The following chapters will discuss the reasons for this (particularly Chapter 5), but the fact remains that the planners' poor forecasting record was one element in the overall decline of the procedure in recent years.

A History of Planning, 1946–81

One can distinguish four relatively distinct phases of planning in France: reconstruction (1946–53), the heyday of French planning (1953–65), the beginning of the decline (1965–75) and the decline (1975–81). It seems likely that the electoral victory of the Socialists in 1981 will herald a new and happier phase in the next few years. These groupings describe the impact that planning had on the French economy, rather than the actual techniques or content of the plans. For example, although the objectives and scope of the procedure changed significantly in 1961, from the point of view of assessment the IVth Plan belongs with the relatively successful IInd and IIIrd Plans. This material is complemented by the detailed numerical history in the fourth section.

Reconstruction, 1946–53
This was the period of Monnet's Ist Plan, the central theme of which was the reconstruction of the war-torn economy. Indeed, it was subtitled 'Modernisation ou Décadence'. Following the stagnation of the 1930s and the severe destruction of the war years, the planners described the 'national consensus' to rebuild the productive base as the 'only favourable factor' in reconstruction (Ist Plan, 1946). The plan took the form of production programmes with associated investment requirements for six 'basic sectors' of the economy – coal, electricity, steel, cement, agricultural machinery, and transportation. It set objectives for the levels of investment and growth in these sectors, drawn up in physical terms, and these were to be largely financed with public funds, approximately half of which were the counterpart of US aid through the Marshall Plan after 1948. It was hoped that this reconstruction would sustain improved living standards, a reduced balance of payments deficit, and full employment. However, the Ist Plan was just a series of detailed investment programmes for rebuilding the heavy industrial sectors (some of which were state-owned) and contained no significant macro-economic or social elements. The plan was extended to run until 1953 rather than the initial 1950, when earlier targets were changed and additional sectors added (fuels and fertilisers) to meet altered circumstances.

Because the Ist Plan was more akin to central than indicative planning, one would not want to assess it in the same way as the later plans, so the limited material available will be discussed at

Table 3.1 The Development of the 'Basic' Sectors of the Ist Plan

Sector	Units	Production				Plan target
		1929	1938	1949	1953	1952/3
Coal	m.tons	55	47.6	49.3	55.1	60
Electricity	m.kW	15.6	20.8	23	41.3	43
Oil Fuel	m.tons refined	0	7	2.8	22	18.7
Steel	m.tons	9.7	6.2	4.4	10	12.5
Cement	m.tons	6.2	3.6	3.4	8.7	8.5
Tractors	000's	20	30	50	230	200
Nitrogenous fertilizers	th.tons	73	177	127	273	300
Railways	b.ton-k	41.8	26.5	41.2	40.4	—

Source: CGP, the IInd Plan.

this point. There was satisfaction with those indicators of development that could be measured over the period (there was no proper national accounting system in this period): an increase in real per capita income from $482 in 1949 to $524 in 1951, and a 500 per cent increase in exports in 1946–53, during which period imports fell. However, as Table 3.1 shows, achievements were more patchy in the 'basic sectors'. Output reached the 1929 level in every sector except the railways, but the plan targets were only realized in fuels and tractors. However, the general impression remained that the Ist Plan was very effective in channelling the necessary funds to the crucial sectors for reconstruction, and the table does reveal rapid development between 1946 and 1953. Indeed, Sheahan (1963) suggests that the plan may have been so effective that the basic sectors were overdeveloped, at the expense of the rest of manufacturing industry.

The Heyday of French Planning, 1953–65

[The IInd and IIIrd Plans (1953–57 and 1957–61) cover the period when the planners are considered to have widely affected public and private sector expectations in favour of modernization, expansion, and international trade.] The process operated largely through the 'Modernization Commissions' (see Chapter 4), and was, for the most part, restricted to the objective of raising industrial production and investment. The IVth Plan (1961–65) saw a major extension in the scope and sophistication of the procedure, with an attempt to describe medium-term government objectives in both the economic and social spheres. We will see in Chapter 4 that the planners saw themselves as writing a coherent manifesto of the government's economic and social objectives at that time, as well as detailing the actions that would be required for their attainment.

The IInd and IIIrd Plans remained primarily concerned with industry, but cast their net somewhat wider than the original 'basic sectors', promoting modernization and growth across the entire economy through 'basic actions' in the IInd Plan and 'imperative tasks' in the IIIrd. The 'basic actions' were a series of reforms to raise productivity and reduce costs by inducing the industrial sector to re-equip; the most important programmes concerned modernizing the capital stock, research and development, labour training, and disseminating new marketing techniques. The 'imperative tasks' of the IIIrd Plan were to ensure a stable balance of payments equilibrium through the planners' stock-in-trade of increased investment, productivity, and efficiency, which were intended to reduce import dependence and improve international competitiveness. These plans did not have the detailed operational significance of the Ist, but the planners and their allies in the public administration are widely credited with imbuing a new spirit of rationalization and expansion across the entire economy (see Shonfield, 1965; Carré *et al.*, 1975).

The IInd Plan operated through a period of weak central government, at least in so far as economic affairs were concerned. The short-lived administrations in the last years of the Fourth Republic were preoccupied with foreign affairs and colonial wars, and it was probably the planners who were instrumental in persuading people, in business, government, and the civil service, that French growth could continue beyond the postwar boom, rather than reverting to the stagnation of the interwar years. Although, as we shall see below, the actual plan forecasts were relatively inaccurate, this does not influence our somewhat favourable assessment of the procedure because the available data and techniques probably meant that the main impact of the procedure could not have come from the detailed targets and projections at this time. In fact, although the plan targets were relatively ambitious by historical standards (for example, GDP was targeted to increase at 25 per cent over the four years, and industrial production by 25–30 per cent; see Tables 3.2 and 3.3 below), the IInd Plan was generally more successful than anticipated in every variable except imports, which had very serious consequences for the balance of payments by the end of the period. Imports, which had been expected to remain constant, rose by 50 per cent over the period, and their coverage by exports fell from 87 per cent in 1954 to 71 per cent in 1957.

The authorities chose to support this very fast pace of development, and allowed the foreign exchange reserves to become depleted to virtually zero by the end of the plan period (Kindleberger, 1967). Although industrial development was very fast (around 45 per cent over the period), to quote MacLennan it was 'a case study in unbalanced growth rather than planned development' (MacLennan, 1963, p. 335). Sectors such as the motor industry, the chemical industry, and housing drastically overshot their targets causing bottlenecks in construction, labour, and particularly capital goods, which were eased by imports. The planners were doubtless partly responsible for this rapid general expansion, although the private sector developed according to the market rather than planners' dictates. However, by the end of the plan period there was a large balance of payments deficit and a 7 per cent inflation rate.

The IIIrd Plan focused on a gradual correction of the balance of payments problem over the following six years. To that end, domestic growth was targeted below that attained in the IInd Plan, with the intention of reducing import dependence and stimulating exports by cutting supply bottlenecks and improving domestic efficiency through further investment. MacLennan (1963) described it as a 'planned variant of the "stop and go" policies' (p. 337) employed at the same time in the UK. In fact, the original plan did not survive the political crisis leading to the demise of the Fourth Republic and the inception of the Fifth under de Gaulle in 1958. The vigorous new government sought to end the balance of payments problem immediately, rather than over the plan period, through the Rueff programme of devaluation and deflation which corrected the balance of trade in nine months at the expense of a major recession. Once the stage had been set again for growth, the planners were invited to participate through an 'Interim Plan' adopted for 1960–61, which sought and achieved a relatively rapid pace of development. The political uncertainties over this period, and the way that the planned path was ignored in the search for short-run equilibrium in 1958–59, limited the value of detailed plan targets. However, the literature attests that the planners continued to be influential in encouraging the cumulative structural changes over the period, which resulted in industrialists moving into export markets and expanding the domestic production of traditionally imported goods.

The French economy was relatively advanced and open by the early 1960s, which meant that the government and private sector had less need for the planners' general exhortations for investment, expansion, and trade. Moreover, the crude material balance-type projections were becoming increasingly inappropriate, even as a point of reference in Modernization Commissions, because they ignored the components of supply and demand coming from outside the economy and the effects of inflation. Finally, there existed a strong and active central government, determined to maintain whatever it perceived to be in the French national interest. The planners reacted in the IVth Plan with a major change in emphasis and scope, the objective being to encapsulate a detailed and consistent picture of French economic and, for the first time, social development by the end of the plan horizon, which would be the agreed basis for government policies and private decisions.

There were all the normal themes of expansion and international competitiveness, with Modernization Commissions covering every sector and a systematic attempt at intersectoral consistency – 'coherence' – through the Horizontal Commissions, as well as consideration of general problems such as the employment creation required to maintain full employment as the post-war baby boom entered the labour market. There was also a commitment to increasing the share of social infrastructure investment in GDP. Finally, the plan selected six sectors for particular expansion (household electronics, building, public works, telecommunications, steel, and chemicals), and proposed modernizing the energy sector.

In practice, the IVth Plan quickly ran into trouble with the unexpected repatriation of refugees from Algeria, and an inflationary and balance of payments crisis, in 1963. The government followed the conservative advice of the Ministry of Finance, headed by Giscard d'Estaing, in introducing a deflationary package: the 'Stabilization Plan' of 1963. Although the government's deflationary policies ran against the overall growth strategy, Carré *et al.* (1975) note that the Stabilization Plan conceded a major point to the planners by safeguarding certain key investment projects. Growth continued to be very rapid over the plan period as a whole, and the domestic aggregate forecasts proved to be very accurate, although the growth of trade, and particularly imports, was again underestimated. Although industrial targets were generally met, there were some problems in the priority sectors, a shortfall of investment for the productive sector as a whole, supply constraints in agriculture, food, steel, and electronics, and major overspending in the public sector. However, despite any misgivings about details, the IVth Plan did represent a high point for French planning, not only because its forecasts were very accurate, but because the planners were actually being allowed to perform the useful task of providing coherent information to decision makers about the medium term.

The Beginning of the Decline, 1965–75

We have discussed the difficulties that can emerge for Meade-type indicative planning when costs constrain the procedure from providing the multitude of forecasts, commodity by commodity and contingency by contingency, that would be needed, and rationality is bounded. Although the French never really attempted anything so specific, the planners did not have the techniques to accurately project the normal progression of the economy in the late 1960s, let alone deal with those events, often with profound economic consequences, that could not be predicted with even the most sophisticated econometric techniques. The 'events' of May 1968 and the oil price crises of 1973 fall into this category, and undermined the basis of the Vth and VIth Plans, respectively (1965–70 and 1970–75). (The repatriation of Algerian refugees in 1963 also falls into this category, but it did not entirely wreck the IVth Plan.) The planners could neither predict these events nor the government's responses to them, and faced an increasing credibility problem with decision makers who wished to remain flexible in the face of unforeseen possibilities.

The Vth Plan sought explicitly to realize Massé's notion of generalized market research (see Chapter 1). It was oriented to the maintenance of international competitiveness ('in pursuance of National Independence') and contained a 5 per cent growth target, generally accepted to be below physical capacity (though above the government's original wishes – see Chapters 4 and 5) so that labour market slack could reduce inflationary pressures. The plan emphasized aggregate goals, denominated in money terms for the first time – price stability, balance of payments equilibrium, and employment – with no normative significance attached to physical output in particular industries. The focus on equilibrium in aggregate financial balances – GDP, investment and savings, foreign exchange, and prices and incomes – led the planners to pay rather more attention to macro-economic policies. Thus, inflation was to be controlled by demand management rather than the planners' more traditional method of inducing structural changes at a micro-economic level. The aggregate objectives presupposed effective counter-inflationary measures (including an incomes policy) and there were targets for wages, incomes, and for the distribution of growth over the period between consumption, investment, public expenditure, and trade. To ensure that short-term stabilization policy would be co-ordinated with the plan, a system of indicators for the macro-economic variables was developed, to alert the Ministry of Finance as to when appropriate measures should be introduced (for further details of this 'clignotants' system, see Chapter 5).

The economy proceeded approximately along the planned course, although with rather more unemployment and less social expenditure than forecast, until the 'events' of May 1968 led the government to abandon its medium-term strategy. The authorities responded to this social unrest by cutting public expenditure in a crisis budget, and devaluing in 1969 to solve the balance of payments problems arising from the renewed growth. This spurt in the last years of the period led GDP to exceed its target, but the plan proved to be quite wrong about the structure of development. In particular, full employment was not maintained, the inflation rate far exceeded expectations (4.4 per cent as against the 'norm' of 1.5 per cent) and public expenditure fell well below target.

The VIth Plan, introduced under President Pompidou, sought very rapid expansion with the overwhelming emphasis on industrial expansion: the 'Impératif Industriel'. The objectives were actually similar to those of the Vth – balance of payments equilibrium, the control of inflation, and full employment – but these were to be attained by providing industrialists with 'supply-side' policies 'to create a favourable environment for industry' (VIth Plan), rather than through the strategy of restricting demand which had been followed previously. The industrial sector was projected to grow faster than ever before (at 7.5 per cent per annum), supported by policies to ease the flow of capital and skilled labour, construct social infrastructure to aid production, and support research and development. The growth of the private and public service sectors was to be restricted 'as a counterpart to this mobilization of resources in favour of industry' (VIth Plan), but private consumption was to grow relatively quickly to provide a strong domestic market for French suppliers. However, the entire strategy had to be abandoned in the face of the quadrupling of oil prices in 1973, when the Western world entered a major recession. In fact, industrial production declined by 10 per cent in 1974, unemployment exceeded one million by 1975, and inflation reached new peaks by the end of the plan period. Following Pompidou's death in 1973, the Presidency was assumed by Giscard d'Estaing, who had been Finance Minister for most of the period since 1961.

Decline, 1975–81

The VIIth Plan (1975–80) had three objectives in the face of severe recession: the restoration of full employment, and also balance of payments equilibrium, and the control of inflation. The emphasis was almost entirely on macro-economic variables. The plan projected a return to full employment based on an upsurge in private investment and exports, but did not specify any policies for the attainment of its economic objectives (for further details, see Chapter 5). In fact, neither world trade nor private investment did pick up sufficiently for the attainment of the plan targets, and M. Barre, who became Prime Minister in 1976, entirely oriented his policies to control inflation and improve the balance of payments, introducing the deflationary 'Plan Barre' in 1976. The general problems to which the VIIth Plan had been directed persisted until 1980, with unemployment reaching 1.45 million, and an inflation rate of 13.6 per cent, though economic growth climbed back above 3 per cent until the 'Second Oil Crisis' of 1979.

The VIIIth Plan saw a revivial of the aggressive industrial imperative of the VIth Plan, based on the development of high technology sectors. This was seen as the best form of defence against what the French perceived as the extreme vulnerability of their economy in the changed world markets after the rise of OPEC, and with increased international competition from both the less developed countries over basic industrial products, and West Germany and America over high technology goods. The election victory of the Socialists in May and June 1981 meant that the VIIIth Plan was abandoned. President Mitterand's government is committed to planning and the 1980s may see a new, and more positive, phase for the procedure.

Interpreting the Numbers

The following sections offer both descriptive statistics on plan implementation and various attempts to assess the actual impact of the procedure between 1952 and 1980. Indicative planning operates through its forecasts so evaluation must be based on some measure of forecasting accuracy and we start by considering aggregate forecast–outcome ratios on the lines of Cohen (1969), Lutz (1969), and Carré *et al.* (1975). However, Massé (1965) has correctly pointed out that it is misleading to draw strong conclusions from plan 'implementation rates' because the impact of the procedure can be felt in a number of ways. Overfulfilment can either be interpreted as the plans having been successful in building confidence, or misleading by creating pessimism. Underfulfilment may also be given a positive interpretation; as in the Soviet Union an impossibly 'taut' plan may still have encouraged greater efforts than otherwise would have occurred. Moreover, in the early years at least, French plans were supposed to embody a programme of government actions to bring about the desired outcome, so the figures cannot be treated as simple projections of the equilibrium growth path.

To sort out the true worth of a plan, as opposed to its accuracy, we would have to construct a model of the entire economy and simulate development with and without plans, but this requires us to know in advance how expectations and the planning system affect the economy. Instead we undertake a series of rather more limited exercises on aggregate data. We study the planners' record over a long time span for systematic errors, and therefore evidence of incompetence. We also develop relative measures of forecasting accuracy, comparing plan forecasts and outcomes with previous long-run trends to see if important changes were foreseen, and with 'Alternative Forecasts' to see if additional information was provided. The disaggregated data are not considered because we have nothing to add to the findings reported in Estrin and Holmes (1980).[4] Since we establish that French planners were successful to some degree on all counts, at least in the early years, we also examine the relative pace and stability of French growth since this is where a demand expectations theorist would expect to observe the impact of the procedure.

The Alternative Forecasts are estimates of the predictions which might have been made at the time each plan was published by an intelligent French market researcher operating without the benefit of a complete macro-economic model.[5] They are derived from an equation estimated for each variable on annual pre-plan period data, and constructed by projecting forward for the duration of the plan. One chooses the equation for each variable separately from a wide class of extrapolative procedures to best describe the movements in each variable prior to the commencement of each plan period. They are estimated equation by equation, rather than from any full behavioural model, because they are intended to represent the sort of projections French decision makers could have developed and used for themselves in the absence of planning. Costs probably inhibited the widespread use of forecasts from sophisticated macro-econometric models, especially in the early years of planning before computers became available, and in fact there has been virtually no independent macro-economic forecasting in France until recently (see Chapter 5). It may also be said that since our assessment concentrates on aggregate data, it excludes the plan information in which firms would be most interested, concerning their own markets. But we have argued that the overall strength of demand is one of the most important factors in private decision-making, with corporate planning often working down from the aggregate forecast to the implications in specific markets. Estrin and Holmes (1980) report that, although the planners did pick up some important additional information at the macro-economic level, this success was not mirrored in the industrial forecasts. These points may explain Carré *et al*.'s observation (1975, Table 14.4) that businessmen's knowledge of the plan forecasts declined with the level of disaggregation of the projections. Thus, our assessment exercises concentrate on important information for decision makers.

Finally, it must be noted that we cannot distinguish between forecasting performance and the effects of planning on development. The plan forecasts were, in part, targets to be achieved by means of state involvement so accuracy must reflect forecasting ability, including over the self-fulfillment effects and the non-informational policy effectiveness of the plan package. The Alternative Forecasts are a guide to what people could have expected to happen in the absence of the information and direct impact of the plan. However well the planners perform relative to the Alternative Forecasts, one can never distinguish the separate effects of these three elements from the data alone, although one may hold independent views on this point. But despite this limitation our criteria can still serve a purpose. We know the planners achieved *something* in the IVth Plan, without knowing to what extent they merely scented in advance the increase in productivity growth or actively brought it about by their intervention. Similarly the anticipated slow-down in growth during the Vth Plan was incorrectly anticipated, whether it was a pure forecast, a pure target, or perhaps the 'natural' equilibrium of the economy which needed intervention to bring it about. The relative accuracy criterion indicates whether a plan had an economic impact without identifying the nature of its effects.

An Assessment of Macro-Economic Forecasts, 1952–80

There have been numerous changes in the definitions of variables since 1946, not least because the French system of National Accounting was only established for the IVth Plan, and was altered in 1976 to conform with UN standards (see Flouzat, 1975). This caused serious problems in constructing the series presented below,[6] and since we have aimed for consistency between forecast and outcome for each individual variable, the tables reproduced may differ from those used by other authors for the early years (e.g. Cohen, 1969).

Forecasts and Outcomes
Table 3.2 presents plan forecasts, outcomes, and implementation rates (percentage outcome over forecast) for GDP,[7] its four main components, and subdivisions of Consumption and Gross Fixed

Table 3.2 Plan Forecasts and Outcomes: Levels

	1953–57 IInd Plan	1957–61 IIIrd Plan	1960–61 Interim Plan	1961–65 IVth Plan	1965–70 Vth Plan	1970–75 VIth Plan	1975–80[c] VIIth Plan
GDP							
Forecast	124[a]	121	108.7	123.9	127.6	133.2	128.8[b]
Outcome	128.9	119.4	112.9	127.6	132.6	120.4[b]	116.4[b]
% Implementation	104	98.7	103.9	103.0	103.9	90.4	90.4
Imports							
Forecast	102[a]	107.9	106.9	123	152.5	159.6	174.4
Outcome	150[a]	118.6	126.6	165.7	180.9	137.6	158.3
% Implementation	147	110	119.4	134.7	118.6	86.2	89.8
Exports							
Forecast	121[a]	127.1	120.7	120	153.2	164.7	176.2
Outcome	141[a]	150	124.7	130.2	171.5	150.6	141.4
% Implementation	116.5	118.0	103.3	108.5	111.9	91.4	80.2
Consumption							
(a) By household							
Forecast		118.7	106.7	122.5[c]	124.6	130	125.8
Outcome		114.8	111.3	126.7	127	124.9	120.6
% Implementation		96.7	104.3	103.4	101.9	96.1	95.9
(b) By administration							
Forecast		109.5	106.5	122[c]	139.6	117.6	110.4
Outcome		106.6	106.3	135.7	124.2	117.3	117.0
% Implementation		97.4	99.8	111.2	89.0	99.7	106.0

(c) Total						
Forecast	122[a]	109.9	123	125.4	129.5	122.3
Outcome	133[a]	118.0	127.2	127	124.1	119.8
% Implementation	109	107.4	103.4	101.3	95.8	98.0
GFCF						
Household						
Forecast	139[a]	111	125	114.2	124	
Outcome			155.1	131	133.5	
% Implementation			124.1	114.7	107.7	
Firm						
Forecast	150[a]	120[a]	128	132.5	137.7	
Outcome		128.8	132.7	150	112	
% Implementation		107.3	103.7	113.2	81.3	
Administration						
Forecast	143[a]	127[a]	150	148.3	144.2	
Outcome		131.5	167.8	144.5	145.6	
% Implementation		103.5	119.8	97.4	101.0	
Total						
Forecast	124[a]	121.8	130	129.2	136.4	133.2
Outcome	147[a]	123.7	142.3	143.2	118.4	113.3
% Implementation	118.5	101.6	109.5	110.8	86.8	85.1

[a] Figures from Carré et al. (1975).
[b] Figures for Le PIB.
[c] Figures from OECD, *France* (Country Surveys).

Table 3.3 Plan Forecasts and Outcomes: Annual Rates of Growth

	1953–57 IInd Plan	1957–61 IIIrd Plan	1960–61 Interim Plan	1961–65 IVth Plan	1965–70 Vth Plan	1970–75 VIth Plan	1975–80 VIIth Plan
GDP							
Forecast	4.4	4.9	4.26	5.5	5.0	5.9	5.2
Outcome	5.21	4.53	6.25	6.28	5.8	3.78	3.08
Imports							
Forecast	0.40	1.92	3.4	5.31	8.8	9.8	11.9
Outcome	8.45	4.36	12.52	13.46	12.59	6.59	9.62
Exports							
Forecast	3.89	6.18	9.86	4.66	8.9	10.5	12.0
Outcome	7.11	10.67	11.67	6.82	11.39	8.53	7.17
Consumption							
(a) *By household*							
Forecast		4.4	3.3	5.2	4.5	5.4	4.7
Outcome	5.04	3.51	5.5	6.09	4.9	4.55	3.81

(b) By administration							
Forecast	3.73	2.29	3.2	5.1	6.9	3.3	2.0
Outcome		1.16	3.1	7.93	4.43	3.24	3.19
(c) Total							
Forecast	4.06			5.31	4.63	5.3	4.1
Outcome	5.87			6.2	4.9	4.41	3.68
GFCF							
Household							
Forecast	6.81	2.64	3.9	5.74	2.7	4.4	
Outcome				11.6	5.55	5.95	
Firms							
Forecast	8.45	4.66		6.37	5.79	6.6	
Outcome		6.53		7.33	8.45	2.29	
Administration							
Forecast	7.42	6.16	7.9	10.67	8.2	7.6	
Outcome		7.09		13.81	7.64	7.8	
Total							
Forecast	4.4	5.05	4.83	6.78	5.26	6.4	5.9
Outcome	8.01	5.46	8.63	9.22	7.42	3.44	2.53

Capital Formation (GFCF) since 1952. Table 3.3 provides the forecasts and outcomes as compound annual rates of growth to avoid any confusion which might arise because the plans are of unequal length.[8] However, it could be potentially misleading to evaluate accuracy using only implementation rates for forecasts denominated in levels. For example, the 90.4 per cent implementation rate for GDP in the IVth Plan, and Administrative Investment in the VIIth, describe an annual rate of growth in the former variable around two-thirds of the target, but around one-half in the latter. The two tables should be read together for a proper indication of forecasting accuracy.

The tables provide a quantitative history of French planning which complements the descriptive material. One can observe from the outcome data the generally fast pace of development before 1970, which was based on the rapid growth of gross fixed capital formation, especially private investment, and exports. One can also see the events described in the historical section: the upsurge of public expenditure during the IVth Plan, the effects of restrictive demand management and public expenditure cuts after 1968 in the Vth, the general tendency for the growth of imports to exceed exports, and the impact of the 1958 and 1959 devaluations during the IIIrd Plan. GDP and consumption forecasts were generally close to the outcome, with the errors rarely exceeding 4 per cent of the forecasts over the four or five years, although the results appear slightly less satisfactory in Table 3.3. However, what is clear is that the remaining variables, and particularly imports, were forecast less accurately than GDP and consumption. GDP is regarded as easier to predict than its components because errors may be offsetting, and this provides a good basis for predicting personal consumption. Even so, the planners appear to have foreseen| the acceleration in growth during the 1950s and early 1960s and its consequences for consumption, although there were serious deficiencies in their projections of investment, government expenditure, and international trade.

Table 3.4 shows the accumulated deviations of plan forecasts from outcomes based back to 1952 (or 1957) and will be used as an alternative measure of forecasting accuracy as well as to search for systematic errors over time.[9] The 'accumulated deviations' are the compounded errors for the whole period since 1946 and are surprisingly small. Thus, the figure for GDP in 1975 tells us that actual GDP in 1975 was within 1 per cent of what it would have been if the economy had followed the planned path since 1952! The table reveals a tendency for the planners to underpredict every variable before the VIth Plan, to a greater or lesser degree, but severely overpredict since then. For example, growth was

Table 3.4 Cumulative Deviations of Plan Forecasts from Outcomes (%)

Year	GDP	Imports	Exports	Household consumption	Administrative consumption	GFCF
1952	0	0	0	0	0	0
1957	3.79	30.93	2.17	0	0	14.84
1961	2.48	37.17	17.1	-3.36	-2.76	16.21
1965	5.34	53.35	23.6	0.05	7.65	23.45
1970	8.94	60.68	31.76	1.9	-3.81	30.92
1975	0.88	54.37	25.35	-2.09	-4.05	20.42

underpredicted for every plan except the IIIrd before 1970, but the resulting cumulative deviation was eliminated by the 10 per cent overprediction of the VIth Plan. Except for household consumption and government expenditure, the accumulated deviations were so large for the remaining variables by 1970 that they were not eliminated by the overprediction which followed. The import forecasts were the most unreliable in almost every plan, with actual imports exceeding targets by 47 per cent in the IInd and by 20 per cent for the next three plans. The cumulative deviation between 1952 and 1970 was 60 per cent, and 54 per cent in 1975. The same pattern can be observed for exports and gross fixed capital formation, though the cumulative errors were slightly smaller. Exports were normally underpredicted by around 15 per cent and gross fixed capital formation by 10 per cent in each plan before 1970, though the Interim and IVth Plans were more accurate. The accumulated deviation of forecast from outcome reached 32 per cent for exports and 31 per cent for gross fixed capital formation by 1970, followed by 9 per cent and 13 per cent overprediction in the VIth Plan. The errors in projecting government consumption and investment differed from the other categories in being unsystematic over time. The implementation rates ranged from 89 per cent to 120 per cent in different plans, but the errors were offset between plans so the accumulated deviations totalled approximately zero. In conclusion, Table 3.4 shows that a process which has been viewed as the engine for French growth actually projected a slower, more balanced growth path than the outcome before 1970, but the opposite in the 1970s as the actual pace of development slowed.

The Accuracy of Plan Forecasts Compared with Long-Run Trends

The discussion in this and the following section is based on Table 3.5, which provides aggregate plan forecasts, outcomes, 'Alterna-

Table 3.5 Forecasts, Trends, and Outcomes by Plan

	1957–61 IIIrd Plan	1961–65 IVth Plan	1965–70 Vth Plan	1970–75 VIth Plan	1975–80 VIIth Plan
GDP					
Outcome	119.4	127.6	132.6	120.4	116.4
Plan forecast	121.0	123.9	127.6	133.2	128.8
Alternative forecast	120.17	119.9	130.4	130.8	—
Compound trends					
Since 1949	122.32	122.02	130.1	130.38	127.4[a]
Last 5 years	118.71	121.63	137.48	131.31	120.2[b]
Last 2 years	124.1	123.75	137.97	134.38	120.7[b]
Imports					
Outcome	118.6	165.7	180.9	137.6	158.3
Plan forecast	107.9	123.0	152.5	159.6	174.4
Alternative forecast	130.2	121.8	160.6	171.0	—
Compound trends					
Since 1949	133.86	127.65	150.39	155.52	156.73
Last 5 years	130.67	128.99	205.5	171.98	161.66
Last 2 years	169.5	127.6	257.9	239.9	158.3
Exports					
Outcome	150.0	130.2	171.5	150.6	141.4
Plan forecast	127.1	120.0	153.2	164.7	176.2
Alternative forecast	121.0	127.5	137.5	146.7	—
Compound trends					
Since 1949	130.78	138.83	145.08	149.72	149.85[a]
Last 5 years	104.5	133.83	145.81	164.54	182.8[b]
Last 2 years	100.0	175.2	144.9	195.38	117.1[b]
GFCF					
Outcome	123.7	142.3	143.2	118.4	113.3
Plan forecast	121.8	130.0	129.2	136.4	133.2
Alternative forecast	115.3	123.5	150.06	146.7	—
Compound trends					
Since 1949	119.74	121.04	135.44	137.91	136.07
Last 5 years	119.65	126.09	156.90	145.61	128.9
Last 2 years	149.83	124.8	163.8	147.56	118.0
Total consumption					
Outcome	114.2	127.2	127.0	124.1	119.8
Plan forecast	—	123.0	125.4	129.5	122.3
Alternative forecast	121.3	117.6	127.1	127.9	—
Compound trends:					
Since 1949	123.89	120.2	128.73	128.24	127.64
Last 5 years	121.11	116.62	135.35	126.79	125.28
Last 2 years	125.80	116.57	137.5	127.6	119.3

[a]These long-run trends are only approximate. They comprise the trend for the old definition of the series until 1973, multiplied by the growth rate of the new series to the end of the plan period.

[b]Based on data from the new system of national accounting.

tive Forecasts', and three measures of the trend.[10] Below, we study the accuracy with which the planners predicted changes in the pattern of aggregate growth from previous trends, which gives an indication of their ability to spot important new developments in the economy.[11] The discussion that follows is based on Table 3.6, which summarizes the relevant information in Table 3.5 by providing deviations of both plan forecasts and outcomes from long-run trends.

The IIIrd Plan predicted relatively slower, more balanced, development than hitherto with production projected to shift from domestic consumption to capital goods and exports and a relative decline in the rate of growth of imports. This was presumably in the hope of avoiding the balance of payments disequilibrium and inflationary pressures which arose during the very fast growth of the IInd Plan period. The projected deviations from previous trends were very large, with imports predicted to grow at one quarter of their previous rate and exports returning to their long-run trend after five years of virtual stagnation. The planners

Table 3.6 Deviation of Forecast (F) and Outcome (O) from Long-Run Trend (T) (% annual rate of growth)

	IIIrd Plan	IVth Plan	Vth Plan	VIth Plan	VIth Plan (outcomes to end 1973)	VIIth Plan
GDP						
F − T	−0.26	+0.4	−0.4	+0.45	+0.45	+0.24
O − T	−0.63	+1.18	+0.4	−1.67	+0.45	−1.88
Imports						
F − T	−5.24	−5.43	+0.3	+0.57	+0.57	+2.5
O − T	−2.80	+2.72	+4.1	−2.64	+3.74	+0.22
Exports						
F − T	+5.0	−3.89	+1.17	+2.10	+2.10	+3.5
O − T	+9.57	−1.73	+3.66	+0.13	+3.10	−1.28
GFCF						
F − T	+0.45	+1.89	−1.0	−0.24	−0.24	−0.45
O − T	+0.86	+4.33	+1.16	−3.20	0	−3.82
Consumption						
F − T	[a]	+0.61	−0.55	+0.2	+0.2	−0.9
O − T	−2.12	+1.50	−0.28	−0.7	+0.3	−1.32

[a]Both components of consumption forecast below long-run trend.

foresaw the signs of the shifts in trends remarkably accurately, but not the scale. As we have seen, the government corrected the balance of payments disequilibrium by devaluation and deflationary policies which cut domestic demand, so shifting production from consumption to exports (and investment). However, the planners underpredicted the increase in the latter two variables and the decrease in GDP and consumption relative to trend, and though the rate of import growth did decline, the deviation from trend was somewhat less than projected. Thus, planners successfully picked up the deviations from trends, and in particular the relative upsurge in exports and investment, although they tended to underestimate their scale.

The differences between plan forecasts and long-run trends in the IVth Plan indicate that the planners foresaw a relative acceleration in the rate of growth, primarily from a further increase in investment and social expenditure relative to trend. Both imports and exports were predicted to grow slower than hitherto, with the change more marked for imports; domestic consumption was projected to grow faster than trend. In fact, the plan correctly forecast the sign of the deviation from trend in every category except imports, although it proved to be pessimistic about the scale of domestic reflation and the growth of exports (however, this was below previous trends). Thus, the planners did correctly foresee the acceleration in growth for the IVth Plan, but made the same errors on trade as with the IIIrd.

The orientation of the Vth Plan can be explained by the domestic and international imbalances at the end of the IVth, and the predicted deviations from long-run trends signalled an intention to allow the economy to grow below potential to correct these problems. Thus, GDP and the components of domestic demand were predicted to grow below long-run trend while the relative growth of exports was projected to increase to finance the continued accelerating import growth. In fact, the government was unsuccessful in its somewhat delayed attempts in 1969 to restrain the upswing that followed the 1968 events, so high growth was sustained in the Vth Plan period. Although the signs of the changes from trend were correct for imports and exports, they were wrong for most of the domestic variables, particularly GDP, investment, and government expenditure. Thus, unlike the IVth Plan, the Vth erred on growth but did anticipate the increased openness of the economy.

The VIth Plan projected that growth would continue approximately on the lines of the previous five years, which was somewhat above long-run trends. GDP, exports, and consumption were projected to grow slightly above trend, investment slightly below it, and it was assumed that import growth would be held down to the long-run trend. In fact, the growth of every variable fell considerably below trend over the plan period because of the recession after 1973, which effectively invalidated the plan forecasts (the only good news was that imports grew more slowly than exports for the first time since the IIIrd Plan). However, it may not be fair to criticize the VIth Plan on this score, since it seems likely that almost anyone else would have made the same forecasting errors about 1975 in 1970 (see below). Thus, Table 3.6 also considers the deviations of outcome from long-run trends until 1973, which tell a very different story than the figures up to 1975. In fact, the VIth Plan correctly predicted the sign of every deviation from trend between 1970 and 1973, and was even superior to the IIIrd and IVth Plans in also projecting the small scale of these deviations in every category except imports. The VIth Plan gave very accurate predictions about how French growth would change from previous trends until unforeseen circumstances altered the situation completely in 1973.

The VIIth Plan projected that French growth would approximately return to the pattern of long-run trends by 1980, despite the experience of recession between 1973 and 1975. Indeed, GDP was forecast to grow slightly above long-run trend over the period (at around the level attained during the 1960s) because of an upsurge in exports and investment (at least, relative to recent experience; investment was projected to grow slightly below long-run trend). In effect, the planners forecast an increase in world demand that would restore the previous pattern of growth without domestic reflation. Since the world boom failed to materialize, the planners' forecasts were excessively optimistic, even when, as with investment, consumption, and imports, the sign of the deviation from trend was correctly predicted.

The Relative Accuracy of Plan and 'Alternative Forecasts'
This section is also based on Table 3.5,[12] and compares the plan and Alternative Forecasts against outcomes for an assessment of the additional useful information provided. The Alternative Forecasts were constructed because we could find no suitable published evidence about private expectations in the medium term.[13] We also consider evidence on short-term business opinion published in INSEE's *Tendances de la Conjoncture*, in the form of differences between optimistic ('up') answers and pessimistic ('down') answers. These are not generally suitable for assessing the precise medium-term plan forecasts, but will provide a useful indication of the way that business expectations were moving after 1973. The relevant material for our discussion is summarized in Table 3.7,

Table 3.7 Evaluation of Plan Forecasts of the Outcomes, Compared with Those of the Alternative Forecasts

	IIIrd Plan	IVth Plan	Vth Plan	VIth Plan
La PIB	X($\approx$)	√	X	X
Imports	√($\approx$)	√	X	√
Exports	√	X	√	X
GFCF	√	√	X	√
Consumption	√	√	X	X

√ means plan closer to outcome than best simulation.
X means best simulation closer to outcome than plan.
$\approx$ means both approximately equal.

which indicates when the plan forecasts were actually more accurate than decision makers could have been expected to produce for themselves at the time.

In the IIIrd Plan, the growth of GDP could have been privately predicted relatively more accurately than it was by the planners, although the plan did project consumption, capital formation, and exports rather better than the extrapolations. Imports were clearly unpredictable at this time, since the two forecasts were almost equally inaccurate on opposite sides of the outcome. Although the plan dominated the Alternative Forecasts for the majority of aggregate variables, one must suspect that the additional information provided by the IIIrd Plan was limited by its relatively inaccurate growth forecast. On the other hand, the IVth Plan was probably very useful, since it predicted every aggregate considered, except exports, better than the Alternative Forecasts. The planners successfully foresaw what decision makers may not have foreseen for themselves at that time – the relative acceleration in the pace of development and investment – although they were relatively less accurate in forecasting the rate of growth of world trade. This accords with our previous evidence and suggests that the IVth Plan must have increased the useful information available in the French economy in 1961.

The Alternative Forecasts were generally better predictors of outcomes than the plans after 1965. The Vth Plan was particularly unsatisfactory on this criterion, with its forecasts inferior to the extrapolations for every variable except exports. The plan projected a change in the pattern of development which did not occur, and the relative superiority of the Alternative Forecasts reflects the fact that decision makers would have done better to base their predictions on previous experience.[14] It might appear from the absolute magnitude of the forecasting errors that the VIth Plan would have been even less useful than the Vth, but in fact it provided less misleading information than its predecessor. Both sets of 1970 forecasts predicted that previous trends would continue until 1975 (although the precise figures differed slightly) and they were invalidated to approximately the same degree by the post-1973 recession. Plan forecasts were generally slightly further away from the outcome because the planners were slightly more optimistic about growth prospects than would be justified by a long-term look at previous experience, but this was understandable in the light of the accelerating trends in the very recent past. It may also have been a response to the apparent pessimism of previous plans observed above. As we have seen, French growth approximately followed the plan forecasts before 1973; the problem for the VIth Plan was that, like the market, the planners failed to foresee the oil crisis and its effects on world trade.

One cannot use this approach to evaluate the VIIth Plan because, with the change in national accounting, formal Alternative Forecasts could not be developed. However, there is considerable evidence that the plan forecasts provided a less accurate picture of the outcome than that which decision makers could have constructed at the same time. As we have seen, the VIIth Plan predicted that the economy would grow approximately along the path described by the long-run trends of French growth since 1949. In fact, French development had apparently entered a relatively new phase after 1973, with every aggregate growing rather more slowly than hitherto. It seems highly unlikely that the VIIth Plan projections could have represented decision makers' best guess of growth over the period, since the unhappy recent experience would have to have carried some positive weight. The differences among the various trend measures were so large, because of the sudden upheaval in 1973, that decision makers would probably have projected somewhere between the extremes, and thereby been more accurate than the planners. In fact, the VIIth Plan was widely regarded as unduly optimistic at its time of publication, both within and outside France (see Chapter 5 for further details).

The surveys of short-term business opinion (which are reproduced in the OECD's annual surveys) do provide a useful indication of private expectations at this time, since they reflect how businessmen felt about growth prospects after 1973. There was no great movement in the series between 1972 and 1974, second quarter, when a positive balance of around 10 per cent in forecasts of short-term employment prospects took a big dive to a more than 20 per cent negative balance. Although this pulled up slightly in 1975, it remained far below the level attained in the early 1970s, which suggests that businessmen would have attached rather more weight to recent experience than long-run experience in projecting forward in 1975. Thus, it is unlikely that the VIIth Plan could have provided additional useful information.

French Growth by International Standards

We have seen that French plans could have affected resource allocation, particularly before 1965. We conclude by considering one area in which the impact might be measured – economic growth. The demand expectations school argues that, if the planners can influence business expectations, the rate of growth can be increased and stabilized and we consider primarily the latter issue by comparing the French and international experience.[15] However, strong conclusions cannot be drawn from our findings because it is impossible to compare actual French growth with what would have occurred in the absence of planning, and this is not evaded by the inference that the alternative path can be represented by progress in countries which do not plan. We concentrate on stability rather than growth because it has been the relatively less explored issue.

On the relative growth issue, we shall content ourselves with noting that French growth was relatively fast by international standards. Real GDP grew by 4.86 per cent p.a. on average between 1949 and 1977[16] and exceeded 5.5 per cent per annum between 1958 and 1973 with a slightly rising trend over the period. This was one of the fastest rates of growth in the developed world, far in excess of relatively mature economies like the UK or the USA, comparable with West Germany, and not too far short of Japan. In consequence, France now has the second greatest GDP in the European Community, and had a per capita GDP of $8,850 in 1978, as against $5,530 in the UK. Like all other countries, French growth has been relatively slower since 1973, but the economy has still maintained an average rate of growth in excess of 3 per cent p.a., which is quite respectable by international standards. Thus, the performance was impressive though, of course, it is impossible to judge the extent to which this can be attributed to planning.[17]

Indicatively planned economies should also suffer relatively fewer disturbances around the mean of any given growth path. To investigate this, Table 3.8 provides a common measure of the disturbances around the average compounding rates of growth in six developed economies: the coefficient of variation[18] of the average annual growth rate. The data are derived from OECD sources for the period 1963–77 which ensure consistency of definition. In

Table 3.8 The Stability of French Growth by International Standards, Measured by the Coefficient of Variation (%)

Period	USA	UK	Italy	Holland	Germany	France
1963–77	73.0	96.0	67.0	51.0	74.0	35.0
1963–73	50.0	56.0	39.0	30.0	52.0	14.0
1963–70	57.0	40.0	29.0	30.0	57.0	17.0
1970–77	112.0	153.0	104.0	63.0	88.0	46.0

Source: OECD, Country Surveys 1963–1979.

fact, over the whole period French growth rates vary least from year to year out of the sample, while British rates vary most around their (relatively low) mean. The findings are even stronger for the period 1963–73, when the French coefficient of variation was only 14 per cent, around one quarter of the level attained in the USA, the UK, and West Germany, despite the events of May 1968. The growth process was more disturbed everywhere between 1970 and 1977, but the French economy was still more stable than the others. The differences in the stability of growth between France and the other countries, fast or slow growing, mature or developing, holds for all the periods examined.

The findings are striking, but we still cannot draw any conclusions from them about the impact of planning; numerous other forces could be at work. The relatively greater stability of French growth could reflect the steadiness of private expectations, innate properties of the economy, or the effectiveness of short-term counter-cyclical policies. Even so, our findings are not inconsistent with the hypothesis that indicate planning acts to stabilize the growth process.

Summary

The continuity in French planning since 1946 rests more with the name than the activity itself. In the chapters which follow, it will be useful to remember that each plan was constructed in a particular environment to meet a specific set of circumstances, and faced its own unique problems of implementation. Even so, we can trace four relatively distinct phases of French planning, with the process rising in prestige and significance after the relatively successful Reconstruction period to reach an apex in the early 1960s, after which decline set in, especially after 1975.

At first sight, the quantitative material does not appear to tell the same story. The simple forecast–outcome ratios confirm that planners were relatively optimistic about outcomes before 1970 and optimistic after that, and that they encountered more difficulties in correctly projecting international trade and private investment than in the other aggregates. But except perhaps for GDP and gross fixed capital formation, there was no marked deterioration in the implementation rates over time. The more sophisticated assessment exercises tell a different, and more historically consistent, story. They suggest that the planners were fairly effective during the 1950s and early 1960s, but provided little information of value to private agents after the IVth Plan. The IIIrd and IVth Plans, for all their inaccuracies, correctly foresaw important structural changes in the economy such as increased openness and acceleration in the underlying pace of growth. This information had real economic value because private agents could not have discovered these developments for themselves. It would seem that the praise lavished on French planning in the 1960s was not altogether undeserved.

In the information-provision sense, things have never been quite right since then, except perhaps during the VIth Plan until 1973. The Vth and VIth Plans, disrupted by major unpredicted events, and the VIIth Plan, which judged the economic climate incorrectly, all failed to foresee the important changes or provide agents with additional information about outcomes. Even so, the evidence on the relative stability of French growth by international standards suggests that the planners could still have been contributing something in these years, though the findings are hardly conclusive. The problems which have emerged since 1965 should not surprise people who have read Chapter 1; they would already be suspicious of single variant plans, particularly in a period when exogenous uncertainty was becoming relatively more significant with the increasing complexity and openness of the economy. The following chapters offer numerous reasons and justifications for those forecasting errors, which must also reflect poor judgement on the part of the planners, if only for attempting to undertake single variant exercises in an uncertain world, which places upon them some responsibility for the declining credibility of the procedure.

Notes

1   Some of the data in this chapter are discussed in Estrin and Holmes (1980), which concentrates on evaluating both the aggregate and disaggregate information in the plans from 1952 to 1978. The relevant sections of this chapter

evaluate only the aggregate data, but up until 1980. The reader is referred to the paper for further information about the sectoral and industrial forecasts.

2   There is already a large historical literature on the early years of planning which we, at best, hope to summarize (see MacLennan, 1963; Hackett and Hackett, 1963; Drèze, 1964; Kindleberger, 1967; Cohen, 1969; Lutz, 1969; Seibel, 1975).

3   There have been other assessments of the planners' forecasting accuracy for an earlier period, such as in Cohen (1969), Lutz (1969), and Carré *et al*. (1975). Vasconcellos and Kiker (1969) also carried out a quantitative evaluation and Wasserman and Wiles (1969), reporting on their comparison of the relative accuracy of French and Soviet plans, do not find much difference in performance. Our exercises are undertaken on a longer data set, and throw light on the relationship between forecasting accuracy and the more general performance of the procedure over time.

4   This is not to suggest that the micro-economic forecasts are uninteresting, but merely that the material is available elsewhere. Estrin and Holmes (1980) provide sectoral and industrial 'implementation rates' from 1952 to 1970, and although these forecasts cannot be evaluated in the same way as the aggregate ones because the scope of industrial coverage constantly varied, it reports the results of related assessment exercises on the disaggregate forecasts of the IVth and Vth Plans.

5   They therefore go one step beyond the 'naive forecasts' used for many years by the UK's NIESR as a benchmark in their *Quarterly Review* (see Posner, 1978).

6   The sources for the forecasts were the relevant plan documents, rather than the later revisions. These were confirmed with reference to Carré *et al*. (1975) and the relevant OECD French surveys, with the latter sources employed in the absence of primary data. For the aggregate material, outcomes were derived from the French National Yearbooks, and checked against Carré *et al*. (1975), OECD data, and alternative authors' figures. The disaggregated outcomes were derived from the data reproduced by planners at the end of the relevant period or the National Yearbooks, and confirmed against the above-mentioned sources.

7   GDP is 'le produit intérieur brut' in the Standard National Accounting System. The French used their own measure 'la production intérieure brute' before 1976. These are referred to as 'Le PIB' and 'La PIB' in the text where the distinction is relevant.

8   The exact dates of each plan are ambiguous because the targets were generally presented as indices for a final year based on an initial one that differed according to the variable. Since the plans also generally contained annual compound growth targets for the period, the forecasts can be presented based on a single year. The plans lasted for four years between 1953 and 1965, but five years since then.

    Plan targets referred to the four or five years following their publication so, for example, the IVth Plan, 1961, covered development in the four years until 1965.

9   This table cannot sensibly be extended beyond 1975 because of the changes in the National Accounting System, which means that the same headings refer to somewhat different variables.

10 The 'trend' is constructed by expanding to an index forecast for the plan period the annual compounding growth rate over the relevant period, from a base in 1949, and five and two years prior to the commencement of each plan.

11 Many other assessment exercises could be undertaken on the basis of Table 3.5, for example, combining the three trend measures in some way to form an intuitive 'alternative forecasts'.

12   The data series are not long enough to construct Alternative Forecasts before 1957. Changes in definitions prevent the construction of Alternative Forecasts for the VIIth Plan, so a weighted average of the trends is used as a substitute.

13   A large number of autoregressive and trend equations were estimated separately for each variable. Generally, the best fit was provided by an autoregressive form with a one-, two-, and three-period lag, although alternative specifications proved superior intermittently. The data series were derived from the French National Yearbooks, commencing with 1949.

14   Estrin and Holmes (1980) observe the same phenomenon in the industrial forecasts.

15   An empirical literature emerged during the 1960s to examine the impact of planning by comparing international growth rates, such as Wickham (1963).

16   All data are drawn from the OECD Country Surveys for the relevant years.

17   Vasconcellos and Kiker (1969) offer a more systematic treatment of the growth issues.

18   The standard deviation of each series normalized by the mean.

4 The French Method of Planning

Introduction

This chapter gives an introductory overview of French planning. We commence by introducing the main agencies involved and their roles, notably the Planning Commissariat and the Finance Ministry. The following section describes the process of constructing a plan in France and the technical instruments available. We go on to review the substantive content of the plans and the manner in which attempts were made to execute them, thereby introducing the subject matter of the following three chapters, before reviewing the reactions of business and trade unions to the way the process had evolved by the late 1970s. Finally, we raise some broad political issues and consider the scope for planning in the 1980s.

We have tried to describe the institutional arrangements as they stood in late summer 1981 after the arrival of the Mitterand–Mauroy government, but most of the analysis concerns the situation in the late 1970s, when the VIIth and would-be VIIIth Plans were being drafted. We have felt it necessary to delve back into the early history of planning at various points to emphasize that the position of the planning system in France has been a continuously evolving one, the successes and failures of one plan affecting the organizational structures for the next one. What we have not done here is to attempt to trace the roots of planning further back than 1946. Shonfield (1965) suggests that Monnet was building on a tradition of 'étatisme' that goes back to Colbert in the seventeenth century. This appears to be an erroneous interpretation, however. The era immediately preceding the Second World War, the Third Republic (1870–1946), was a period of economic liberalism on the whole, despite the fleeting efforts of the Popular Front government of Léon Blum (1936–38). If there are any historical antecedents of the planning system of postwar France they would lie in the corporatist arrangements of the wartime Vichy régime.[1]

The Actors

Economic planning in France has a number of facets. We deal here with the process of elaborating and implementing the national

89

five-year plan which is the responsibility of the Commissariat Général du Plan (CGP). Many other kinds of planning take place in France alongside the national plan. There is regional planning by the central government, operational policy planning by the government, and corporate planning by state and private enterprises. The task of the CGP was never to carry out all these functions, but its aim has been to try to co-ordinate the planning activities of other bodies, where possible bringing them together and facilitating coherence. Nor has the CGP had any executive functions except for its influence over the use of Marshall Aid Funds after the war.[2] Its role is supposed to be that of the missing 'Walrasian auctioneer' discussed in the first two chapters. It acts as an information broker during the construction of the plan, but from that point has to rely exclusively on persuading those with the responsibility for making decisions to implement the plan. Government agencies and firms may heed the planners' advice as they seem to have done up to the mid-1960s, but they do not have to, and the influence of the CGP and the plan itself on actual policy-making has diminished considerably since about 1965.

It is sometimes convenient to speak of 'the plan'[3] as in: 'Under the IVth Plan the government gave priority to education', as if to imply that all policy carried out during the time period formally covered by the plan was in some sense part of it. This is slightly misleading, however. Strictly speaking, the plan is a law voted by parliament on the recommendation of the government, which lays down a general orientation for policy and a series of objectives, which in recent years have been increasingly loosely defined and have left the mechanisms of implementation to be specified later. Commissaire Ripert (1976) likened the plan to a 'party platform'. The plan itself has always been the 'Plan of the Government', however influential the CGP may be in drawing it up. Implementation, in so far as the plan will not be self-implementing, is also the responsibility of the government.

Even in the early years, when production targets were defined for individual industries, it was never anticipated that these would be implemented using Soviet-style administrative methods. It was originally intended that state intervention should take place whenever important objectives were not being achieved spontaneously as a result of the information disseminating activities of the planners in showing people what actions corresponded best to the realization of their own aims. However, the underlying aim of the planners for most of the postwar period was the establishment of a healthy capitalist market economy with free trade and intervention unnecessary, or at least confined to narrow areas of market incompetence. In a sense, then, the eclipse of planning in the 1970s could be regarded as simply the successful completion of the original task of reconstruction. In practice, government intervention in the economy continued through the 1970s, but the role of the plan became negligible. Since 1961, the plan has ostensibly had wider aims than fast-growing industrial production; it has sought to put together an integrated framework for the country's overall social and economic objectives on the basis of widespread consultation. The decline of French planning that we observe since the early 1960s, which the Socialist government has vowed to reverse, is therefore not simply a gradual replacement of planned dirigisme by a free market. The most striking element is the elimination of the co-ordination function of the CGP within what remained an active administration on the economic front.

The Commissariat Général du Plan

From its creation in 1946 to 1981, the CGP has always been fairly small, with about 140 white-collar staff, including secretaries, in 1979.[4] It has no executive power and its only funds are to finance its organizational and research operations. The main job of the CGP is to orchestrate the process of consultation and deliberation on national problems and priorities which leads up to the drafting of a five-year plan. This can take nearly two years and involve hundreds or thousands of participants in 'modernization commissions'. Once the government has decided what to include in the plan, the CGP's role becomes the much lesser one of producing internal reports on the progress of the plan and background papers for the start of the next one.

The CGP has always had a somewhat ill-defined status in the French administrative system.[5] Set up in 1946 as a quasi-autonomous non-ministerial body, its influence has always depended on the prestige and personal status of its staff and in particular of its head, the Commissaire du Plan. Under the Socialist government the CGP is responsible to a Minister of Planning and Regional Policy (Michel Rocard),[6] whereas in the years before the 1981 elections the Commissaire reported to the Prime Minister (Raymond Barre from 1976 to 1981), an arrangement which had operated since 1962.

The Commissaire is a senior civil servant. The first postwar Commissaire, Jean Monnet, was a somewhat unorthodox personal ally of de Gaulle. The most famous of his successors, Pierre Massé (1959–66) was a distinguished economist who had headed Electricité de France. The Socialists appointed Hubert Prévot, a former official with the Finance Ministry's Forecasting Division (the Direction de la Prévision) who had for several years been on secondment to the Socialist trade union confederation (the CFDT) as chief of their economics department.

Being small and lacking resources of its own, the CGP was

always effectively dependent on the Ministry of Finance with whom it has had an uneasy relationship. Shonfield (1965) suggests that there was fairly close collaboration during the 1950s, but during the 1960s the Finance Ministry did all it could to clip the wings of the plan. The apparent success of the planners in the early years has been attributed to their non-ministerial role, working through existing agencies rather than seeking to usurp others' authority.[7] The Hacketts (1963) also point out that by 1963 there had been twenty-two Finance Ministers since the war but only three Planning Commissaires, with strength coming from the continuity at the top of the CGP. In bureaucratic terms the Finance Ministry remained supreme, however, and after 1963 it was under the almost continuous control of Valéry Giscard d'Estaing, first as Finance Minister, then as President, while after Pierre Massé's departure in 1966 there was a series of less distinguished figures as Commissaires: François Ortoli, René Montjoie, followed by an eighteen-month interregnum in 1973–74, then in quick succession, Jean Ripert, a personal ally of Giscard, and, up to 1981, Michel Albert. Up to the time of Massé, the Commissaire's position had retained a certain political neutrality as well as some autonomy, but later conservative governments sought to turn the Commissaire into a rather minor functionary of the government who did exactly what he was told without arguing. (He always had to do what he was told, but until the mid-1960s was expected to argue!)

Within the administration the Commissaire and his staff have always had to operate by using informal pressure and by mobilizing their access to the Prime Minister and, at certain moments, the President, with whom ultimate authority rests. In the past, especially before 1966, this was often effective, but the logic of it rested on the CGP's not having its own policies to advocate in competition with those of other ministries. It had to remind the Finance Ministry or other bodies to carry out policies that on paper the government was fully committed to. While the government declared that it did not wish short-term macro considerations to undermine the long-run growth strategy, the planners were acting entirely in the spirit of government policy by urging the Finance Ministry to bear this in mind, and in pressing industrialists to continue to invest in modernization with assurances that the state was backing them. In a situation of imperfect information this function is extremely useful. Each Ministry pays attention to its own sphere but the job of the planners is to draw attention to the implications of one ministry's policies for the overall objectives of the government. The Planning Commissioner sat on a number of important committees and, as we have noted, the CGP was often asked to draft policy proposals for specific areas, including incomes policy in 1965–67, and certain aspects of industrial policy.[8] The CGP was also given the specific task of co-ordinating all aids to industry in the 1960s, but here as always basic control remained with the Finance Ministry, and these specific tasks were strictly ad hoc. The CGP was not subsequently invited to participate directly in policy-making.

The need for a co-ordinating body was evident in the criticisms made by internal observers of the degree of co-ordination within the French state (see Milleron *et al.*, 1979, and Chapter 6; Stoffaës, 1978; Stoléru, 1969, and Chapter 7). But circumstances did not permit the CGP to carry it out. In the late 1960s the Finance Ministry and its political head, Giscard d'Estaing, managed to severely reduce the status of the plan. Whenever counter-inflation became a pressing issue it was either written into the plan (as in the Vth Plan) or subsequently declared to be a supreme objective overriding anything that may have been in the main plan text (as with the Plan Barre of 1976 which effectively superseded the VIIth Plan). The CGP's task of co-ordinating industrial policy was given by Barre to the Industry Ministry, together with block funding that gave real power. In addition, the modernization commissions of the plan ceased to be the main channel of contact between industry and the government, and the CGP's institutional role in this respect passed to the Industry Ministry.

Attempts were also made to reduce the status of the CGP in the country at large, to make it clear that no distinction existed between the 'plan of the government' and the 'plan of the nation'.[9] In fact, after 1960 only the IVth Plan really presented the planners with the opportunity to engage in widespread consultation in order to produce a set of national priorities that were not simply those the government had already set. De Gaulle came to office in 1959 with firm ideas of foreign policy and a desire for national solidarity and renewal, but he was willing to let the planners influence the details of economic and social priorities in a way that does not seem to have happened since.[10] Successive governments have tried to curb the autonomy of the plan and its consultative process. In 1975, Giscard established a Central Planning Council of ministers who would meet to monitor the implementation of the plan. While critics said this just furthered government control of the plan, it seems to have been only a symbolic recognition of the subordination of the plan to the government that had anyway existed for many years.[11]

We asked a Finance Ministry official, quite close to a minister, whether it was true that the Finance Ministry had 'killed the plan'. He agreed that it was probably true but not entirely fair to say this. In the 1960s, Gaullist governments 'talked long term but thought short term'; in the late 1970s the government seemed preoccupied with the current year's inflation rate but it had an underlying long-term strategy and did not need the plan's help to work it out or implement it. 'Le plan est sur un terrain déjà occupé.' Of course, the commitment of the Gaullists to planning stemmed positively from an attachment to the use of state power as well as negatively from the lack of faith in the market mechanism to solve the long-term problems of the economy, and in many ways the decline of planning is related to the replacement of Gaullist governments by the more orthodox conservatism of Pompidou and Giscard. Gaullist leaders Chirac and Debré were very critical of the way Giscard d'Estaing had shunted the plan to the sidelines of economic policy-making.

The position of the planners was indeed very marginal by the late 1970s. They formed a separate group almost 'cut out of the rest of the administration'[12] and Nizard describes them as 'deprived of all power' (Nizard, 1979, p. 129). Their actual activities can best be illustrated by examining a report on their budget compiled by the Finance Committee of the National Assembly.[13] The CGP's budget for 1977 was 40 million francs (about £5 million), of which 17 million francs paid for the CGP's own staff. The rest was used to pay for research carried out in a series of related centres in the rest of the administration, or by outsiders and funded via a committee for this purpose, CORDES.[14] The CGP's main research centres were CEPREMAP, a centre for the application of mathematical methods to planning, where much theoretical research of great interest has been produced; CERC, which gathers data on household income distribution and was set up in the wake of the CGP's brief involvement in incomes policy; and CREDOC, which does research on consumption patterns. In 1978 a new body, CEPII,[15] was added to the list to act as a focus for the collection and analysis of data on developments in the world markets, the need to keep abreast of which was one of the themes of the Barre government. Another body related to the CGP is the BIPE,[16] a business association sponsored by the state through which the CGP began in 1979 to market commercially economic forecasts prepared largely within the Finance Ministry, but as pure forecasts only. In the case of these, the 'projections détaillées glissantes' (PDGs), and the work of CEPII it can be said that the CGP was beginning again to carry out the role of 'collective market research' advocated by Massé.

The National Assembly report was critical of the way the research material was produced, however. They point out that the CGP relied heavily on outside bodies, and in particular they queried why it sometimes had to *pay* ministries to carry out studies instead of having access to internal government research automatically. There was certainly no indication of the CGP being commissioned by other government bodies to do their research for them as one might have perhaps expected. In fact, all the CGP's forecasting material is supplied to it by the research divisions of the Finance Ministry, the Direction de la Prévision (the DP), the forecasting department of the Finance Ministry, and INSEE, which is also the National Statistical Institute.

The report also raised the question of the institutional status of the planners. In 1957 a civil service 'corps' of 'conseillers du plan' was established, comparable in institutional status to the prestigious corps of engineers or the inspecteurs des finances (the inner élite of the civil service). But after the initial recruitment in 1957 no one else joined it. The result was that while Shonfield (1965) may speak of the planners in the early 1960s as being part of the inner elite of French civil servants, able to use their old school links (of the École Polytechnique or ENA (École Nationale d'Administration)) to press their case with Finance Ministry officials, this was certainly not the case in the 1970s. We were given a CGP staff list in July 1979, dated July 1978. This made clear that the overwhelming bulk of the staff were young, low rank officials on short-term contract ('agents sur contrat'), often on secondment from universities or other parts of the civil service. Only about a dozen of the 140 or so staff were either Conseillers du Plan or *permanent* members of other civil service corps. Turnover was also very fast, as was evident in the number of amendments that had already been made to the document which was nevertheless still not up to date. Staff have again been reshuffled following the arrival of the Socialist government.[17]

The CGP staff was well to the left of the Barre administration. One official estimated that a majority had voted for Mitterand in 1974, while another observed: 'Right-wingers prefer to go where the real power is.' That is of course the Finance Ministry, but in the apartheid that had sprung up between the planners and the rest of the administration, the 'confraternité de la planification' as it was described to us did include certain of the technical staff of the Finance Ministry who did the CGP's forecasting work for it. There was considerable interchange of personnel and identity of outlook between the staffs of the CGP and of the DP and INSEE where the econometric modelling was mainly done. These sections of the Finance Ministry were evidently more allied to the CGP than the rest of the Finance Ministry.

The Ministry of Finance

The Finance Ministry has always been the most powerful agency of the centralized French state (see Hayward, 1973). For certain periods, the Ministry of the National Economy was a rival, but this was absorbed and for most of the period covered the body had the formal title of 'Ministère de l'Economie et des Finances'. Between 1978 and 1981, it was divided into an Economy Ministry and a Budget Ministry, but both shared the same building on the Rue de Rivoli and the overall tutelage of Premier Barre. Although retaining a commitment to administrative decentralization and a separate Minister for the Budget, the Socialists have recombined the ministry.

All executive power stems directly from the President under the Vth Republic (that is, since 1958). The Finance Minister only exercises authority over and above his colleagues because it has been delegated to him by the President. Giscard d'Estaing had a fairly free rein from Presidents de Gaulle and Pompidou during his term as Finance Minister (1962–66 and 1969–74), although de Gaulle apparently intervened personally in 1968 to prevent a devaluation (see Prate, 1978). The Prime Minister can be totally excluded from economic decision-making, as appears to have happened to Chaban-Delmas from 1969 to 1971 and Chirac from 1974 to 1976 (see Mariano, 1973; Cerny and Schain, 1980). President Giscard exercised authority through the agency of Finance Minister Fourcade between 1974 and 1976, but for the remainder of his term in office effective power was delegated to Prime Minister Barre, who also held the Finance portfolio until the division of the Ministry in 1978 (after which he continued to exercise effective control). President Mitterand was reported to have delegated economic authority to Prime Minister Mauroy (*Le Monde*, June 26, 1981), who was expected to share it with Finance Minister Delors.[18]

The reunification of the Finance Ministry was apparently welcomed by civil servants who had been worried about the possible threat to their supreme power from the division of the ministry. This power rests on a number of factors. First and foremost, the Finance Ministry had absolute control over the spending of other ministries, each of which had a financial controller who reported to the Finance Ministry as well as to his 'host' ministry (see Hayward, 1973). The network of personal contacts and influence to which senior Finance Ministry officials belong extends further than this. Members of the corps of Inspecteurs des Finances occupy the most senior administrative (and often political) positions of state, and graduates of the Ecole Polytechnique and the ENA find a ready welcome in industry after even a few years in government service.[19]

The Finance Ministry for a long time maintained a quasi-monopoly of information. Its forecasting division (the DP) was originally set up as a rival to the CGP and although this aspect was not significant in the late 1970s, one DP official told us that they were only allowed to give the CGP such information as the Finance Minister authorized. He added that the Finance Ministry was always able to exploit the fact that other ministries (unlike the nationalized industries) were able to carry out very little research work of their own and were therefore all the more easily controlled. This official commented that the splitting of the Finance Ministry into two ministries had to some extent reduced its power but not all that much because it meant that any disagreement between the Budget and Treasury divisions of the old Finance Ministry perforce became an interministerial conflict, and while it was always possible for a policy-maker to yield to a colleague in the same ministry, ideas would become hardened if there was any suggestion of rivalry from another ministry. In fact the Finance Ministry was always, in Hayward's term, a 'federation' of sub-departments. The two most powerful divisions, the Budget and Treasury sections, managed to keep effective control of public spending and macro-economic policy entirely to themselves. The Treasury administered all aids to industry until the decision to give block funding to the Industry Ministry in the 1970s, and tolerated no interference from the CGP (or even its own forecasting division).[20]

We have already noted that the CGP is closely tied to two of the Finance Ministry's Divisions, the DP and certain departments of INSEE, the National Statistical Institute. Both of these bodies maintain an extremely high standard of technical expertise, and each has been headed by Edmond Malinvaud at various times. Their members, like the CGP staff, are often on short-term contract rather than being members of the permanent corps of the Finance Ministry. INSEE and the DP both operate several econometric models and INSEE is the main source of forecasts for the CGP.

Other Bodies Involved in Planning

Civil servants from all ministries are among the members of the modernization commissions for the plan, but the Industry Ministry is more involved with the planning system than any other, apart from the Finance Ministry. In fact, in the 1970s it effectively took over the original main function of the CGP – the co-ordination of industrial policy. In the 1960s this Ministry ranked low in the administrative and political pecking order and was even less able to stand up to the Finance Ministry than was the CGP, but its status was significantly raised in 1969 when it was also given responsibility for scientific research, and it was later given financial autonomy under Barre.[21] The Industry Ministry has had a much closer identification with business interests than the CGP. (One planning official said to us: 'Whenever the industry minister comes into a meeting we can hear big business outside the door.') Writers associated with it, such as Stoléru (1969) or Stoffaës (1978), have been severely critical of traditional planning methods and the ambitions of the planners.

The strategy of this ministry in recent years has been the anticipation of market developments and the building up of 'industries of the future'. The situation here was complicated under the Socialist government by the establishment of a separate Ministry of Research and Development,[22] but, as we note in Chapter 7, the Socialists object more to the dissociation from the plan than to the substance of the ministry's policy.[23]

Other institutional bodies involved in the planning process include representatives of nationalized industrial and financial concerns, who participate in the construction of the plan and are in principle responsible for plan implementation. Another body that liaises with the CGP is DATAR, the agency responsible for regional planning, which unlike the CGP is endowed with modest executive authority.[24]

Methods of Plan Construction

There are two elements in the construction of a French plan: the quantitative forecasting exercise, which included the selection of targets in earlier years, and the institutional process of discussion and consultation around the figures. We commence by discussing how the forecasts were made and used (see also Drèze, 1964; Liggins, 1975; Seibel, 1975).

Quantitative Techniques
Nowadays we take the use of econometric methods for granted, but far more elementary statistical methods had to be used in the immediate postwar period, and no formal models were used until the 1970s. There was not even an effective national accounting system in the 1940s, so targets had to be constructed independently for each sector. Simple input–output techniques became available in the 1950s, and National Accounts were properly established around 1956–59 using a rather unconventional system which was replaced by the ESNA system in 1976 (the Extended System of National Accounts; see Flouzat, 1975).

The input–output techniques enabled the planners in the IIIrd and IVth Plans to develop 'coherent' targets for individual industries implied by a given overall growth rate for industrial production taking account of inter-industry linkages. The Vth Plan made use of elementary econometric methods for the first time, and also attempted to make output forecasts by value as well as by volume, reflecting the government's preoccupation with inflation. Quantitative techniques were described at the time as follows (Lutz, 1969):

> The projection is based on an evaluation of the productive possibilities of the economy during the plan: labour, productive equipment, technical progress. There is worked out correspondingly an image of 'final demand', or of what is expected to be demanded in the terminal year for purposes of consumption, various types of investment and export, account being taken of the social objectives of the plan. Given this image of demand and assuming internal and external equilibrium, a detailed table of supply, i.e. of production and imports is drawn up. To these tables of demand and supply are added tables which describe the way in which incomes are distributed and used, and in which savings pass from savers to investors.[25]

Little attempt was made to model behavioural relationships during the 1960s, though the methods applied had advanced greatly on the earlier work. Ironically, the status of the figures was reduced from objectives to forecasts when the forecasting became more sophisticated in the 1970s.

The VIth and VIIth Plans employed formal and somewhat rigid econometric methods. This emphasized the fact that the resulting figures were only technocratic projections, without the earlier elements of social and political choice. However, the greater simplicity of computing meant that virtually unlimited numbers of scenarios could be simulated on a variety of models and assumptions, as occurred for the ill-fated VIIIth Plan (see Chapter 5). The central element in forecasting for the VIth and VIIth Plans was the FIFI model,[26] developed in the late 1960s under R. Courbis on the basis of his small open economy model (see Courbis, 1975), which assumed that output was determined by world demand and relative competitiveness alone (see Liggins, 1975, and Chapter 5). This assumption proved to be highly controversial, the forecasts having become intensely politicized during the 1970s,[27] and was relaxed slightly for the VIIth Plan. A large number of other models were also developed in the 1970s for use in government non-plan forecasting carried out in the DP and INSEE. As will be explained in Chapter 5, none of these models could track a path through time or consider more than a limited number of variants. In the late 1970s a new forecasting model, DMS,[28] was developed that overcame these limitations, which was convenient for the Barre government which wished to drop the notion of a central forecast in the plan, let alone a quantitative objective. However, DMS also had more Keynesian properties than FIFI, which militated against the Barre regime using its forecasts. These factors meant that the plan forecasts came to have substantially less operational significance in the 1970s than hitherto. Although the macro-economic and implied sectoral projections continued to be made, they were essentially just one input into the process of discussion rather than a direct basis for action. The formal properties of the models came to have more ideological overtones in France in this period than might be expected elsewhere.

The Consultative Process

We now consider the institutional structure of the plan's consultative apparatus. The main element in this is an array of committees (usually described in the past as 'Modernization Commissions') whose members are appointed by the government, sometimes on the advice of the CGP. Membership is drawn from business, trade union officials, and outside expert interests.[29]

The Ist Plan created only 'vertical' commissions for specific industrial sectors. Gradually the number of 'horizontal commissions' (concerned with across the board matters such as finance or trade) began to increase, so that by the time of the VIth Plan there was only one commission for the whole industrial sector, with lower status sectoral working parties reporting to it. Pascallon (1974) reports the number of commissions increasing from ten to thirty-two between the Ist and Vth Plans, and, while the VIth only had twenty-five 'commissions', it had forty 'committees' or subcommissions. Membership of commissions for the Ist Plan totalled 500, for the Vth 1,950, and for the VIth 2,500, plus another 2,500 in committees. In this respect, as well as in regard to its technical sophistication, the VIth Plan was a high point, though the consultations were in fact becoming increasingly irrelevant politically. The VIIth Plan had only thirteen commissions and the abortive VIIIth Plan only seven, with a corresponding reduction in the number of people involved.

It is widely argued (e.g. by Cohen, 1969(1977a), 1977b) that the representation was always biased toward business. Pascallon's data supports this view: for the Ist Plan unions made up 17 per cent of the commission members, and business 22 per cent. The figures were 11 per cent and 13 per cent for the IVth Plan (the most balanced) and 21 per cent and 29 per cent for the VIth.[30] In the 1970s the Employment Committees for the VIIth and VIIIth Plans, for example, had 5 out of 31 and 6 out of 40 representatives, respectively, from the main union groups and about the same numbers directly representing business interests.

Cohen (1969) complains that there was little for the union representatives to do in the years before 1960, since the plans were mainly concerned with the needs of industry. But there does seem to have been mutually profitable negotiation between business and government (see Shonfield, 1965). Critics saw the operation as having a 'corporatist' character. As we shall see in Chapter 7, there was no equivalent to this in the planning system of the 1970s, the whole emphasis of which began to evolve during the 1960s.

The activities of the commissions changed over the years as the concerns came to be more general and relevant to the whole economy. The early 1960s saw an attempt to use the 'concertation' process to define a national consensus on social priorities, and to reconcile conflicting class and group interests. This succeeded quite well with the IVth Plan, which is still regarded by many as the high point of French Planning.[31] For the Vth Plan, the government steered the 'consensus' away from the concern for social policy that emerged in the IVth. This led to the production of a 'Counter Plan' by the unions, a proposal for faster growth rather than the concern to curb inflation espoused by the government (see Ensemble, 1965). The consultative process was much weaker, and the unions refused to participate in the VIth Plan, seeing the 'industrial imperative' as 'the imperative of the industrialists'. They attended the meetings for the VIIth Plan commissions but withdrew before completion and refused to sign the reports. They did attend the VIIIth Plan deliberations but submitted minority reports.

The Planning Cycle

Before one plan has ended it is time to start work on the next. Initially, INSEE supplies some preliminary projections for the end year of the new plan to the CGP and the government lays down a set of guidelines about the kind of plan it wants. Once the government gives the go-ahead (which used to be two to three years before the start of the new plan but has been less in the 1970s) the CGP sets up the two stages of the planning process. The second stage results in the production of the plan itself, while the first is known as the 'Options Phase', though the label refers to the choices already made rather than a set of alternative possibilities from which the consultative process may select. A small number of 'commissions of the first phase' are set up (four for the VIIth Plan, one for the VIIIth). Taking as given the basic government guidelines (such as the industrial imperative of the VIth Plan, or adaptation to world market forces for the VIIIth), they define what they see as the main problems and policy objectives for the next five years, reporting to the government in published texts that appear in the name of the commissions. The government then produces (with the aid of the Commissaire) a 'Report on the Options for the Plan' in its own name, which takes as much or as little notice as it wishes of the advice given and which states in more precise terms (but not too precisely) the objectives of the plan. The commissions of the second phase will then have to reflect on how to achieve these general goals.

The first phase thus defines a set of general objectives. For the VIIth Plan[32] these were stated as: the restoration of full employment and national economic freedom of manoeuvre; controlling inflation, reducing social inequality; decentralization of decision-making. The text of some of the first phase commission reports implies that the initial guidelines had stressed the balance of payments; in fact priorities changed again for the plan itself. For the VIIIth, the options were given as: reducing dependence on imported energy; the development of competitive industry; strengthening agriculture and food processing; specific actions on employment; improving the efficiency of the social security system (i.e. cutting costs); improving the quality of life ('cadre de vie').[33]

For the second stage of the process, a larger number of commissions are formed to help draw up the final plan. This is the planning process proper, to which the numbers of participants quoted from Pascallon (1974) refer. The job of the Phase 2 commissions for the VIIth Plan was to consider ways of achieving the objectives laid down in the Options Report given the central macro-economic forecasts (they would have been targets in earlier years) which had been supplied by INSEE to the CGP. They worked out the implications of the overall growth rate for their own sphere of competence, to highlight problems that might arise. For the VIIIth Plan there were no central projections carrying official blessing, but a large range of simulated variants, all of which nevertheless showed rising unemployment under the Barre government's policies.

The commissions *may* make proposals for specific actions, but in recent years have been expected to discuss general issues. For the VIIth and VIIIth Plans there were heated debates about macro-economic strategy despite the government's desire to regulate the activities of the commissions as tightly as it could without being seen to strangle the process. At the same time the government made clear that no notice would be taken of any proposals that did not fit in with what it wished. More than one official commented that during the VIIIth Plan deliberations, government representatives met privately to draft proposals to ensure reports that reflected the government's view. Substantial care had in general been taken in choosing 'independent' members to avoid dissension, though not always successfully. Occasionally a group produced a report critical of government policy, such as the Employment Committee for the VIIth Plan. The government could also influence the proceedings by its manipulation of the forecasts offered to the commissions when there was a central projection or target. When a formal model is being used, there is limited scope for this, but the government could tell the technicians what assumptions to make about exogenous variables, such as changes in productivity or the financial implications of its policies. Many participants in the VIIth Plan were critical of the forecasts, and indeed of the whole concept of the FIFI model (see Chapter 5). The commissions produce reports which make recommendations, and for the VIIth and VIIIth Plans these were synthesized by the Development Commission and published, together with a mountain of research studies. The VIIth and VIIIth Plans also contained a limited number of specific public spending proposals (known as PAPs, see below), but these were largely decided after consultation among ministries.

It is the job of the Planning Commissaire to write a draft plan, on the government's instructions, that will incorporate such of the recommendations of the commissions as the government desires, in rather general terms. The Commissaire gives the plan to the government before it is published so that it may make any further desired changes. In 1965, Commissaire Massé was able to persuade the government to raise its target growth rate by 0.5 per cent per annum at this point, but in 1980 when Commissaire Albert complained that the published version of the plan played down all reference to unemployment, and had an additional chapter praising the government's record, he was publicly rebuked (see *Le Monde*, September 23, 1980).

The published version of the plan (with glossy covers) is still officially only a draft. It is submitted to a permanent consultative body, the Economic and Social Council (see Hayward, 1973), before being voted by parliament into law, with no more than the most minor changes of wording after its initial publication. Parliament has debated each plan since 1961, but never acquired any say in its construction. The quinquennial planning cycle is complete and the CGP is left with the tasks of collating material on the implementation of this plan and for the initial discussions with the government on the next one. The progress of the VIIth Plan was supposed to be monitored by the government's Central Planning Council, but this was not a major operation.

The Substance of the Plans

The first three plans were essentially concerned with raising industrial production, but in the 1960s the plans embraced attempts to programme public spending and to integrate social and regional priorities. From the mid-1960s onward macro-economic considerations became more important, but by the late 1960s, the government began to lose interest in the plan and in making long-term commitments, and in the 1970s it consisted almost exclusively of forecasts rather than objectives. The complexity of the forecasting exercise for the VIth Plan somewhat obscured the fact that its political relevance was very limited, though this was made quite explicit for the VIIth Plan. The macro-economic orientation however fitted in with the new forecasting tools and compensated for the fact that there was little to do in other fields. The status of the plan as a set of forecasts rather than objectives is one of the main criticisms made by the Socialists, who hope to reverse this state of affairs.

The overall quantitative success of the plans of the 1960s should not lead one to forget that there were no formal implementation procedures. Until the establishment of the somewhat irrelevant Central Planning Council under Giscard and the PAP expenditure programmes, the only forces to secure implementation were the lobbying activities of the CGP within the administration, and the tendency for 'self-implementation' so beloved of P. Massé. If firms and the public authorities had correctly stated their objectives and expectations, and exogenous events had turned out as anticipated, everyone would indeed have carried out the plan quite spontaneously, assuming always that the planners had done their calculations correctly. But, as we have seen, external shocks kept hitting the economy, and to implement the plan decision makers would have had to work out what would have been recommended for those circumstances, a much harder task which added to the pressures for ad-hoc policies. We should take note of the point made in a book authored by a group of planning officials that the plan had by the 1970s become merely one minor instrument of public policy, rather than government policy being arranged to implement the plan (see Atreize, 1971). The planners had a heavy task if they were to act as genuine co-ordinators. They were helped in the 1960s by the Commissaire's membership of important committees but hindered in the 1970s by the much lower status of the Commissaire and the CGP itself within the administration. Albert and Marcillac (1978) suggest that the limitation of the scope of the plan was a way of making it more operational, echoing the claims of the government, but this does not seem to have been the case in practice at all.

Macro-Planning

Though the first four plans had targets for national aggregates and the balance of payments, they did not pay attention to specifically macro-economic or monetary considerations, viewing the aggregates as merely the sum of a set of micro-economic components. The Vth Plan was elaborated at a time of government anxiety over the inflation rate and the GDP growth target was deliberately set below what was feasible.[34] Commissaire Massé made an undertaking to organize negotiations for an incomes policy in exchange for an increase in the target growth rate. The scheme eventually foundered, though the planners have since been advocates of an incomes policy. However there is some doubt about whether responsibility for the incomes policy can be said to have come under the scope of 'Le Plan' per se or whether it was a personal task assigned to Massé. If one believes the distinction to be meaningless (as Massé argues it to be in his preface to McArthur and Scott, 1969), the relevant observation is that the attribution of responsibility for counter-inflation strategy to the CGP was a strictly once and for all event.

The planners continued to be interested in macro-economic questions but there was little formal attempt to integrate the plans and macro-policy. The commitment to link the budget to the IVth Plan did not prevent the 1963 Stabilization Plan from being introduced, with its halving of monetary growth between 1961–63 and 1963–67 (see Chapter 5). Although Massé persuaded the government to adopt an official growth target of 5 per cent for the Vth Plan the short-term forecasts or 'economic budgets' being used as the basis of government policy in 1965 and 1966 were still 4.3 per cent and 4.5 per cent (see Carré *et al.*, 1975, p. 386). The Vth Plan contained a formal attempt to integrate the plan and macro policy, with a set of indicators, 'clignotants', drawn up, supposedly to monitor the progress of the economy and indicate the need for corrective action if development veered too far off course. The clignotants were supposed to indicate *when* action was needed, but not what the Finance Ministry should actually do. In fact, the Ministry would never have tolerated such an infringement of its autonomy and only accepted the clignotants in the knowledge that they would be ineffective. In a paper presented to the 1970 World Econometric Congress, G. Olive of the French Finance Ministry (Olive, 1970, p. 22) notes that all the medium-term forecasting to date had assumed even growth. Thus, cyclical fluctuations had been ignored and, in particular, no attention had been paid to major exogenous shocks like the 1968 events. This meant that the Finance Ministry always had to act on its own initiative. Carré *et al*. (1975), writing from a Keynesian perspective, praise the Ministry of Finance for the results of such stabilization policies as they did carry out up to the 1960s, pointing out that France had few built-in stabilizers, with limited revenue being collected in the form of a progressive income tax, and little counter-cyclical spending on unemployment pay. Even today the system remains rather narrow. In fact, though there were many 'external' shocks, the internal workings of the economy and the final outcome before 1973 display very little instability (see Chapter 3) so there was not a lot of work for the Finance Ministry to do.

It was perhaps fortunate that other stabilizing factors were as powerful as they were in the 1960s, for it is not clear that the Finance Ministry would have been willing to deviate from the desire for balanced budgets, which was only abandoned briefly during Michel Debré's spell at the Finance Ministry in 1966–68.[35] Giscard d'Estaing believed in slow growth of the money supply, but indicative planning did not cover monetary policy. After steadily declining monetary growth rates averaging 7.7 per cent between 1963 and 1969, the delayed response to the 1968 crisis took the form of a devaluation and monetary contraction of −1.6 per cent in 1969–70.[36] This was followed by expansion in double figures for the whole period of the VIth Plan, which in one respect can be said to have been accompanied by accommodating monetary policies.

Monetary growth slowed down under Barre. The oil crisis led, perhaps involuntarily, to the development of a budget deficit which averaged about 1 per cent of GDP[37] over the period of 1974–80, but in 1980 the Barre government succeeded in its declared aim of restoring a budget surplus. There was therefore no attempt to implement the VIIth Plan in the sense of employing budgetary stimulation but the text of the VIIIth Plan was able to claim that with an annual output growth over the period 1976–79 of 3.7 per cent p.a. (VIIIth Plan, p. 54), the VIIth Plan had indeed been successfully implemented. In fact, ironically, the VIIth Plan had suppressed all mention of growth rate targets for GDP and instead had set the restoration of full employment as an official objective. Unemployment rose continuously between 1975 and 1980, and it cannot truly be said that effective efforts were made to implement the macro strategy of the VIIth Plan. The Socialist government continued the macro-orientation of planning by promising a two-year Interim Plan for 1982–83 that would concentrate on the restoration of full employment,[38] with a quantitative target of 400–500,000 for the reduction of unemployment over the period. Wider goals were to be deferred until 1984–89. These issues are developed in detail in Chapter 5.

Social and Budgetary Planning

Relating as they did to industrial production, the first three plans were not concerned with the national budget except in so far as funds were wanted to promote industrial objectives. With the IVth Plan, the entire economy came under the purview of the planners and it was natural that in the IVth and Vth Plans there were programmes laid out for public investment by category (education, housing, etc.). The figures involved were targets for overall 'budgetary envelopes', rather than being funding authorizations, and specific projects were not, in general, written into the plan unless they had particular political significance. The plan was supposed to articulate national priorities at the time of its elaboration, and the only subsequent power available to the CGP to ensure that actual spending respected the priorities laid down was to lobby within the administration, especially the Finance Ministry, which it did with some success in the early 1960s when the shift of public expenditure toward social infra-structure heralded by the IVth Plan did materialize (see Chapter 6). But both the Vth and VIth Plans declared their priorities to be for industry, and in line with its greater technical sophistication but lower status the VIth Plan (1970–75) gave projections of expenditures by very fine budgetary categories, but these were strictly forecasts and had no normative status at all. Instead, the VIth Plan offered six small expenditure programmes ('programmes finalisés'). The VIIth Plan involved only highly aggregate figures on public spending.

The VIIth and VIIIth Plans used the term Programme d'Action Prioritaire (PAP) to denote the programmes written into the plan, which were claimed to be the most vital expenditure projects of the nation for the period, to be realized at all costs; they involved about 15 per cent of state expenditure for the VIIth Plan. The programmes finalisés and PAPs were somewhat oriented toward social objectives (e.g. reduction of infant mortality in the VIth Plan, care of the elderly at home in the VIIth) and were also supposed to be directly related to attempts at cost–benefit analysis and programme budgeting taking place elsewhere in the administration (known as RCB),[39] but this does not seem to have been the case.

Though the IVth Plan's emphasis on social priorities was respected, the quantitative targets and forecasts for the Vth and VIth Plans were both less ambitious and less well implemented; the VIth was more open in declaring that there was no commitment to its forecasts. The VIIth Plan PAP budget was maintained, but in the wider sphere of social policy its promises of reformist social policies never materialized and in this sense it was less well-implemented than the VIth Plan. Cohen (1977b) is generally critical of this experience, though it is not always clear whether he is accusing the government of putting too low a priority on social spending in the plans or of not fulfilling their stated priorities, or both.

One important innovation in the field of social planning in the 1970s was an attempt to incorporate social indicators into the plan, in particular for the monitoring of the progress of the PAPs. Much of the initial work on this was actually organized by J. Delors (Finance Minister since 1981) when he worked as an adviser under the brief reforming premiership of the Gaullist J. Chaban-Delmas (see Delors, 1971). Jobert (1978) reports on ambitious attempts to construct social accounts to monitor the integration of social and economic policies. They were ultimately stopped, he suggests, because the planners seemed to be presuming rather too much to dictate social priorities and because their calculations seemed likely to show up the social costs more than the benefits of government policies. The election of President Giscard in 1974, with a reformist element in his programme (see Giscard, 1977), led to a flurry of interest in this aspect of the plan in 1975, when officials described the aims of the VIIth Plan as 'macro economic and social'. As a result, one of the commissions for the first phase of the VIIth Plan was on social inequality; chaired by J. Méraud of CREDOC, its report (*Rapport de la Commission: Inégalités Sociales*) (CGP, 1975d) was widely quoted, and the public debate brought the issue very much to the fore, though its main observations were actually on the inadequacy of statistics. In the second phase there also was a Committee on Incomes and Transfers reporting to the Development Commission, which collated a lot of data, although its final report emphasized the difficulties of major action to redistribute income. (Interestingly, it considered wealth taxation, a measure which President Giscard actually proposed but then withdrew). In general, the social priorities explicitly laid down in the Options phase of the VIIth Plan were simply not followed up[40] as the President lost interest in social reform in his later years in office. Thus, the VIIIth Plan devoted one chapter to the social security system, but was entirely concerned with reducing its costs. (The Report on the Adaptation of the VIIth Plan had argued that international competitiveness would suffer if social security benefits grew faster than national income, as it claimed was happening, and great stress was laid on the priority of reversing this trend and cutting down the total outlay.) At a technocratic level the planners, especially at INSEE, continued to concern themselves with the measurement of non-economic objectives under the auspices of the VIIth Plan (see, for example, *Les Indicateurs Economiques et Sociaux*) (CGP, 1976i), but the government was not interested. The VIIIth Plan did not follow up this lead at all but it is an area that is likely to be of considerable interest to the new government. Apart from the personal commitment of Finance Minister Delors to social indicators, there are significant micro and macro reasons for the government to have an interest in them.

The Socialists would wish nationalized industries to take account of social goals rather than to merely maximize profit at market prices,[41] so alternative criteria would be needed to measure success. Some of the doubts about the market expressed by the Socialists are those of 'mainstream economists' such as Samuelson (1976): maldistribution of income, monopoly, neglect of social or environmental considerations, and the informational problems stressed above; but Attali (1978), for example, also implies that preferences are distorted by the culture of the market and advertising. In our interview with him in 1977, H. Prévot, then with the CFDT union organization, also argued that, while there would always have to be a big role for the market, social pressures influenced demand, and he, like Attali, would want to see the production of more public services, with fewer highly advertised consumer goods.

On the macro-economic side, the Socialist Party programme puts its initial stress on employment and output in a traditional Keynesian manner, but the ultimate objectives of the new regime are toward far-reaching reforms in society. If such measures have adverse repercussions for private business confidence, France could find itself experiencing setbacks in the recorded values of indicators such as GNP. Rational planning would then require the evaluation of the social gains to be set against narrower concepts of economic welfare. Chapter 6 examines these issues in more detail.

Industrial Planning

As time went by, the industrial projections also became forecasts instead of objectives, with only the aggregate figures having the status of targets after 1965. Before this date there were objectives for industrial branches as a whole and some firms reported their specific investment proposals to the modernization commissions, but there were never any targets for the output of individual firms in either the private or the public sector.

In the IVth Plan, a declaration was made that the entire

apparatus of the state would be used to construct any programmes necessary to ensure its fulfilment. This was believed to require the realization of the figures for 'basic' industries but not necessarily of those for consumer goods output. The Vth Plan stated that the pattern of output was to be decided by firms, not the state, and the objective of the plan became that of 'competitive' growth. This sat uneasily with the vast array of sectoral programmes and incentives that were supposed to be co-ordinated with each other and the Plan but in fact were not, though a few 'planning contracts' were signed.[42] The VIth Plan denied the need for a generalized industrial policy and instead sought to identify three or four sectors which it said should be the object of programmed interventions not outlined in detail, but which in the event did not coincide with the pattern of intervention actually adopted. From 1975 to 1981 plan texts appearing in the government's name proposed a strategy of promoting rapid adjustment to follow world market forces, which in so far as it was implemented followed a 'plan' but one that involved neither the spirit nor the institutions of traditional French Planning, the co-ordination role being given to the Industry Ministry.

The traditional arrangement had been for the CGP Commissaire to use his membership of important committees to seek consistency between industrial policy and the plan. He was a member of the council of the FDES, which made loans to industry, and in principle the CGP continued to be asked for an opinion whenever the government authorized a major loan to industry, but his opinion was not worth much after 1970.

In the late 1970s, the aims of industrial policy became to anticipate world market forces and strengthen the most promising *firms* rather than whole sectors, though there may have been little change in practice.[43]

As far as the direct effect of the plan on the *private* sector is concerned, we have seen the results in overall quantitative terms in Chapter 3, but it is not possible to infer directly from this to what extent firms were consciously implementing the plan. McArthur and Scott (1969), after extensive interviews with firms, insist that they were not paying attention to the plan: 'An overall appraisal of the direct influence of the national planning process on corporate stategies must note that the degree of influence was small, regardless of sector, and that the steel sector is the only one where it was clearly discernible' (p. 441).

Carré *et al.* (1975) report on a survey of 2000 firms carried out by INSEE in 1967 (see Tables 14.4 and 14.7). The firms were asked what their knowledge of the Vth Plan forecasts was and whether this had influenced them, with the answers reported by size classes. The largest firms (over 5,000 employees) *all* knew the Vth Plan's overall growth target, as did a majority of firms even down to the smallest size class (10–99 employees). Awareness of the detailed industrial forecasts was much less widespread, however. A majority of firms of all size classes except the smallest were familiar with the production forecast for their own industry, but while a majority of the larger firms (over 1,000 employees) knew the investment forecasts for their industries, most smaller firms did not. The use of this knowledge does not seem to have been all that great, however. When asked about the impact of the plan on their production decisions, a majority of firms reported a 'slight' or 'zero' impact. For investment decisions the same was true for smaller firms, but 51 per cent of firms with over 5,000 employees reported a 'significant' effect of the plan. If anything, these figures probably overstate the impact; Carré *et al.* noted that the survey was in fact carried out among firms who had chosen to attend an INSEE conference on economic information, and were already supplying data to INSEE. A slightly greater degree of interest in the plan figures is however reported by Schollhammer (1969).

We also have evidence of the influence of the plan on business decisions in the 1970s in a poll carried out for the CGP in 1979 (SOFRES, 1979a, 1979b). Respondents were asked whether they had taken account of the VIIth Plan in defining the objectives of their firm. Overall, 80 per cent said no, and this did not differ significantly across industries, though the influence on larger firms (over 1,000 employees) showed up as being marginally greater (66 per cent no). As to the productive side of the public sector, the day-to-day unplanned character of government intervention in the running of state firms gave rise to concern in the late 1960s and the Nora Report (Nora, 1967) proposed a system of long-term 'contrats de programme' to be signed between the state and each nationalized industry to programme public investment in a way that was coherent with the rest of the plan. In fact, only two were ever actually signed. It is therefore clear that French firms, private or public, did not in any·sense attempt to implement the plan directly. If this is to happen, it can only be if they are led to it indirectly through the implementation of plan-related government policies and incentives or contractual arrangements in the context of a national plan.

The Socialist government announced its intention to bring industrial policy back into the realm of national planning[44] and in particular to use a newly expanded public sector to achieve its aims. This will obviously involve attempts to pre-programme nationalized industries' investments, in a way that had never really been tried in the past. Chapter 7 outlines in more detail the relationship between industrial policy and planning.

Regional Planning

France has always been a highly centralized state, all the more so under the Vth Republic (see, for example, Hayward's *The One and Indivisible French Republic*, 1973) but there has been a consistent worry about regional imbalance, dating back to Gravier (1947), and an interest over the last twenty years in regional planning or 'aménagement du territoire'. There have been limited attempts to regionalize the activities of the national plan. Active regional planning has been conducted since 1963 by DATAR[45] whose role both parallels the CGP in that it has responsibility for proposing regional plans, and goes beyond it in that DATAR had some funds of its own in the form of the FIAT[46] which was part of the special budget of the Prime Minister, to whom DATAR was directly responsible. It also had some executive powers on specific regional aids, though it was never in a position to direct the regional use of general funds being administered from the centre which were of course the prerogative of the Finance Ministry. Being attached in a more direct way than the CGP to the Prime Minister's office, DATAR was always more a politicized body, and critics claimed that its main function was to announce public investments in any area where a sudden by-election cropped up. Hayward (1973, p. 170) refers to 'aménagement éléctoral du territoire'.[47]

The first three plans had no specifically regional objectives at all. Some separate exercises in forecasting regional levels of employment and public expenditure were carried out between 1955 and 1962, but they were however quite unrelated to the national plan (Cavallier, 1977). In keeping with the sweeping ambitions of the planners in the 1960s, the IVth and Vth plans took upon themselves the task of developing programmes to solve the nation's regional imbalances. The CGP acquired a regional division in 1963 but any specific executive responsibility was given to DATAR. The role of the CGP seems to have been to organize the regional aspects of the national plan while DATAR was allowed to develop a modest system of regional aids of its own. Large spending decisions always rested with the Finance Ministry. The CGP also organized consultation with regional representatives on national planning problems, and for this purpose the government set up in 1964 non-elected regional consultative bodies known as CODERs (Commission de développement économique régionale).

Within the framework of the national planning system regional objectives were of three kinds: there were overall objectives regarding geographical imbalances of income and development at a fairly broad level (e.g. Paris vs. the rest; backwardness of the Southwest); there were attempts to regionalize the programming of the national budget; and the plan also identified certain regionally specific projects that had particular political significance (e.g. the Rhône–Rhine Canal in the VIIth Plan). Details of land use planning were not included. There was also a certain amount of regionalized econometric modelling in the 1970s.[48]

The main manifestation of the regionalization of the plan was that in the IVth and Vth Plans there were targets for the breakdown of total public expenditure by region as well as by national functional category, but although these were objectives, the figures had little operational significance since there was no way of translating overall totals into individual regional expenditure decisions. No power was transferred to the regions. The VIth Plan tried to get round one part of the problem by including not just budgetary envelopes but fully worked out regional programmes (Programmes régionaux de développement et d'équipement – PRDEs). These projections were very detailed but were officially given the status of 'forecasts', not targets, and had little impact. For the VIIth Plan, the lack of forecasting of public spending in any sort of detail applied also to regional spending. There was a commission for 'aménagement du territoire' for both phases of the plan, and a report on consultations with the regions. The latter provided responses of regional representatives to a questionnaire on expenditure priorities sent out by the CGP. The VIIth Plan promised that in parallel with the PAPs of the national budget, there were to be similar safeguards for a limited number of 'programmes of local initiative' (PAPIRs).[49] The head of the regional division of the CGP observed that the VIIth Plan marked the end of the attempts to 'regionalize' the national plan and expressed anxiety as to whether even the limited promises on regional development would be kept. In fact, the PAPIRs did not even begin until 1977. Cavallier (1977) echoed the criticism of other CGP officials (see Mignot and Voisset, 1977) who urged that greater power should be devolved from Paris, with the plan acting as a co-ordinator among autonomous regional entities.

In many ways, regionalization of the national plan was just a substitute for genuine decentralization in an overcentralized state. Regions were 'consulted' on matters which elsewhere local elected representatives might have been free to decide on anyway. An indication of the degree of central control over decisions is given in Milleron *et al.* (1979, pp. 100–1), where the approval of fourteen separate state agencies is shown to be required before a local school can be built even after general budgetary authorization has been given. (The sum involved would be 1 to 5 million francs and several hundred such decisions would be taken each year.) It is probably the high degree of centralization rather than the influence of the CGP over public expenditure that caused popular identification of the plan and the regional distribution of public spending, and explains the experience of a mathematical economist at CEPREMAP: visiting relatives in the country he was immediately urged to get a swimming pool for the village written into the plan once it was revealed that he was 'something to do with planning'. It is ironic that in the survey of business firms carried out by SOFRES for the CGP in 1979 the primary domain of influence of the plan was thought to be regional development even though the activities of the plan in this sphere had been virtually eliminated. Though recent plans never did carry any specific public expenditure proposals for particular towns or projects unless they were of national significance, a DATAR official told us it was helpful to get a pet project, such as the Rhône-Rhine Canal, or the Fos complex near Marseilles, written into the plan because it did make it more likely that it would be carried out, though by no means certain.

Thus, the link between national and regional planning became very tenuous in recent years. We do not seek to cover the other aspects of regional planning undertaken in France in the present study but will be content to just mention the conclusions of French sources. Pascallon (1974) sums up the experience to that date by observing (pp. 135–7) that in so far as regional planning operated through the same circuits as the rest of national planning it suffered the same difficulties as the CGP. To the extent that it operated through its own mechanisms, these were no stronger in relation to the main centres of power than were those of the CGP, despite DATAR's small budgetary allocation. Grémion and Worms (1976) suggest that the experience of the 1960s can be summed up by saying 'in a phrase: planning did not transform the traditional institutions or administrative practices; it is these institutions and practices which transformed the regionalization of planning' (p. 232). We ourselves were able to ask one DATAR official in 1977 the extent to which DATAR pays attention to the national plan in its decisions; the answer was that there are no operational links at all.

It was a natural response to such a situation for the Socialist Party to make major decentralization of the state a primary goal. G. Fuchs, appointed a government adviser under Mitterand, put the case for a major decentralization of the planning system (see Fuchs, 1977). He argued for a multiplicity of corporate plans to be drawn up by the different levels of government. The role of central planning should be to co-ordinate the regional plans and those of central agencies, and to enable contractual arrangements to be drawn up between them.[50] The technocrats should merely advise on what is possible rather than impose their priorities. The establishment of a Ministry for Planning and Aménagement du Territoire was a major gesture. M. Rocard[51] stressed the importance that regional initiatives would have in future planning, although more so in the eventual five-year plan of 1984–89 than in the Interim Plan for 1982–84. Some steps were taken at once however to allow regional assemblies to decide the disposition of certain discretionary aid funds.

The limited extent of the devolution for the Interim Plan should not be interpreted as lack of willingness to decentralize decision-making. It is too soon to evaluate the success of the concept, but it seems likely that if decentralization fails it will not be through lack of commitment by the government, many of whose members built up their political careers as mayors of large towns and who retain strong local ties. One leading Socialist economist, a member of a working group responsible for public finance aspects of decentralization, observed that the government appeared quite sincere in its desire to overcome the inevitable arguments of the Finance Ministry that fiscal devolution is impossible. He also remarked that President Mitterand had far more to gain by going down in history as the architect of a reform of the structure of the French state than by short-sightedly trying to retain all the levers of control in the hands of his government in Paris during his period of office. The role of the plan as a co-ordinator among autonomous entities could be very fruitful.

Union and Business Reactions to Planning

We have accumulated interesting evidence on the views of both the unions and business about the planning system in the late 1970s.[52] Worried about its status in 1979, the CGP commissioned France's leading opinion poll firm, SOFRES, to survey business leaders and trade unionists about their attitude to the planning process. The resulting reports, each about 100 pages long, do not appear to have been published. SOFRES interviewed fifteen national and local officials of the main union groups, the Communist CGT, the Socialist CFDT, and the smaller FO (Socialist) and CFTC (Catholic). All the union representatives showed a keen interest in the idea of planning, but the CFDT and CGT were extremely critical of the way it was then being carried out. They saw considerable erosion of the planning process which had gone further in the VIIth Plan, and regretted the lack of any attempt to articulate real priorities other than the need to submit to world market forces. They saw the reduction of the scale of consultation in the 1970s as an attempt by the state to short-circuit serious debate, but they felt the need to go on participating, primarily because of the access to information that the planning process provided. The CGT was slightly suspicious of some of the data emanating from the CGP, but otherwise it was clear that the unions still had a high regard for the CGP whose officials seemed keen to listen to union views and to transmit them to the government, whom they blamed for ignoring them in the final plan. The unions felt the CGP had lost all significant power within the administration. They also regretted the lack of influence of Parliament in the planning process. A pre-condition of any serious reform of the planning procedure was seen to be a willingness on the part of the government to give the plan a greater role. The main unions (but not the FO) saw a basic incompatibility between the 'liberalism' of the Barre government and any serious attempt to plan: forecasting market demand was something business did perfectly well for itself in Germany. However, the unions appear not to have been insisting that real planning was only possible under a left-wing government; SOFRES reports a 'nostalgia' for the Gaullist IVth Plan period.

These views were also reflected in an interview we had with H. Prévot, when he was head of the CFDT economics department. He argued for radical reform across the whole of society, being opposed to centralized planning, and arguing instead for what he described as a 'politique contractuelle permanente' in the context of a wider degree of self-management in society. But the unions would in principle be prepared to discuss an incomes policy with any government that was prepared for serious negotiation.

We therefore see that, while there came to be total disillusionment with the outcome of the planning process in the 1970s, the unions retain strong sympathy for the concept and even the institutions. There seem to be fewer apparent obstacles to the genuine revival of wider consultative planning than, say, would have faced an attempt to revive an incomes policy in the UK in the late 1970s.

It is slightly ironic that though Cohen (1969) and the trade unions saw the plan, if not the CGP, as having become the creature of business, SOFRES found a distinct lack of interest in the operations of the plan among the 1,100 'chefs d'entreprise' who replied out of the 5,000 to whom they sent questionnaires. A majority of respondents thought the plan was unimportant, only 9 per cent believing the plan was 'very important' in France in the late 1970s. They saw a distinct shift having come about over the years, but

with rather more believing this was due to an increasingly unpredictable economic environment than to the increased extent of
political 'liberalism', which was the second most supported answer
to this question. It is interesting to note that these two elements
were ranked inversely by unions and business.

The businessmen agreed with the trade unions however in replying by a 2:1 majority that the plan itself was largely the outcome of
government directives rather than of a process of joint deliberation, but 57 per cent of them felt that the government was at the
same time hardly at all committed to what was in the plan. Eighty-
two per cent declared themselves not very interested in the
activities of the plan, with large firms slightly more interested than
small ones. SOFRES remarked that polling usually tends to
exaggerate the degree of interest of respondents in the subject of
the questioning. Two-thirds of the businessmen had never consulted a plan document, and, very strikingly, of the minority
that had, less than a third of these had done so in a professional
capacity rather than out of personal interest.

Curiously, the businessmen interviewed by SOFRES did express
the same potential interest in planning as the unions. Asked what
the role of the plan should be in the future, 72 per cent called for a
greater not a lesser role, wanting more clearly defined objectives
and being apparently willing to accept implementation mechanisms with the degree of dirigisme that this might imply. There was
a certain division of opinion here, SOFRES noted. Firms in sectors
and areas most affected by the general economic recession were
keenest to see an extension of the role of planning; the largest
firms (over 1,000 employees) were least keen, but even there
more respondents wanted more than wanted less planning.
SOFRES found that 82 per cent of businessmen interviewed
would be interested in participating in plan commissions. (One
rather sceptical CGP official remarked to us in this context that
she was always surprised how easy it was to get people to attend
plan meetings; perhaps it made them feel important.) The
businessmen, however, were anxious to see firms represented
directly rather than via employers' organizations, as had increasingly happened in recent years.

The other surprising result was that although the firms indicated
a lack of interest in the CGP's activities they responded strongly in
favour (94 per cent) of being given more information by the CGP.
Three-quarters indicated that they would be willing to buy from an
independent agency forecasts of trends in the national economy,
industrial branches, and product markets. This was taken by the
planners as a sign of interest in their proposal for a system of
'Projections Detaillées Glissantes', macro and micro forecasts with

no normative status at all to be distributed through the BIPE (see Chapter 5). Interestingly, when asked what was the main source of economic information, the bulk of firms replied that it was the national press and only a small minority reported relying on their own economic research department.

The SOFRES survey does not report on the extent to which the firms saw the planning exercise as simply a way of lobbying for favours, but it is clear from the general answers and from our own discussions that in general big firms did not see the Planning Commission as a significant channel of influence for extracting favours from the government in the 1970s. Both unions and business recognize that though they may be able to get the CGP to listen to them this will not influence the government much, although the unions had no one else to talk to before 1981.

The Broader Political Context

We have been explaining the decline of planning in France in terms of the inappropriateness of rigid five-year commitments worked out in fine detail in advance, combined with bureaucratic and political rivalries which made it impossible for the CGP to develop a more useful role under the conservative governments of Presidents Pompidou and Giscard. An ideological hostility to planning was obviously part of it, as well as an identification of the government with business interests. There are those who would go much further however and claim that French economic policy was not merely run *for* business interests but also *by* business, and that underneath the apparent desire not to plan there was a hidden capitalist logic. (See, for example, Herzog, 1971,[53] or Nizard, 1976). This argument is reasonably plausible but unilluminating if taken to mean merely that lack of co-ordination is an inevitable consequence of a situation in which business firms insist on being free to call on the government to bail them out whenever something goes wrong even at the expense of wider goals. It is unlikely that underlying the open espousal of the goal of higher industrial profitability there was another coherent hidden plan that actually was implemented, though Hayward (1973) remarks that the government was not always keen to reveal what its true objectives were, remarking: 'However while seeking to bamboozle its opponents the government must not mislead itself. So, like a systematic tax evader, it must keep more than one set of accounts of its activities.' (p. 180). This was probably true in the late 1960s, for which the true role of planning is more apparent in retrospect that it seems to have been at the time, but in recent years the governments were fairly ruthless about making clear their real goals. The desire to bolster industrial profitability and restrain the growth of wages and social security spending was no secret.

But it is not clear that the interests of big business or multi-national firms were particularly enhanced by the disappearance of the traditional planning system and the emphasis on the market-place. Marxist writers have the theory of State Monopoly Capital-ism to cover the phenomenon of increasing state support for capitalist firms in crisis, but this concept is in opposition to the declared aims of the Barre government, of only giving help to the strongest firms with the best growth prospects, with payment by results using contractual schemes. Of course, in practice steel was the main recipient of aid in the late 1970s, but there was a serious effort to move in the opposite direction. It is reasonable to suppose that what big business wants is a form of risk participation by the state. A situation where the state does not try to control firms in advance but gives generous help whenever an investment fails at the taxpayers' (or workers') expense is precisely what would suit business, as would a policy of promoting concentration rather than competition.

In many ways, the ideal state policy from the point of view of domestic business is precisely what preceded the aggressive market-oriented approach ostensibly adopted in the 1970s. Marx-ists savour the idea of a contradiction between the ideological desire of business for stress on the virtues of competition with the practical desire for monopoly profits. The argument would be that the stress on competition was needed to 'sell' the idea of inter-nationalization, but that the real goal was just more power to business. But this is hard to swallow. What made the FIFI model and the trade liberalization strategy politically unpopular are pre-cisely those features that private industry would itself dislike, namely, the intensification of competition and the shouldering of additional risk by the capitalists as well as the workers. The Left in France is always very critical of multinational firms. H. Prévot put to us the argument that, by organizing the international division of labour in component supply, multinational firms were depriving France of vital inter-industry linkages that were needed to promote technical progress. However, it is implausible to view multinational firms as having dominated the policy of the Gaullist governments during the years in which trade was liberalized.[54]

We propose therefore in the present work to take it for granted that the government before 1981 favoured business but do not adopt a perspective which sees the state as the mere puppet of private interests. The large size of the state's own industrial hold-ings and the continuance for many years of family control rather than joint stock enterprise in many firms (Peugeot, Citroën, Dassault, Michelin, etc.) made it quite possible for the state tail to wag the capitalist dog whenever the politicians wished it to.

If this view is correct, it suggests that the socialist aim of a dramatic reform and renewal of the planning system is not as over-optimistic as an initial reading of the last two decades' experience would seem to suggest. There will of course be the same internal obstacles to planning. The Socialist government had internal divisions[55] and even included a small number of Communist ministers in 1981. There could indeed be scope for disputes between the ministers responsible for Finance, Planning, the Budget, Industry, and Research and Development. There were already personal, ideological, and interministerial rivalries.[56] However, the commitment to some form of planning was at least as central to the socialist programme as was the extension of nationalization, and in his speeches to the National Assembly, Prime Minister Mauroy repeatedly stressed the desire of the government to use some form of planning to give coherence to its policies. It will not be until the late 1980s that the effectiveness of the commitment will be clear, however. The new government did not aim to introduce a sweeping new system of planning until 1984, when a full five-year plan was to be launched; the Interim Plan of 1982–84 was intended to be mainly a framework for the government's previously agreed macro-economic strategy.[57] Whether the inevitable difficulties that will face this policy can be overcome, however, may determine how easily the government can conjure the spirits of the IVth Plan out of the mists of time in order to recreate a new form of planning for the 1980s.

Notes

1 On the roots of planning see Kuisel (1981), Chs 1 and 7. Recent French accounts include Pascallon (1974) and a semi-official account in Pagé (1975).
2 The funds were largely channelled through the FDES (Fonds de développement économique et social), a body then closely linked to the CGP.
3 In French, 'Le Plan' is also often used to refer to the CGP itself or the consultative process it organizes.
4 Source: list of personnel given to us, July 1979.
5 The UK's National Economic Development Office was apparently modelled on the CGP, and the short-lived Department of Economic Affairs on the equally moribund French Ministry of the National Economy, which has had a precarious but unimportant existence at various times. See Leruez (1978).
6 The joint responsibility for 'planification' and 'aménagement du territoire' is a break with tradition, as is the nomination of a very senior minister to supervise the plan alongside the commissaire. For details of earlier arrangements see Pascallon (1974).
7 But Kuisel (1981, Ch. 8) argues that the CGP was weak even in Monnet's day.

8 See Bonnaud (1976, p. 98) and the discussion in Chapter 7.
9 See Lutz (1969) on this distinction.
10 See Prate (1978) on de Gaulle's views on economic policy.
11 Pascallon (1974) notes that in 1946 a 'Conseil Supérieur du Plan' was set up, but it remained inactive.
12 This description is by John Zysman in a seminar at the LSE in 1980. We are grateful to Anne Stevens for drawing our attention to it.
13 See Assemblée Nationale (1976) for this report.
14 The numerous acronyms are defined in the index, but in any case are used in the abbreviated form in French.
15 Centre d'Etudes Prospectives et d'Informations Internationales. See Chapter 7 for more details on this body.
16 Bureau d'Information et de Prévision Economiques. Some of BIPE's activities are discussed in Chapter 5.
17 We were told by one socialist economist that while many former CGP staff moved on to senior advisory positions in the new government, the Commissariat itself was once again restocked with new and relatively inexperienced personnel after the 1981 elections. M. Rocard, the Planning Minister, had supporters in many parts of the government but they were scattered rather loosely.
18 There is potential for internal conflict here. The Industry Minister, P. Dreyfus, former head of Renault, was also reported to be a close confident of the Premier. It is not clear where this leaves the Budget Minister, let alone the Minister for Planning (Rocard) and Research and Development (Chevenement). In an inteview (*Le Monde*, June 30, 1981), Chevenement discusses his role in the government.
19 See Anne Stevens (1980). The incestuous nature of the 'old boy' network meant that in his years at the CFDT before his appointment as Planning Commissaire in 1981, Hubert Prévot was in fact on secondment from the Finance Ministry under a scheme for support of union officials.
20 The gap between the decision makers and the 'services d'études' is the theme of Milleron *et al.* (1979). Milleron subsequently became head of the CGP's economic service.
21 See OECD (1974) on the administrative structures and interministerial committees in the early 1970s.
22 This may have just been a political manoeuvre to find a post for J.-C. Chevenement, one of the Socialist Party's leading left-wingers.
23 See the interview with P. Joxe, in *Nouvel Economiste*, June 15, 1981 on this point.
24 The activities of the regional planners are not considered in great detail in this book, but are discussed briefly below.
25 This quotation is actually from the *Report on the Principal Options for the Vth Plan* (1964), but is quoted in translation by Lutz (1969).
26 The acronym stands for Modèle Physio-Financier.
27 In retrospect, the forecasts of the Vth Plan were the only ones that were similarly the subject of intense political debate in the earlier years (see a critique in the *Contre-Plan*, Ensemble, 1965).
28 The 'Modèle Dynamique Multi-Sectoriel', see Chapter 5.
29 Left-wing critics argue that government officials were also representatives of business interests before 1981.
30 The rest of the members were from other social interests, the administration, and outside experts.
31 See, for example, Delors (1978). This point was made to us by H. Prévot.
32 See *Rapport sur l'Orientation Préliminaire du VIIème Plan* (CGP, 1975e), which was the relevant report for the VIIth Plan, first phase.

33   See *Rapport sur les Options Principales* (CGP, 1979), which was the relevant first phase report for the VIIIth Plan.
34   As explained in Chapter 3, the government was seeking a rise in unemployment to stem inflation.
35   See Mariano (1973) on this issue.
36   Money supply data from Federal Reserve Bank of St. Louis (1981). See also Table 5.1 in Chapter 5.
37   Budget data from Bank for International Settlements (1981). See also Table 5.1.
38   See P. Mauroy's speech to Parliament, reported in *Le Monde*, July 10, 1981.
39   Rationalization des Choix Budgetaires. See Ullmo (1978) and Chapter 6.
40   Andréani (1978) argues the need for much greater effort in the future to develop social planning and social indicators.
41   The nationalized industries were to be in the forefront of social advance; see Mauroy's speech to Parliament (*Le Monde*, July 10, 1981).
42   See Shonfield (1965, Ch. V) on contrats de programme. This issue is also discussed in Chapters 5 and 7.
43   This point is discussed in Green (1980), Stoffaës (1978), and EEC (1981), and the findings are surveyed in Chapter 7.
44   P. Mauroy's speech to Parliament (*Le Monde*, July 10, 1981) confirms this position, held in opposition.
45   Délégation à l'aménagement du territoire et à l'action régionale.
46   Fonds interministeriel d'aménagement du territoire.
47   In an interview with *Le Monde*, September 9, 1981, the new Planning Minister M. Rocard explained that the Socialists could set the CGP into action easily by appointing a new Commissaire. It had not been possible to appoint a head for DATAR immediately, as this body needed rather more reorganization. M. Rocard was in charge of both national and regional planning. Eventually, B. Attali, brother of J. Attali, was given charge of DATAR (*Le Monde*, October 16, 1981).
48   See Liggins (1975) on the REGINA model and also Pascallon (1974).
49   Programme d'action prioritaire d'initiative régionale.
50   For a discussion of the possibility of contractual arrangements between different levels of government, see Breton and Scott (1978). Canadian Federalism involves extensive arrangements of this sort. Eight of the ten Canadian provinces pay for Ottawa to supply police services through the RCMP, while other services are provided by the provinces in return for payments by Ottawa (e.g. Medicare).
51   See a lengthy interview in *Le Monde* (September 9, 1981), and a speech at Nantes (*Le Monde*, July 8, 1981), warning of the dangers of centralized bureaucracy. M. Rocard became a dedicated opponent of excess state power during the 1970s, a view shared with M. Delors.
52   The VIIth and VIIIth Plan Commission reports also contain union memoranda of dissent.
53   Herzog is a former DP official turned communist politician.
54   For a study commissioned by the CGP on multinationals see Bertin (1975), which argues for tight monitoring of multinational penetration by the industrial sector.
55   There is known to have been intense debate within the government over nationalization, with Rocard and Delors opposing Mauroy and Mitterand's wish for a 100 per cent stake in newly nationalized firms. (See *Le Monde*, September 15, 1981.)
56   Although nominally one of the four senior 'Ministers of State', Rocard has identified himself with currents of opinion opposed to those of Mitterand. This

could severely jeopardize once again the political position of the planners within the administrative–political hierarchy.

57 M. Rocard acknowledged that for the interim plan the broad strategy had already been decided: 'But this plan will not simply be putting decisions already taken into coherence. It will also contain announcements of inter-ministerial policies' (interview in *Le Monde*, September 9, 1981). *Le Monde* (July 8, 1981) had described the interim plan as intended to 'reset the counters to zero'. For details of the interim plan see *Le Monde*, October 22 and 25, 1981.

5 Macro-Economic Policy and the Plan

Introduction

In this chapter we discuss macro-economic planning. In the last years of conservative rule, the planners were forced to concentrate on macro-economic issues, in the face of a public commitment to non-intervention at the micro-economic level. Unfortunately, the desire of the government to appear to avoid interfering with the market, and the analysis the planners themselves adopted of the way the economy worked led to a certain self-contradiction: a five-year programme of no five-year macro programme.

In order to see how this came about, we begin by discussing the models used by the planners to forecast the evolution of the French economy. It is important to begin with such an account, since the assumptions of the main econometric models used by the planners constitute a distillation of the Weltanschauung or ideology of planning in the 1970s. In the third section we consider how far, under ideal institutional arrangements, macro planning and policy could have been integrated in an optimizing framework, drawing on an exercise known as 'Optimix'. We then turn in the fourth section to the actual experience of planning between the oil crisis and the end of the Giscard era in 1981. We look in detail at the preparation of the VIIth Plan; then consider how the subsequent 'Plan Barre' counter-inflationary strategy affected developments, as well as the formal 'readaptation' of the VIIth Plan, and the preparations for the abortive VIIIth Plan. Finally, we draw on French experience and our own analysis, particularly that of Chapter 2, to consider the role macro-economic planning of the sort attempted in France could have in an environment favourable to planning but lacking the ideal circumstances needed for pure intertemporal policy optimization; that is the situation prevailing in France in the 1980s.

The Econometric Models Used for Planning

Formal macro-economic models have been an integral part of French planning since the late 1960s. The VIth Plan forecasts were based on the macro-economic projections emanating from the FIFI model, which was developed from Raymond Courbis's original work on small open economies; his theory of the 'économie concurrencée' or 'competitioned economy'.[1] FIFI was somewhat modified for use in the VIIth Plan (see Roux-Vaillard and Vignon, 1976), and ultimately abandoned in favour of DMS, a model with more conventional Keynesian properties,[2] which was used as the centre-piece of the simulation exercises for the VIIIth Plan. Below we briefly outline certain features of each model,[3] which clarifies their broader implications within the administration and for the wider public. As the planning exercise became increasingly the concern of quasi-academic econometricians, the nature of the models themselves became more controversial.

The basic elements of FIFI play an important role in the analysis of macro-planning discussions which took place during the 1970s. Courbis's original model (see Courbis, 1972), which forms the economic heart of FIFI, assumes a fixed exchange rate, no international factor mobility, and certain crucial behavioural conditions. Thus, the economy is assumed to have a domestic sector which can set prices to cover costs and an exposed tradeables sector which is a price taker on world markets. Wage inflation is assumed to be determined by tightness in the labour market, giving rise to a Phillips curve. Variations in profitability determine the level of investment because the self-financing ratio is assumed to be fixed, and capacity is assumed to determine output in the medium term. However, competitiveness *vis à vis* the rest of the world determines supply capacity and hence employment possibilities in both the short and medium term. One of the immediate implications of such a model is that government stimulatory policies will do very little for employment (which ultimately depends on profitability in the world market), but will certainly worsen the balance of payments. FIFI encapsulates Courbis's preconception that disturbances on world markets will have a differential impact between sectors, with the implication that reflationary policies would primarily act to redistribute employment and output between the exposed and sheltered sectors. The precise causal mechanisms are not clear in the approximately 2,000 equations of the full FIFI model, or even in the 44 equations of the simplified version of Courbis's book, but one can see how such a model constrains policy options. The only obvious policy instrument the planners can offer the government is to act to raise profits by holding down wages. The FIFI model was the subject of intense political controversy. It may have reflected the general opinions of the Pompidou régime, but it was described to us by J. Delors as 'un modèle réactionnaire', and the discussions in the course of the VIIth Plan preparations showed how reluctant the unions were to use policy simulations from it.

There were serious economic and technical weaknesses in FIFI which led to revisions for the VIIth Plan projections, and its ultimate replacement by DMS. The original FIFI model was inappropriate for the flexible exchange rate system operating after 1971, since prices could no longer be treated as effectively exogenous in the exposed sector. Moreover, the strict complementarity of the modelled production process did not allow for capital–labour substitution and the emergence of structural unemployment, a much discussed issue in this period. Roux-Vaillard and Vignon (1976) outline the important changes of assumption for the VIIth Plan: replacing the assumed perfect substitutability of domestic and foreign tradeable goods by a conventional marginal propensity to import function (implying some degree of complementarity) and representing the industrial sector production function in Cobb-Douglas form permitting factor substitutability. But the central technical weaknesses remained. FIFI could not trace out a path for the economy through time, but only gave a static picture of the outcome in the end year of the plan. In that sense, it was more like a 'Tableau Economique' or input–output model than a dynamic behavioural system, which severely restricted its usefulness. Moreover, the number of alternative policy variants and scenarios which could be explored was very limited, a serious weakness in this increasingly uncertain period. Finally, despite the revisions, the handling of floating exchange rates remained unsatisfactory.

Work began on DMS in the early 1970s when an INSEE team visited Canada to study the Candide model, itself an offspring of the Keynesian Klein–Goldberger model. The model builders were particularly concerned to overcome FIFI's central weaknesses, and DMS became operational around 1978. It has in the region of 2,000 equations and is dynamic in the sense of plotting a path for the economy in the medium term over time. Its main analytic innovation is the explicit modelling of the growth of capacity year by year using a vintage capital approach which combines complementarity between labour and capital in the short run, when capacity is fixed, with long run substitutability as labour shifts to equipment of a newer vintage. It also offers great flexibility, allowing INSEE and the planners to simulate the consequences year by year of a vast number of variations in policy instruments and to calculate the implications for the main industrial sectors rather than just the aggregates (see Charpin *et al.*, 1979).

The modelling of short-term output determination incorporates much of the traditional Keynesian approach to effective demand and imports. Short-run production and employment depend on aggregate demand, though the process of capital accumulation moves the model from period to period. This leads to major differences in the policy recommendations stemming from the model, compared to FIFI. Moreover, DMS adopts a rather different approach to the self-financing of private investment, assuming that prices are determined by a mark-up on costs including a certain profit necessary to service old as well as new equipment. This has the 'radical' result of the model suggesting that reflation can provide a double bonus in a situation of 'stagflation'. Stimulatory policies increase output and employment which restores profits and reduces the need for firms to increase prices in order to cover fixed costs. Hence, despite the element of wage inflation that comes from reflation in simulations of DMS, traditional Keynesian policies act to raise output and mitigate one of the causes of inflation – the attempt by firms to improve failing profitability.

Thus, the econometricians built the planners a much more flexible and useful tool than FIFI, but one based on an unashamedly Keynesian perspective of the world. There were some technical problems as well; the lack of precise National Accounts data before 1959 caused problems in estimation. Ordinary least squares was, in general, employed, and the resulting estimators proved rather sensitive to minor changes in the data base, as occurred when France changed its national accounting system in 1976 (see Flouzat, 1975). DMS was also unfashionable in other ways. The model ignored the impact for better or worse made by monetarist theorists in the fields of economics or politics; there is no significant role for financial variables, whether domestic or international, with the exchange rate taken as exogenous and the money stock not entering any of the equations.[4] This did not reflect the views of the Barre administration, which was keen to control the money stock and stressed 'supply side' economics. Nevertheless, DMS (along with another short-term model, METRIC) was extensively used by the planners in the debates over the VIIIth Plan, and also by the Socialists before taking office to simulate the effects of their policies. It was designed to be used by outsiders as well as the government (in conjunction with the input–output model PROP-AGE in the system known as Projections Detaillées Glissantes (PDG)). The government had had a virtual monopoly on economic forecasting for many years, a situation that satisfied neither the opposition nor the Barre government with its liberal German-style views about the economy. Thus, virtually everyone supported the opening up of the model and the PDG system. The only source of independent econometric forecasting in the late 1970s came from Professor Courbis, who continues to run an independent unit at the University of Paris, Nanterre: the Groupe d'Analyse Macro-économique Appliquée (GAMA).

All this led to an intense politicization of what may seem to be rather technical econometric issues, as the debates on the VIIth and VIIIth Plans revealed. For many, the FIFI model came to have the ideological status accorded in the UK to the doctrine of monetarism itself, rather than being treated as a mere technical instrument, such as the London Business School Model. The issues of fundamental ideology are always much closer to the surface in France than in England or the United States, but the ideological content of the economic analysis we will be discussing operates at various levels that take different forms. We must be careful to distinguish the different perspectives of the various actors: the politicians, the planners (who themselves are not totally homogenous in their views), and other civil servants who actually make policy. One should in fact go further and distinguish between the underlying vision of the economic system held by the actors, and its manifestation in formal models, which are normally rather more ad hoc in assumptions and different from the original theories from which they were derived. The planners were probably more radical in orientation than was implicit in the FIFI model during the mid-1970s, though the model encapsulated fairly well the general views of Pompidou and Giscard. However, as the Project Optimix discussed below shows, it is not always possible to infer the true ideological beliefs of politicians from what they say or do.

Thus, during the early 1970s there was a congruence between the views of some of the planners, their forecasting model, and the government, which allowed the VIth Plan to proceed relatively successfully from 1970 to 1973 within the tightly circumscribed notion of planning that it represented. In the late 1970s, the planners had an econometric model that formally articulated their views and allowed the choices as seen from the CGP to be quantified, but there was a total disjunction between the planners on the one side, and the politicians and important civil servants on the other. Needless to say, decision-making authority did not rest with the planners who, in consequence, became increasingly isolated in the last years of Giscard. Paradoxically, the incoming government in 1981 held views which could be readily assimilated within the perspective of the planners' model, with the result that the Socialist government on coming to power was able to announce an Interim Plan that closely resembled the advice previously passing from the CGP to Barre, and the likely outcome of which had been simulated on the government's own forecasting model before the elections and circulated to business in order to assure them of the security of future profits under Socialist policies.

Formal Policy Optimization before 1975: 'Project Optimix'

One very interesting analytic exploration of the issues we have just touched on occurred during an attempt, carried out in the context of the VIth Plan at CEPREMAP, to see whether econometric models could be used to trace out optimal policy programmes for the economy; the 'Project Optimix' (see Guesnerie and Malgrange, 1972, and Deleau, Guesnerie, and Malgrange, 1972a). The first problem faced by the Optimix team was to deduce what the government's objectives must have been, to use them as the maximand in a constrained optimization problem. (Heal, 1973, discusses constrained optimization as a description of the planning problem.) Guesnerie and Malgrange observe that the *arguments* of a macro-economic objective function may be elucidated by interviews with decision makers, but the relative valuations placed on them (the marginal rates of substitution) cannot be so readily evaluated. Thus, within the heart of the planning system, the researchers had to devote considerable efforts to discovering the government's actual objectives. The Optimix exercise was not set up by the state to ensure optimization of its policies; it was a quasi-academic exercise commissioned by the operational end of planning from their mathematical colleagues to see if optimal planning was feasible.

The researchers decided that, since they could not formalize the preferences of the public decision maker ex ante they would adopt the method of revealed preference to deduce what the preferences of the government would have been if it made certain observed choices subject to known constraints. In the complex macro-economic optimization studied by Optimix, the idea was that if the model used (FIFI) was linear (or at least approximately so for small variations about the chosen outcome), knowledge of the marginal impact of any policy variable would allow one to deduce the implicit marginal valuations of the state. Thus, the FIFI model was used in reverse, with the analysts taking the policy options chosen for the VIth Plan and working back to what the implicit objectives must have been for the chosen outcome to be preferred to any alternative.

Guesnerie and Malgrange (1972) pause to reflect on the nature of government objectives, classifying them into variables with an immediate impact, a present and future impact, and variables that are not really objectives at all but which the government has to worry about because of the inadequacies of the model, known as proxy targets. If the prime objective is inflation control, one need not express direct preferences about the money stock if one believes the model's prescription of the best counter-inflation strategy will automatically print out an appropriate monetary target, but if one suspects the model understates the effects of monetary expansion, there will be an extra penalty on monetary growth in the objective function. Certain conditions had to hold for the revealed preference method to work, such as the government having actually referred to the model in formulating its objectives, and having confidence in the forecasts of the model and the effects of the variation. As Guesnerie and Malgrange note, these were not necessarily satisfied, even in the late 1960s, and we know that the Barre government had little faith in the model by the late 1970s. Oddly enough in a technical exercise of this type, Guesnerie and Malgrange also suggest that the government's underlying objective may actually have been support of profit and the ruling class for its own sake, though the point is not followed up and they instead stress the practical problem of distinguishing between final and proxy objectives. Thus, they note that the budget balance, although in principle merely a proxy target, because of the sensitivity of the balance of payments to the government deficit clearly became a goal in its own right in the early 1970s, irrespective of what was happening to the macro-economy.

The Optimix exercise went on to show how, with the deduced objective function and constraints imposed by the model, something like an optimal dynamic response to an unfolding uncertain path of the economy could be developed (Deleau, Guesnerie, and Malgrange, 1972a). They show that under certain conditions, knowledge of the government's past decisions would enable planners to calculate policy solutions that would be considered optimal by the state for future oriented choices. But the entire exercise assumes that the state has been able to choose optimal strategies in the past, and can presumably do so in the future. Knowledge of the objective function simply allows the planners to *predict* what the government would do anyway, possibly a superfluous activity. However, the exercise would make sense if the government told the planners to run their model, for example, to maximize employment subject to predetermined limits for the balance of payments deficit and inflation. Here it would be assumed that the state knew explicitly what it wanted, but was ignorant of the workings of the economy and hence would not have always chosen correctly in the past. In a world of environmental uncertainty, a government that could instinctively solve its problems in the past may not be able to do so in the future if increasing uncertainty is making things more complex.

The flaw in this particular technocratic approach to planning will be appreciated by anyone versed in Lindblom's analysis, or the effects of informational imperfections on individual and public decision-making (see Chapter 2). In the fog of ignorance surrounding actual choices, it makes much more sense for models to be used hesitatingly in exploring the potential of possible approaches, and to try to discover new options, rather than attempt to select the optimal policy using what purports to be a well-defined account of the government's objectives and a correct model of the economic system. The Optimix project was very interesting in exploring the deepest questions of policy optimization in a technocratic context. But the validity of the exercise is enhanced if we suppose that the state cannot itself search through all possible policy mixes each time around without help. The planners will then be looking for fairly robust objective functions, and searching for policies that might not easily be spotted by the authorities and which, while not necessarily optimal, nevertheless give high values for a number of objective functions that might appeal to the state.

Macro-Economic Policy and Planning, 1970–81

Problems in the 1970s

We begin with a brief outline of the problems with which the French authorities had to come to grips during the 1970s. Some long-run structural problems began to emerge in the French economy in the late 1960s, and were aggravated by the post-1973 crisis. Our discussion focuses around Table 5.1 which summarizes the main macro-economic data for the periods 1949–70 and, in more detail, 1970–80.

French economic growth was fast by international standards until 1973, with the highest rates toward the end of the period, due in part to a steadily rising share of investment in GDP. GDP grew consistently by more than 5 per cent per annum and investment by more than 7 per cent p.a. after 1955. Exports did even better (growing at an average rate of 9.8 per cent p.a. between 1952 and 1970) but without outrunning imports (which grew at 9.85 per cent p.a.) so there was no systematic improvement in the trade balance despite a good performance in the early 1960s. Although inflation was relatively high by international standards in the 1950s and early 1960s unemployment was consistently low.

Serious difficulties began to emerge in two areas in the late 1960s: unemployment and declining profitability, which was held to threaten future investment and growth. Unemployment roughly doubled between 1963 and 1970; though the absolute level was probably still below 300,000 it had previously been seen as a

Table 5.1 Macro-Economic Indicators, 1949–80

Year	Annual % change in: Real GDP	Investment[a]	Prices[b]	Levels of: Unemployment[c] (000's)	Balance of payments[d] ($b.)	Policy Variables Budget surplus[e] (% of GDP)	Monetary growth (%)[f] (annual rate)	Period
1949–55	5.0	2.4	6.1	226–283			16.7	1961–63
1955–60	5.0	7.8	6.1	161–254			7.7	1963–65
1960–65	5.5	7.4	3.8	97–142				
1965–70	5.6	7.9	5.1	148–262			−1.6	1969–70
1971	5.4	4.8	5.5	337	0.5			
1972	5.9	7.1	6.2	380	0.3	0.8	12.2	1970–73
1973	5.4	5.9	7.3	394	−0.7			
1974	3.2	1.1	13.7	498	−6.0			
1975	0.2	−3.4	11.8	840	−0.1	−0.7	12.4	1974–76
1976	5.2	4.5	9.6	933	6.1			
1977	2.8	−0.7	9.4	1,073	−3.3	−0.8	7.4	1977
1978	3.6	1.4	9.1	1,167	3.8	−1.8	11.2	1978
1979	3.2	2.6	10.8	1,350	1.2	−0.6	12.3	1979
1980	1.3	−0.8	13.6	1,451	−7.8	0.3	8.0	1980

[a] Gross fixed capital formation.

[b] Implicit GDP deflator up to 1970; then consumer price index.

[c] Carré et al. figures used up to 1960; OECD thereafter. Earlier figures are not strictly comparable. Range given for 1949–70.

[d] Current account in $US: deficits (−), surpluses (+).

[e] General government surplus as percentage of GDP. Negative figures indicate borrowing. See BIS, *Annual Report* 1981 (p. 36) for exact definitions.

[f] Annualized rates of growth of narrow money supply (i.e. equivalent to M_1). Data from FRB St. Louis, *International Economic Conditions 1961–81*, based on IMF statistics and definitions.

Sources: Pre-1970, Carré et al. (1975); post-1970, OECD, BIS, FRB St. Louis.

negligible problem. The planners believed that technical change and the rising cost of labour relative to capital was causing a substitution of machinery for men. In turn, the higher capital–labour ratio seems to have led to an apparent decline in the rate of return on investment and profitability. The planners were worried about structural unemployment as a problem in its own right, and because of the implications for capital formation and growth. Many of these ideas found numerical expression in Sautter (1975), who clearly influenced thinking in the VIIth Plan deliberations (much of his data were reproduced in the text of the report of the VIIth Plan Committee on Employment, discussed below). He reports that the overall capital–labour ratio had risen by 2.4 per cent p.a. during 1950–59, but by 5.5 per cent p.a. during 1964–73. Value added per unit of capital had risen by 2 per cent p.a. during 1950–57 but had fallen by 1 per cent p.a. over 1964–73. His calculations also suggest a marked drop in the rate of profit on industrial investment, though this was substantially offset by a cut in profit taxation. In fact, French profitability seems to have held up reasonably well by international standards, with labour's share in total domestic income rising from 60.4 per cent in 1960–64 to 67.5 per cent in 1974 and 73.0 per cent in 1980. The comparable rise in the UK was 74.7 per cent to 81.4 per cent and for Germany, 62.9 per cent to 71.8 per cent.[5] The rate of increase in total factor productivity is estimated by Sautter to have fallen from 3.8 per cent p.a. in 1950–57 to 3.0 per cent in 1964–73. Whatever the significance of the exact numbers, there was a clear doubt in the planners' minds in the mid-1970s as to whether high levels of industrial investment could continue to sustain growth in the way it had done in the past. However, as we shall see, the official projections underlying the VIIth Plan took no account of these doubts, and postulated a high and further rising share of investment in GDP, an assumption about which the OECD, among others, expressed severe scepticism (see OECD, 1976, *France*, p. 38).

These problems were severely compounded by the post-1973 recession. Unemployment, which had risen slightly despite the rapid growth between 1970 and 1973, nearly trebled to over 800,000 by 1975. The balance of payments also became an acute concern as the oil bill rose. Although Chirac reflated slightly in September 1975, it would appear from the published documents (such as *Rapport de la Commission: Relations Economiques et Financières avec l'Extérieur*) (CGP, 1975b) that the French did not accept a 'Keynesian' analysis of the proper response to the oil crisis.[6] It was seen as inevitable that the industrialized nations would have to adopt deflationary policies, and the planners feared severe recessionary problems before a full recovery. The French general government borrowing requirement, 1974–76, was 0.7 per cent of GDP, as against 4.6 per cent in the UK and 3.6 per cent in Germany (Bank for International Settlements, *Annual Report*, 1981, p. 36). Even this was clearly involuntary (due to falling tax receipts and higher social security spending) and efforts were made to reduce it, which provoked great arguments in the planning debates. In the end, a surplus of 0.3 per cent of GDP was recorded for 1980.

There was a temporary upturn in several indices, though not employment, at the time the VIIth Plan was launched in 1976 (see Table 5.1). GDP and industrial production rose sharply in 1976 after a dramatic fall of the latter in 1974–75, exports had held up surprisingly well, and non-oil imports were down. The government used this development as a basis for longer-term optimism but the planners did not share the official view that full employment could be restored easily by 1980.

Thus, by the mid-1970s, France was broadly facing the traditional symptoms of the 'British Disease': unemployment, inflation, and a balance of payments problem. The optimism of the 1960s and early 1970s, reflected, for example, in the 1973 Hudson Institute Report, *L'Envol de la France*, which foresaw France rapidly overtaking Germany as Europe's major industrial producer, gave way to extreme pessimism. The unemployment problem was all the more severely felt because, despite the gradual rise before 1973 and the fears it had led to, France has always had very low levels of recorded unemployment and the new levels represented a bigger proportionate increase than, for example, in the UK. The limited coverage of unemployment insurance also aggravated the social impact. Inflation, too, while nothing new to France, was more of an obsession with even French Socialist politicians than was the case until recently in the UK. The balance of payments problem was made more worrying by the lack of indigenous oil, and the longer-term fear that France would be hard put to find niches in the international division of labour between low wage countries and the most advanced technological exporters (see Chapter 7). The congruence of these medium-term problems in 1975 might lead one to have expected an important role for the national planning exercise in the search for solutions.

The Preparation of the VIIth Plan
In fact, the VIIth Plan was a wasted opportunity because the government chose not to use the exercise in the formation and articulation of its priorities. The VIIth Plan experience is interesting in its own right, highlighting the impossibility of the procedure operating effectively against the opposition of a determined

government. Moreover, a detailed study of the documents indicates what the exercise could have offered a government with a less well-defined sense of the appropriate direction in which to move.

The mood we encountered at the CGP, INSEE, and the DP in the summer of 1975 was one of intense gloom. Nobody we spoke to thought that the CGP's 'pessimistic' projections at that time, of over 1 million unemployed in 1980, were at all unrealistic. One typical response came when we asked an official of the DP how he saw the outcome of the VIIth Plan; 'Mal', he replied. The planners' spirits were not improved by an eighteen-month period with no Commissaire until Jean Ripert was appointed in late 1974, with the VIth Plan due to end in 1975. The planning cycle was then put into accelerated motion, with the VIIth Plan actually produced in July 1976.[7] This unseemly haste gave rise to many complaints about lack of time for consultation.

It is interesting to trace in detail the shifts and evolutions of official and technical opinion during the course of the planning process, to see how the long-term specialists' pessimism was converted into the optimism of the VIIth Plan.[8] In addition to our own discussions over subsequent years, there are two published accounts of the way the forecasts for the VIIth Plan gradually changed: Roux-Vaillard (1976) and the *Rapport du Comité: Emploi et Travail* (CGP, 1976e).

The planners did not know what was going to happen to Western economies in 1974, nor even what exactly had happened in France. But by 1975, the current state of the world was quite evident. The alternative scenarios run on the FIFI model, even as modified, emphasized the importance of exogenous world demand for French growth; in fact the alternative plan variants for the 1st Phase were basically alternative growth paths for the world economy. The French consistently predicted higher growth in France than in her trading partners, as had been the case before 1973, but lower growth elsewhere was still reflected in virtually identical reductions in French growth. Therefore, it seems very strange that the government and the planners should have stuck so firmly to GDP growth forecasts in excess of 5.0 per cent per year, 1976–80, when there was such uncertainty about world economic recovery, As Cave (1981) suggests, this outcome was clearly determined primarily for political reasons.

There were two scenarios for the simulations undertaken in spring 1975, optimistic ('rose') and pessimistic ('triste'). In the optimistic one, the world was assumed to have mastered the problems of stagnation and inflation, and could absorb whatever France had to export. The need to sell enough abroad to pay for costlier oil affected domestic consumption and investment but the effect on output was far less. The pessimistic scenario saw a continuing but relatively unsuccessful fight against unemployment and inflation, both of which were projected to be higher in this case. But neither scenario foresaw an elimination of the unemployment problem during the VIIth Plan. The report of the Commission on Growth and Finance for the 1st Phase of the plan[9] estimated unemployment at around 600,000 on the optimistic assumption of 5.2 per cent p.a. growth (the growth rate in 1970–73 had been 5.9 per cent p.a.). The pessimistic assumption of a 3.8 per cent p.a. growth rate led to projected unemployment of between 1 and 1.2 million by 1980.

But even in the 1st Phase, these unemployment figures were seriously questioned. In Annex III of the same Growth and Finance report, the figure of 600,000 unemployed quoted in the main text was queried on the basis of what were proposed as more plausible estimates of labour force participation: 'In 1980 for an ex-ante labour supply of 23.2 million people, employment will rise respectively to 22.2 million (Projection 1) and 21.2 million (Projection 2).' Thus, the annex predicts unemployment rising to between 1 and 2 million by 1980. The technical annex to another report was even more sceptical. 'Even from a "pedagogic" point of view, it seems that these two scenarios give an excessively optimistic view relative to under-employment: the unemployment forecast in scenario 1 seems seriously under-estimated; the hypothesis of "variation in the activity rate" minimizes the true impact of the problem especially in scenario 2 which could undermine the reasoning concerning the means and consequences of restoring external balance' (*Rapport de la Commission: Relations Economiques et Financières avec l'Extérieur* (CGP, 1975b), p. 97). These figures were all published in the official documents, though the manner of presentation could lead a casual reader to overlook the unemployment forecasts. Unpublished papers (such as *Deux Projections pour 1980*, INSEE, 1975) confirmed that high levels of unemployment were robustly forecast by all the variants consistent with government guidelines.

All the projections contained alternative hypotheses about not only real growth rates for the world economy, but also rates of inflation in the rest of the world, as if they could be expressed in the same units. Measures to reduce inflation were assumed not to reduce growth, even in the short run. The planners were working with the most rigid assumptions of a fixed effective exchange rate, though the connection between domestic inflation and employment breaks down if we have a floating exchange rate with flexible real wages. There appears to have been no consideration of a scenario in which the exchange rate was deliberately lowered; both the planners and the political authorities considered devaluation to be ineffective. The *Rapport de la Commission: Relations Economiques et Financières avec l'Extérieur* (CGP, 1975b) sums up the official view (Chapter 3, part II (6)), which is worth quoting in its entirety as virtually the only consideration of the matter in 82 pages of main text:

> Finally, it seems necessary that the average parity of the franc should remain relatively stable against other currencies during the period considered. The Commission considers that a depreciation of our money would immediately present serious problems: effects on the commercial balance which would risk deteriorating, putting at risk the primary objective of seeking a surplus; threats on internal prices; alteration of confidence in the franc of a sort as to make foreign borrowing harder and costlier; raising the franc value of foreign currency debts. It is by the moderation of domestic price increases that the necessary gains in competitiveness must be obtained. (p. 75)

Thus the situation at the end of the 1st Phase of the VIIth Plan was that even relatively optimistic assumptions about world economic recovery projected unemployment to be higher in 1980 than the already serious levels of 1975, with policies of macro-economic stimulation or devaluation ruled out. Somehow the government had to get out of this mess. The planning exercise had in fact carried out a rather useful task; it had shown within the limits of forecasting techniques available that unemployment was going to remain a major problem for France in 1980 under any sort of existing policies, even on favourable assumptions about world trade. This could have provoked a serious re-examination of policy, perhaps with the FIFI model being used to discover policy mixes with favourable outcomes in a variety of circumstances. Instead, the government chose to suppress or massage the figures until a set of acceptable projections emerged.[10] We have seen in Chapter 3 how far this led the VIIth Plan projections away from the actual outcomes.

The 'massage' operation was rather complex, and reflected the government's concern for external balance. First, the VIIth Plan was given the stated objective of restoring full employment, but all figures were suppressed from the plan itself. They were put into an accompanying *Dossier Quantitatif*, whose normative status was even less than that accompanying theVIth Plan which at least had macro-economic objectives. The *Dossier Quantitatif* also managed to avoid including any statistics at all on unemployment, the reduction of which was stated to be the prime goal of the plan. However, the projections that were published were not those of the 1st Phase reports, and Roux-Vaillard (1976) gives an account of how they were altered, with Table 5.2, reproduced from their paper, showing how the forecasts actually changed between November 1973 and April 1976. Ostensibly, the final version incorporated into the *Dossier Quantitatif* was an average of the optimistic and pessimistic variants of the earlier simulations but this interpretation conceals a lot. As we have seen, many forecasters in 1975 already thought the pessimistic version was too optimistic so that averaging the two would not give a certainty equivalent. In fact, the averaging was done for some variables but not for others so that by assuming a slowdown in productivity growth the final projection had employment growing at a rate much closer to the earlier optimistic projections though GDP was to grow more slowly. Productivity projections fell steadily over 1973–76. Perhaps, more subtly, it will be noticed that the quoted growth rates are for the whole period 1970–80. By 1976, the 1975 figures were, it is true, not fully known but it was already clear that they were very poor so that to forecast the *same* growth rate over 1970–80 in 1976 as

Table 5.2 The Evolution of the VIIth Plan's Growth Rate Forecasts, 1973–76

			For 1970–80[a]					For 1975–80[b]
	Nov. 1973	May 1974	April 1975 opti- mistic	April 1975 pessi- mistic	Oct. 1975 No. 1	Oct. 1975 No. 2	April 1976	April 1976
Gross domestic production	5.7	5.7	5.3	4.5	5.1	4.4	4.6	5.7
Household consumption	5.6	5.2	5.1	4.5	4.7	4.4	4.6	4.2
Productive investment	6.8	7.6	6.6	4.7	6.3	4.5	5.4	7.5
Apparent hourly productivity of labour	5.7	5.6	5.5	5.0	5.3	5.1	5.0	6.0
Total employment	0.9	0.9	0.8	0.5	0.7	0.6	0.7	1.2
Price of GDP	5.9	6.9	7.7	8.0	8.4	8.4	7.9	7.5
Average hourly wage	10.3	11.3	12.4	12.4	12.9	12.7	13.4	12.3
Inflation among France's partners	5.8	7.0	8.3	8.3	8.5	8.5	8.5	7.5
Growth of France's partners	4.2	4.5	3.5	2.7	3.6	2.8	3.2	4.2

Source: [a]Roux-Vaillard and Vignon (1976). Their figures are rates for 1970–80, because the initial estimates were made before the oil crisis, and also because 1975 data were still provisional in 1976.
[b]VIIth Plan, *Dossier Quantitatif* (1976).

in 1975 was to implicitly project a rate about one-fifth higher for the 1976–80 part of the course.

The Employment Committee for the VIIth Plan was severely critical of the projections in the final *Dossier Quantitatif*, and their 400 page report (*Rapport du Comité: Emploi et Travail* (CGP, 1976e)) is one of the most illuminating documents about French planning in recent years. Five of the thirty-one committee members were trade unionists, and their views must have influenced the final report, though the two each from the socialist CFDT and communist CGT formally resigned six weeks before the deliberations ended. The committee used FIFI as a basis for discussion, but took the opportunity to record a battery of criticisms (see page 63), some of which related to the need for a finer degree of labour market disaggregation but many of which attacked the fundamentals of the model. The report objected to the wages–prices–unemployment link of the open economy assumption ('L'existence d'une relation salaires–prix–chômage peut-être incriminée en elle-même'), the result of which was that any policy measure raising unit costs reduced employment. It was particularly dissatisfied with the message from FIFI that reductions in working hours would only raise measured employment if pay fell with hours worked. Though not strictly part of the model, the committee also objected to the way that labour force participation was always assumed to fall as unemployment rose, absorbing part of the excess supply. Despite these reservations, the report is emphatic that an intelligent and critical use of a formal model was a vital intellectual discipline.

The report also provided a detailed scrutiny of the quantitative basis for the actual numerical projections used in the plan calculations (see Chapter 14). Table 5.3, reproduced from the report, traces the evolution of the labour market between 1960 and 1974, and of the forecasts between April 1975 and May 1976. It shows how the 1975 projections of the 1.4 million and 1.0 million unemployed were turned into a 'gap between resources and employment' of 738,000, which was then transformed into an unemployment figure of 617,000 by assuming a greater variability in the participation rate. A substantial part of the 'improvement' was obtained by postulating a growth of employment in the (sheltered) service sector of 3.2 per cent p.a. over the whole 1974–80 period (i.e. significantly faster than this for the remaining 1976–80 stretch), which compared with an outcome of 3.5 per cent p.a. for 1970–74. A specific section of the report queried the government's employment figures (pp. 357–9), and commented that behind the rapid growth of the service sector was assumed to be growth of value added at a rate never before experienced. They were especially

Table 5.3 Employment Growth 1960–74 and VIIth Plan Projections for 1974–80

	Levels ('000s of persons)						1980ᵃ			Annual % growth rates			1974–80ᵇ		
	1960	1965	1970	1973	1974	1 Apr. 75	2 Apr. 75	Feb. 76	1960–65	1965–70	1970–74	1 Apr. 75	2 Apr. 75	Feb. 76
Population	45,184	48,633	50,225	51,618	52,045	55,879	55,879	54,400	1.5	0.7	1.1	1.0	1.0	0.7
Labour force	19,294	20,236	21,133	21,772	22,040	23,187	22,951	23,014	1.0	0.9	1.1	0.9	0.7	0.7
Withdrawals from labour market³	−192	−195	−145	−145	−135	−145	−145	−145	—	—	—	—	—	—
Unemployment	−239	−269	−356	−450	−501	−730	−1,010	−617	—	—	—	—	—	—
Total employment	18,863	19,772	20,632	21,177	21,404	22,312	21,796	22,252	0.9	0.8	0.9	0.7	0.4	0.7
By sector:														
Agriculture	4,011	3,316	2,729	2,397	2,294	1,827	1,827	1,827	−3.7	−3.8	−4.2	−3.7	−3.7	−3.7
Food Industry	664	684	655	643	638	622	642	651	0.1	−0.3	−0.7	−0.4	0.1	0.3
Energy	386	376	346	330	326	239	233	312	−0.5	−1.6	−1.5	−5.0	−5.2	−0.7
Industry	4,589	4,903	5,051	5,252	5,320	5,429	5,315	5,337	1.3	0.6	1.3	0.3	0	0.1
Transport & Telecommunication	923	1,029	1,089	1,125	1,156	1,150	1,099	1,215	2.2	1.1	1.5	0	−0.8	0.8
Housing	63	67	78	85	88	90	90	85	1.2	3.1	3.1	0.4	0.4	−0.6
Building & Public Works	1,590	1,940	2,075	2,048	2,050	2,014	1,933	1,936	4.1	1.4	−0.3	−0.3	−1.0	−0.9
Services	1,992	2,239	2,732	3,017	3,132	3,717	3,551	3,792	2.4	4.1	3.5	2.3	2.1	3.2
Commerce	1,951	2,145	2,366	2,491	2,535	2,791	2,673	2,614	1.9	2.0	1.7	1.6	0.9	0.5
Total of above	16,169	16,679	17,121	17,388	17,539	17,879	17,363	17,769	0.6	0.5	0.6	0.3	−0.1	0.2
Other	2,694	3,093	3,511	3,789	3,865	4,433	4,433	4,483	2.8	2.6	2.5	2.3	2.3	2.6
Total Employment	18,863	19,772	20,632	21,177	21,404	22,312	21,796	22,252	0.9	0.8	0.9	0.7	0.3	0.7
Of which self-employed	5,655	5,009	4,474	4,118	4,015	3,329	3,266	3,249	−2.4	−2.2	−2.8	−3.0	−3.5	−3.5

ᵃProjections for 1980 made in April 1975 (1, the 'optimistic' scenario; 2, the 'pessimistic' scenario), and in February 1976 for the final plan.
ᵇAssumptions made for the projections which are queried by the report.
Source: Rapport: Emploi et Travail (CGP, 1976e).

critical of the supposed flexibility in the participation rate, which was not based on behavioural experience or stated policy, and noticed the absence of policies to bring an assumed reduction in the working week, which exceeded extrapolations very substantially. Finally, they questioned the unspecified mechanism of industrial policy that was assumed to create 50,000 jobs (though, as we see in Chapter 7, the Industry Commission Report (1970) did make some precise suggestions here) and queried whether the assumed 100,000 public sector jobs the government was promising to create was consistent with announced budgetary targets. The Employment Committee report pins down for us many of the data manipulations which took place in the 2nd Phase of the VIIth Plan.

As we have seen, the report was also very critical of the forecasts of government action. It referred continually and sceptically to the fact that, under its terms of reference (given by the Gaullist Chirac government), the restoration of full employment was declared to be the main goal of the VIIth Plan. Chapter 9 of the report discussed the overall strategy that could have been, and seemed to have been, adopted. Considering the sectors nominated for particular assistance in the draft proposals of the plan's Industry Commission, it expressed concern that these had not been picked for their ability to contribute to the employment problem: 'It seems that the studies done have concentrated on the possibilities for production in each sector and especially on the external market, rather than the effects on employment of a deliberate ('volontariste') reorientation of final demand, especially internal demand' (Employment Committee Report (CGP, 1976e, p. 175). The report considered three possible ways to reduce unemployment other than strictly macro-financial policy measures: reduced immigration, shorter working hours, and earlier retirement. On immigration the committee was mindful of the benefits, often overlooked, that immigration brought to France, but broadly favoured a greater use of domestic workers for jobs done by immigrants, on a phased basis. The discussions of shorter working weeks and earlier retirements illustrated the interactions between the politics and the econometrics of economic policy analysis. The committee wanted to see some form of work sharing and, as we have seen above, was annoyed by FIFI's projections on this subject. It observed (p. 316) that if other countries were carrying out the same policies, France's relative competitive position would not be affected, and in fact proposed specific policies to shorten working hours. On the retirement age, the committee again used FIFI, and while deploring the 'brutality' of the model (p. 333), they observed that it was valuable to have attention drawn to the adverse macro-economic consequences of higher social security levies on those still in employment in order to finance more pensioners.

There is no need to go into the other proposals in the report, though they were very detailed and paid attention to numerous micro aspects of the labour market designed to monitor and improve its functioning. As one of the CGP staff on this group told us later, this kind of exercise brings people together for a process of reflection that would not occur in any other form in France, and the willingness of the unions to participate just up to a point where they begin to feel compromised by the final reports is an indication of the interest they have. The VIIth Plan Employment Report went further than any similar document in touching on the real controversies. Having said all this, the report of the Employment Committee was completely ignored. One planning official commented to us that the more work that went into plan reports, the less attention they got from the government.

We should note that not all the planners to whom we spoke shared the scepticism of the Emploi-Travail committee about the VIIth Plan's contribution. One forecaster stressed the apparent upturn in 1976, when industrial production rose by 9 per cent having fallen by 8 per cent in 1975. The mild reflationary stimulus given in 1975 may have helped, but Barre's policies put this into reverse and the recovery did not last. On the whole, however, we did not find many people who were happy with the final macro-economic forecasts of the VIIth Plan. Certainly the OECD, also writing in early 1976 with access to at least as good information on the coming upturn in world trade, expressed very severe doubts as to whether the VIIth Plan could be realized. Commenting on the two variants' figures they said, 'Either way this represents a brisk and steady growth, and, with the means of intervention at present available to the authorities, it is hard to see how it could be achieved', (OECD, *France*, 1976, p. 38).

The VIIth Plan and the 'Plan Barre'

The replacement of the Chirac administration by Barre's in September 1976 gave a new twist to macro-economic planning. Barre, an economist of considerable political experience, had his own ideas about economic policy, and his first act was to introduce the 'Plan Barre', a programme of fairly orthodox conservative anti-inflationary measures. This effectively put the full employment goal of the VIIth Plan to one side, though there were modest proposals to reduce unemployment, the Pactes d'Emploi, which started in 1977 incorporating reductions in social security levies for newly recruited young people, and some training expenditures. The government's aim was to reduce the budget deficit, and targets for the money stock (M2) were adopted from 1977. Table 5.1 shows that the tightening of the budgetary stance continued up to 1980, with a deflationary response to the 1979 oil price increase. Although the government modified its initial desire to restore immediate budget balance in 1977–78, with some deficit anticipated in 1978–79, French fiscal policy in the late 1970s was much more restrictive than in other OECD countries. In fact, the Barre government went as far as it could to renounce the objectives of the VIIth Plan in presenting a *Rapport sur l'Adaptation du VIIème Plan* (1978), which foreshadowed the approach of the VIIIth Plan and explicitly committed the government to non-interventionism to an even greater extent than hitherto.

The results of the Plan Barre were mixed. Table 5.1 indicates an initial success in 1977 in holding down the growth of the money supply from the levels recorded in 1970–76, but Giscard as President never approached the monetary rigidity of his Finance Ministry days in the late 1960s. However, the Barre government felt able to claim, in the VIIIth Plan (Chapter 1), that its policies had been successful, and growth certainly did exceed 3.0 per cent p.a. over 1977–79, with an overall annual average growth rate of 3.7 per cent during 1975–79. But growth slumped sharply in 1980 in the wake of the 1979 oil price rises. The overall growth performance may appear to be relatively good by the standards of other OECD countries (though far worse than VIIth Plan projections, even if these were not targets), but it cannot be said to constitute an implementation of the VIIth Plan, which after all had set full employment as its goal.

There was an attempt to evaluate the impact of the employment policies actually carried out under the VIIth Plan in the report of the VIIIth Plan Employment Commission (see *Rapport de la Commission Emploi et Relations de Travail*, (CGP, 1980b), pp. 93–7). Ostensibly each of the three Pactes d'Emploi schemes between 1977 and 1980 had subsidized between 300,000 and 500,000 workers in its period of operation. The report estimated total expenditures related to unemployment to have risen from 0.76 to 1.56 per cent of GDP between 1974 and 1979, including both unemployment pay and subsidies to promote jobs. Some 74 per cent of this was unemployment pay, which emphasizes how small the macro-economic stabilization effect of this social insurance is in France. The commission estimated that the Pactes d'Emploi had actually created fewer than 100,000 jobs net, allowing for the OECD estimate that around 70–80 per cent of such 'new jobs' are displacements from elsewhere. The report also criticized the fact that the Pactes only catered to young people and were generally taken up by the better educated.

The Strange Fate of the VIIIth Plan

The planners were continuously at work during the late 1970s preparing forecasts and simulations, despite their peripheral position within the administration. These activities were at first undertaken under the auspices of the VIIth Plan, and later for the preparatory work on the VIIIth. For example, the VIIth Plan Energy Commission continued to meet after 1976, producing a report in 1979 (see Chapter 7). The VIIth Plan Development Commission made proposals for the *Rapport sur l'Adaptation du VIIème Plan* (1978), Barre's statement of intent for the rest of the plan period and beyond. This report could be seen as Barre's formal repudiation of the VIIth Plan, but is more usefully interpreted as the first steps in the construction of the VIIIth. It stressed the need for France to adapt to changing world market forces and insisted that reflation always did more harm than good, and that government intervention should only be in the direction of promoting the faster adjustment of resources toward the strongest sectors.

The formal 1st Phase of the putative VIIIth Plan began in 1979. The social affairs division of the CGP had continued to analyse the employment situation, and produced a detailed 'Dossier sur l'Emploi' (1979) for the VIIIth Plan Development Commission (1st Phase). The Commissariat's economic service concluded that classical methods of macro-economic stimulation could reduce unemployment, but not to pre-1973 levels, and would also risk 'inadmissable' internal and external financing problems. In February 1979, INSEE presented its rather gloomy prognostications for 1983 in 'Un Jeu de Projection de Référence à l'Horizon de 1983' (1979). The Development Commission, in its report to the government (*Rapport: Phase des Options*) (CGP, 1979), gives a somewhat watered down account of what must have been an intense debate. 'Some members' of the commission are reported as urging more expansionary policies, but 'a majority', like loyal MPs in the UK, see the need to worry about the external balance as paramount. However, detailed exploration of alternative approaches was called for and was subsequently carried out in the second phase.

In addition to its own reflections, the report also summarized evidence given to it by other experts. C. Sautter of CEPII (see Chapter 7) made a number of interesting observations. He insisted (p. 18) that the 'myopia of the market' had to be combatted: first, by internationally concerted Keynesian measures (which would, he said, then be effective); secondly, international competition should be regulated or concerted via the OECD to prevent elimination of jobs that would become viable again in an upturn; thirdly, R & D needed more support; and finally, there was a grave danger that the firms best equipped to survive the recession would not necessarily be the best and most dynamic from the point of view of long-term growth, young firms often being heavily indebted. Sautter argued that a macro-economic approach to these problems would be inadequate on its own; finding the right international specialization in each sector was crucial, but he did not believe that the market alone could achieve this. Intervention to improve efficiency and data collection were very important. The micro-economic aspects of Sautter's argument, which were echoed in the Development Commission's proposal for detailed 'programming' of industrial adjustment and conversion, were not too far out of line with the Barre government's own stated aim, though they implied a greater commitment to overseeing the market than the régime was prepared to undertake. However, the macro-economic ideas were anathema.

Advances in computer simulation techniques in the late 1970s greatly assisted the work of the VIIIth Plan commissions. Brunhes (1980) notes that the commissions dealing with social policy had access to econometric models that allowed them to virtually instantaneously simulate the economic and financial consequences of any proposed measure, whereas hitherto social and economic deliberations had been rather separate. Gauron and Maurice (1980) and Maarek (1980) also report on further post-Optimix experiments to simulate mathematical optimization programmes. Most strikingly, the commissions made use of the far greater flexibility, simulating on DMS alternative dynamic time paths and policy proposals. The Development Commission requested INSEE to run DMS 'in reverse', trying to work back from a target of lower unemployment to the implied policy orientation, producing a comparative analysis of twenty-seven scenarios (three budgetary policy variants in three states of the world on three assumptions about the scope for flexibility in social policy for the labour market, i.e. hours worked and pay).[11] The Development and Employment Commissions explored possible paths to higher employment in as much detail as they could, but the dissenting minority report of one CFDT representative on the employment group complains that these efforts were hampered by the pressure put on the commission by the government, and that it had been 'virtually put to sleep' between January and May 1980. Yet some very interesting work did emerge from the VIIIth Plan deliberations, despite the obstacles and the unwillingness of the commissions to draw conclusions from the studies presented to them that would be damaging to the government.

All the macro-policy variants showed a reduction in unemployment coming from higher government spending. The simulations considered some quite subtle variants and concluded that the favourable impact on employment was significantly greater and the unfavourable impact on the balance of payments was less if any reflationary stimulus concentrated on direct employment creation or the purchase of goods and services by the public sector rather than if household consumption were boosted via tax cuts or higher transfer payments. The simulations also showed substantial potential for cuts in recorded unemployment figures, from reductions in working hours accompanied by corresponding reductions in earnings. The actual outcome here was said to depend crucially however on the response of firms on the investment side; if they were more affected by aggregate demand than current profitability the impact would be much more favourable.

The 'scenarios of departure' for the VIIIth Plan, published in *Economie et Statistique* (1979), and the Employment Commission report, showed unemployment rising from around 1.5 million in 1981 to between 1.8 and 2.2 million in 1985, depending on the evolution of the world economy. Barre did not take kindly to these calculations, and in a speech to the Economic and Social Council, presenting the Report on the Options for the VIIIth Plan, he referred to 'the figure of 1,800,000 unemployed which the econometricians have pulled out of their model assuming we sit by with our arms folded' (Barre, 1979). The Employment Commission also tried to check the consistency of its unemployment forecasts by examining the projections for the eleven industrial sectors of the DMS model against the projections at the same level of aggregation from the inter-sectoral model PROPAGE, inviting 'expert opinion' to pronounce on the relative merits of the two sets of forecasts. Inconsistencies between the forecasts made the commission wary of making firm predictions. However, the commission noted that the assumed relationship between unemployment and labour force participation which acted to make unemployment grow more slowly than employment fell (the subject of severe criticism by its VIIth Plan predecessor) had been retained in DMS although the effect had not manifested itself during the course of the VIIth Plan. The basic conclusions from the analysis of the base scenarios was that, while service sector employment would grow, the rate would be insufficient to absorb the future decline in employment in the rest of the economy. The commission called for policy action to reduce future unemployment.

In fact, the final recommendations of this Employment Commission were much more in line with government thinking than had been the case for its predecessor. Despite the implicit backing for a reflationary strategy evolving from the DMS simulations, the recommendations were carefully couched in terms that were not directly critical of the government's policies. Stress was laid on the need to orient government expenditures toward those items that stimulated employment, rather than concern with overall financial orientation of the state, and space was devoted to themes popular with the government, such as the need to reduce labour costs. Finally, it is worth noting that the VIIIth Plan deliberations excluded any variation in the exchange rate from consideration. The report on trade and exchange policy (*Rapport du Comité Economie Internationale et Exchanges Extérieurs*) (CGP, 1980a) explicitly ruled out both devaluation and protectionism.[12]

This point takes us to the heart of the problems for planning in the late 1970s. Despite the technical advances which seemed to presage a new lease of life for the exercise, ultimately the government did not care what any of the participants had to say if it conflicted with the administration's pre-existing strategy. Macro-economic stimulation was rejected out of hand by the Barre government in its Report on the Adaptation of the VIIth Plan (1978) and the Report on the Options for the VIIIth Plan (1979). In the end, the only detailed forecasts in the VIIIth Plan itself were demographic; all reference to the simulations undertaken by the CGP were omitted. The plan document, of course, ruled out any reflation but stressed that the French budget deficit (which we have seen was a low proportion of GDP by international standards) was to be cut because of the effects on the money stock and balance of payments. For all the effort and technology applied, the VIIIth Plan basically reconfirmed as an act of faith the policies of the Barre administration since its inception. We asked a number of CGP officials around this time whether they thought their activities had any purpose at all, and there was a distinct unease in the answers we received. One official concerned with employment felt he could not do his job if he had to take the actual policies of the Barre government as given. He offered a 'technician's judgement' that superior policies were available to deal with unemployment, including micro-economic measures. He added that only the plan paid attention to certain detailed aspects of the employment statistics, such as duration and breakdown by age, which would normally be overlooked by the 'classe politique'. Another official in the macro-economic section of the CGP was more optimistic, thinking some progress was being made toward convincing M. Barre of the need to reflate.

The planners' ideas found favour with the new government. The

Socialist government promised a two-year interim macro-economic plan for 1982–83, aiming to reduce unemployment while maintaining financial prudence and without devaluing the franc.[13] In a simulation of the impact of these policies using their own models (MOGLI and PROTEE), R. Courbis and his associates at GAMA estimated[14] that the effects on unemployment would be 'spectacular' with a reduction of 640,000 as compared to the likely outcome for 1982 under the Barre policies. The budget deficit, Courbis calculated, would stay under 4 per cent of GDP, the same order of magnitude as the likely German deficit. Courbis estimated that if the franc was allowed to fall the effects on employment would initially be adverse due to deteriorating terms of trade. Courbis's group, however, did worry that the balance of payments was likely to be a serious problem, given France's \$7.8 billion deficit in 1980, a situation which they contrasted unfavourably with that of 1975–76 when there was a slight reflation by Chirac and Fourcade before Barre's arrival.[15] The GAMA analysis retained FIFI's approach in warning the government that the effects of demand stimulation can only be short-lived and that structural policies to improve competitiveness would be needed.

It is too early to predict the outcome of the Socialist Party's reflationary programme. An initial commitment was made to stabilize the franc and interest rates were raised, but only time can tell whether moves to restore full employment will be thrown off course by financial crises on the one hand or measures to prevent such crises on the other. The Socialist Party had circulated simulations of its policies made on DMS to business interests to maintain 'confidence'. If the announcement of its policies had created expectations of disaster to come, one would have probably seen a larger and a quicker fall in the value of the franc than the 3 per cent devaluation of October 1981. Probably the most worrying aspect of this event from the point of view of macro-economic planning and coordination is the report (*Guardian*, October 8, 1981) that Finance Minister Delors did not tell Budget Minister Fabius that a devaluation was imminent, together with other measures that would render the draft budget for 1982 obsolete.[16]

Projections Detaillées Glissantes

We have noted that the absence of any economic forecasts in the VIIIth Plan was part of a systematic trend that had begun in the late 1960s on the part of the government in not wishing to give hostages to fortune. The Barre government gave this a new twist however in insisting that the provision of macro-economic information was no longer the function of the plan. Forecasting exercises were to be carried out in the process of plan construction to illuminate the discussions but the idea of a central forecast in the plan became as objectionable as a growth *target* had been for the VIIth. It was Barre's view that 'pluralism of economic information was to be sought'. The Report on the Adaptation of the VIIth Plan echoes Vera Lutz in its reference to this point. Therefore, the government decided to proceed with the system of forecasting known as 'Projections Detaillées Glissantes' (PDG). It had been intended all along that new DMS model would not be used exclusively by the administration, but would be available to outsiders much in the same way as the Treasury's econometric model in the UK.[17] The planners too had become worried about the fact that plan forecasts were excessively compromised as a result of their politicized character. We have seen how sceptical the CGP officials were of the employment forecasts behind the VIIth Plan. Most of the over-optimism came from deliberate government manipulation, but in a report introducing the PDG system, the CGP remarked[18] that at a sectoral level firms and trade unions have had an incentive to be over-optimistic, and they cited the example of the steel projections for the VIIth Plan, where the sectoral working group had insisted on retaining a forecast of steel output in 1980 of 34 million tons, with an unchanged labour force; at the same time a 'serious' government committee was working on the hypothesis of 29 million tons and major redundancies.

The decision to set up the PDG operation was announced in the VIIth Plan. The intention was that while the administration would use the DMS model as it chose, there should also be a commercial marketing of its services through the nominally independent business research organization BIPE. An indication of the prevalent mistrust of government forecasts was the proposal of an independent committee to supervise the procedure, whose job it would be to certify that any forecasts were guaranteed to be free of manipulation.[19]

The methodology of the PDG system recalls Massé's 'collective market research'. The system has three layers. The DMS macro model will be used to make projections on whatever assumptions about exogenous factors the users care to specify. This will give forecasts of macro-economic variables and disaggregated forecasts to the level of the nine industrial branches that are recognized in its equations (e.g. manufacturing industry divided into consumer goods, investment goods, and intermediate goods). Another model, PROPAGE will then calculate the implications of the industrial production forecasts of DMS for sectors in detail. It distinguishes 40 sectors and uses an input–output approach. Initially PROPAGE will simply translate the DMS forecasts into an internally consistent set of industrial and inter-industrial projections: the aim is to use these calculations to check for any implausibility or implied inconsistency in the DMS calculations. The last step in the process is to produce very finely detailed forecasts for sales of 200 individual product categories, chosen for their particular relevance to business. Here formal models will not necessarily be used.

The macro forecasts gain circulation in the press, but it is intended to disseminate the detailed forecasts on a subscription basis with small and medium firms particularly in mind. It will be recalled that the survey of business opinion carried out for the CGP in 1979 asked firms if they would be interested in buying such a service, with 75 per cent replying that they would. The PDG operation began to operate in 1979, and, taken together with the decision to promote the international economic analysis centre, CEPII, with a view to providing information about developments in world markets (see Chapter 7), we can see that the steps at 'déchiffrage' ('denumericalization') of the plan had at least some positive counterpart.

The Plan, Macro-Economic Policy, and Uncertainty

We have seen that the increasingly macro-economic orientation of French planning went hand in hand with the decline in the procedure. We must now try to summarize the lessons from this discouraging experience. French planning lost relevance in part because of the nature of the exercise itself, particularly in the 1960s and early 1970s when only single-variant end-point forecasts were produced (see Chapters 1 and 3). However, many of the more recent problems have institutional and political causes, and these prevented the technical and consultative developments from being exploited. We have focused on some of the interesting things that French planners were doing in the 1970s, despite their irrelevance for practical decision-making, precisely because they indicate the ways that planning could help in an uncertain world. We conclude by discussing the potential impact of strategic co-ordination and consultation.

The institutional elements in the decline of macro-economic planning have been considered in Chapter 4. There was a general hostility between the plan and the Finance Ministry, and rivalries within both the civil service and the Cabinet left the planners with no terrain over which to determine policies. More generally, there is a permanent tension between policy-makers concerned with the short run and the longer term, although in France authority always rested with the former group, which has been reflected in an unwillingness to pre-commit budgetary policy to the growth targets of the plan. Even so, before 1973 the unwillingness to adopt macropolicy to the plan in order to keep public hands free did not conflict unduly with the aim of steady growth except for the severe monetary contractions of 1963–65 and 1969–70. The matter only came to a head after the oil crisis, when the Finance Ministry's concern with inflation and external balance pointed permanently against the longer-term view. The late 1970s, despite the magnitude of the problems, can be seen as one bad situation that refused to progress.

This point underlies certain elements of the 'politicization' of planning during the 1970s. It is very awkward for the government to publish unambiguously pessimistic medium-term forecasts. In the 1950s and 1960s, the government was only too happy to let the planners say just how good the next five years were going to be, and to take some credit for 'concerting' this state of affairs. But the other side of the coin was politically unacceptable. What government would forecast, let alone target, a marked deterioration of the economy over the foreseeable future, even when all its own actions had been taken into account? Hence the concern to eliminate the numbers from the plan, and massage the data. But to be fair, ideology must also enter here. French administrations in the late 1970s simply did not believe that the economy operated in the way described by the planners (or their models), and therefore altered the forecasts in line with their preconceptions. Moreover their objectives – inflation, external and budgetary balance – were not those of the planners – unemployment and growth. This brings us to the final political point, already stressed in Chapter 2. The planning exercise has considerable value in an uncertain world, discovering and co-ordinating through analysis and consultation the preferred development path. It has nothing to offer a government whose objectives and implementation path are already known. The planners can either disagree with the government, to no good effect since they lack any decision-making authority, or publish the government's predetermined programme as a public relations exercise. For the most part the planners were too dispirited to fight very hard by 1975; the latter phenomenon predominated.

Yet there were also numerous potentially productive developments in macro-economic planning during the 1970s. On the technical side, the new models permitted the provision of far more useful information to the state and private sector, dealing with numerous variants, plotting out time paths, and simulating the impact of various policy packages. This enabled the planners to offer a more fruitful framework for consultative discussions, in which we have seen both enterprises and the unions wished to participate. So what are the prospects for planning in the 1980s, with a new regime committed to the exercise and therefore willing to take advantage of the possibilities which have been opened up? Their positive attitude automatically solves some of the problems, but the outcome depends on what sort of planning they actually choose to do.

The need for policy flexibility clearly restricts the scope of the planning exercise. Governments are not behaving irrationally in trying to keep their hands free, though the conservative administrations in France may have gone too far in that direction. J. Delors argued that 'navigation by visual aid has been substituted for navigational science' (Holland, 1978, p. 27) because the French government wished to avoid embarrassing commitments. Of course, at that time the Barre government did not trust the planners' radar; but, although it is unwise to make promises that may not be tenable, any action taken now does have implications for the future. Even though the government will be responding to new shocks all the time, planning can track down some consequences of policy decisions, in particular showing how the outcome will vary according to circumstance. As shown in Chapter 2, planning could help us to discover policies which are robust with respect to alternative models of the economy and paths of events.[20] In this respect, the planners would be following the excellent, if unheeded, advice of the VIIIth Plan (p. 10) to define actions that would pay off 'in all states of the world'. They can only ever undertake limited prior analysis, so the exercise cannot tell decision makers exactly what to do in advance, but it can identify contingencies about which it will be useful to have had some prior thought, and possibly counsel against strategies that could lead to severe dangers. The VIIth Plan deliberations seem to have accurately spotted that the final outcome was not all that sensitive to the kinds of policy variations under consideration in 1975–76, and the VIIIth Plan projections suggested a degree of sensitivity to certain variables. One might expect the new regime to actually use rather than suppress such information, and the problem of the government being unwilling to publish pessimistic 'targets' is solved by this approach to forecasting; the planners can revert to the useful task of providing and disseminating information. But there is the danger that the government could go to the opposite extreme, engaging itself in excessive pre-commitments.

Chapters 1 and 2 have stressed the problems associated with fully programming the state's activities in the medium term when the world is uncertain. But there are circumstances when conditional pre-commitments make more sense than perfect flexibility, and it is the planners' job to find them. For example, the ability to negotiate on such matters as pay policy is affected by the government's willingness to make elementary conditional contracts with other 'social partners'. It is futile to retain complete freedom of manoeuvre if other parties can counter your moves. There is also a role for 'planning agreements'. We have seen that firms' medium-term corporate plans are not generally precise enough to be integrated into a formal economic plan (see Chapter 2) and that exact contractual arrangements will only apply in a limited number of cases. But although rigid planning agreements are inappropriate, there is still potential for very flexible ones. It may be in the state's interest to conclude long-term supply contracts in industries where heavy capital investment makes it hard for supply to respond easily to fluctuations in demand, such as the suppliers of power generating equipment. The state shoulders some of the risk in return for lower costs and the beneficial side-effects of a guaranteed market for the producers. There is certainly little sense in varying state purchases from technology intensive industries cyclically, as both France and the UK have done.

The present discussion will clearly cut no ice with a rational expectations monetarist, though the milder version of that approach is consistent with our ideas. Stabilization policies are not necessarily rendered ineffective if they begin to have an effect as soon as they are expected (see Gordon, 1978), though the government must take this into account and firms must know if current policies are temporary or permanent. Indeed, the announcement of contingent policies may be very important. Buiter (1981) has shown that policies which vary in a reasonably predictable way with economic fluctuations are superior to fixed rules. The commitment to stabilizing measures may, in itself, so improve confidence that they are not needed, as Matthews (1968) and Maddison (1976) have argued may have been the case for European private investment before 1970. The planning exercise can discover the relative merits of flexibility and conditional pre-commitments in each area, and disseminate the chosen policy rules to the private sector.

This leads us to the role of consultative rather than purely technocratic planning. The exercise could spot some option or contingency that other decision makers, state or private, had not considered. Costs mean that attention must be concentrated on government policies and the activities of agents who are significant enough to have potential feedback implications, though the planners may have to discover who they are. When information is imperfect, the government's policies can be improved by industry, particularly the largest national and multinational firms, and the unions commenting on the propositions through a formalized consultative procedure. Similarly, the planners can offer a macro-economic evaluation of the major actors' proposals, whether or not commitments are actually made, to highlight likely disequilibria and point out to certain people that what they expected will not happen. This gives an opportunity for a second opinion on schemes which appear to the initiators to have no flaws. Hall (1980) stresses the value of this for project planning and Jones (1981) has argued that the role of the German banking system has been significant for industry in this respect. He also believes that French planners carried out a useful checking role in the early years. Income policy is one example of an area on the interface between micro- and macro-economics. Informationally, it can seek to convince people that the new equilibrium really does have a low rate of increase of nominal variables; contractually, it may reduce at least some of the leap-frogging element of pay bargaining, and allow unions to avoid the prisoner's dilemma of each putting in for high nominal claims in case others do; and politically, it enables the state to negotiate with those bodies large enough to affect the macro-economic outcomes.

The problem remains of motivating everyone to exchange information at a 'fair' price in a consultative exercise. One would hope that private agents stand to gain enough from the second opinion to be favourably disposed, as is confirmed by the SOFRES Opinion poll (see Chapter 4), but the experience of the 1970s leads us to question the attitude of the state. The planning process can be a validation or legitimation device, of particular use when the state's priorities are ill-defined, as during the IVth Plan. It is not clear why governments do not use this device more often, bending on the details of their macro-policy to secure the stamp of approval from social partners and the plan. The reasons are probably political rather than economic. Perhaps the fear on the part of the French Finance Ministry and the rest of the government has been that the end result is bound to be an accretion of power to the agency that ostensibly decides what does and does not command consensus approval. The price of validation may well get driven up if there is a greater demand for it by the state, and the planners can capitalize on their monopoly of the right to pronounce a policy in the 'general non-party' interest. But some governments may also have a relatively greater demand for the appearance of consensus. De Gaulle was willing to go some way to establish his claim to be the embodiment of the entire nation in the early 1960s, when France was living under a real threat of a military coup from the army in Algeria. Barre apparently regarded legitimation of his policies as unnecessary.

Successful planning in France in the 1980s not merely requires the proper use of the new instruments in a loose, flexible exercise, but a commitment by the government to widespread consultation and discussion. It will be interesting to see whether Mitterand regards his election victory as adequate legitimation, so that, despite the greater attachment to planning, the exercise will merely reflect the chosen priorities of the government, or whether the plan will again become the product of a consensus-based consultative process.

Notes

1   We do not intend to explain Courbis's ideas or the FIFI model here in any great detail, though a large specialist literature on the subject does exist. The reader is referred to Courbis (1972, 1973, 1975), a symposium in the *Revue Economique* (November 1973), Liggins (1975), and Cave and Hare (1981). We have written further on the topic in Holmes and Estrin (1976) and Estrin and Holmes (1982).
2   The literature on the DMS model is smaller, but see Fouquet *et al.* (1979), Charpin *et al.* (1979), Cave and Hare (1981), and Estrin and Holmes (1982).
3   There were numerous other models associated with French planning, such as REGINA, integrating regional and national projections; MOISE, on international trade; and DECA and STAR for short-term forecasting (see Liggins, 1975). FIFI and then DMS were the central models for macro-economic planning, however.
4   Thus, DMS has no role for liquid assets in determining consumption or investment, no real balance effects, no 'crowding out' of private by public expenditure, no interest rate effects, no rational expectations effects, and no international financial flows. It effectively ignores the 'new conservative macro-economics' (Akerlof, 1979). Many of these issues are hotly debated (see Buiter, 1980) but the lack of reference to these points makes DMS, though new, appear somewhat dated.
5   Data from BIS, Bank for International Settlements, *Annual Report 1981*.
6   As proposed, for example, by the OECD. Their view is contained in the 'McCracken Report' (OECD, 1977).
7   The five 1st Phase commissions reported in the spring of 1975 and the report on options produced detailed guidelines by the summer. The thirteen commissions of the 2nd Phase met between November 1975 and April 1976, with the final plan appearing in July.
8   For other accounts of this process, see Green (1978), Cave and Hare (1981), and particularly Cave (1981).
9   The *Rapport de la Commission: Croissance, Emploi, Financement* (CGP, 1975a) was chaired by Edmond Malinvaud, and is sometimes referred to as the 'Malinvaud Report'.
10 Cave (1981) offers a very similar interpretation of what went on between the 1st Phase and the publication of the VIIth Plan.
11 See *Le Monde*, June 14, 1980 or Cave (1981) for details of this experiment.
12 There does not seem to have been disagreement between government and opposition on this point. Indeed, the communist CGT's memorandum of dissent in the trade report begins by expressing its support for a policy of maintaining the value of the franc, before going on to condemn policies to redeploy resources toward sectors of international strength while allowing imports into sectors where France was weak.

13 See the interview with Finance Minister Delors in *Le Monde*, June 30, 1981.
14 See *Le Monde*, June 30, 1981 and a correction in July 14. We are grateful to Prof. Courbis for supplying fuller details of his results: see GAMA notes No. 348 and 351 (June 18, 1981). The full text describes the employment-creating effects of Mitterand's policies as spectacular but emphasizes the financial risks.
15 This point was stressed in a private note to the authors from Prof. Courbis.
16 The parallels with the Wilson government in the UK in 1964 are disturbing.
17 In another step toward 'pluralism' of macro-economic information, the Barre government had proposed to establish an independent centre of macro-economic analysis to rival INSEE, l'Institut Français des Conjonctures Economiques (IFCE). The new government has retained this scheme.
18 'Un outil pour la planification d'entreprise: les projections glissantes detaillées' (1979). See also Vignon (1979) and Charpin *et al*. (1979). This point was also expressed to us in discussions.
19 We were told that there was some hesitation on the part of the government in approving the first set of names proposed for this committee.
20 This has been argued by King and Matthews (1977) and Bowles and Whynes (1979) for the UK, and Chow (1976) for the USA. See also Johansen (1978), Ch. 8.

6 The Plan and the Public Sector

Introduction

This chapter is concerned with the relationship between planning and the state sector. As we have seen, before 1961 the plan was actually written to outline the future development of the national economy, especially the industrial sector, rather than being a plan for the state. The first section notes that the planners did not concern themselves with the budget at all until the IVth and Vth Plans, which contained targets for the growth of public investment by category. From then onward, the familiar picture of declining relevance and operational significance began. The VIth Plan merely predicted overall public spending, and even these projections were dropped for the VIIth and VIIIth Plans. An innovation for the post-1970 plans, which was said to herald an important new role, was the inclusion of specific expenditure programmes as plan commitments, but the practice was disappointing and, in general, the implementation rates were patchy. The third section considers the use of budgetary programming and planning techniques in the public sector, an area in which the planners could have spearheaded rationalization in public decision-making. In fact, we find that their use has been highly sporadic, not linked to the overall plan, and that they have had little impact. We then consider the relationship between the plan and the state productive sector, which has actually been the main recipient of industrial subsidies. Once again, whatever the potential in this area, we find the planners have had little say in recent years. The nationalized industries in France in the past have been fairly autonomous, and in so far as any government control has been exercised, it has not been in the systematic framework of the plan. Yet it is the intention of the new Socialist administration to tighten the links between the state and its enterprises, so we must see whether previous experience throws any light on their prospects, and we conclude by examining the political aspects of this commitment.

The Plan and the Budget

In the debate on the VIIIth Plan, R. Barre sneered at those who thought that the plan should be a list of budgetary obligations, claiming that the early planners never had any budgetary commitments in the Ist Plan. This would appear to be a rather misleading description, since the Ist Plan did in fact have a list of public projects and used Marshall Aid funds to carry them out, but the budget and plan have been entirely separate operations in recent years. The CGP was influential in the use of FDES funds during the Ist Plan, but in the 1950s the plan concerned itself with general industrial growth. As we have seen in the previous chapter, it sought to persuade decision makers inside and outside the government to use their money in some ways rather than others, but the planners were not really concerned with the budget as a whole (see Bravo, 1976, p. 21). It was only with the IVth Plan, and its newly defined aim of Economic and Social Modernization, that the overall budget became of interest to the planners. Moreover, they also became increasingly concerned with macro-economic aspects of budgetary policy, which came to be an increasing source of potential conflict between the CGP and the Finance Ministry.

The IVth Plan is still regarded by radicals as the golden era of planning. These include Jacques Delors, Mitterand's Finance Minister, who participated in the plan's construction. This was the first time that the government expressed a commitment to increased spending on public services and social infrastructure in the context of a multi-annual programme; GDP was intended to grow at 5.5 per cent p.a. over 1962–65, and public investment by 10.7 per cent, with further detailed targets. The desire to raise the level of social facilities was fairly unambiguous, but the actual commitments made were of a rather non-operational character and the outcome is somewhat hard to interpret. Different data tell different stories, but the overall picture is roughly that public investment as a whole held up well, being more or less on target, despite the introduction of the counter-inflationary Stabilization Plan of 1963–5. Bravo (1976) observes that, although the plan was referred to in budgetary decision-making, it was not considered 'imperative'.[1]

We can see with reference to Table 6.1, which provides the overall fulfillment rates for the public sector for the IVth, Vth, and VIth Plans, that the actual priorities accorded to the various areas of public expenditure did not in the end coincide perfectly with the quantitative objectives laid down in the plan. The fulfillment rates for the nine budgeting heads for the IVth Plan range between 78.5 and 110.3 per cent. However, the general ranking looks sufficiently close, with educational expenditure in particular growing as scheduled, for us to accept Bravo's observation. In budgetary matters, as in so many others, the nostalgia for the IVth Plan would seem to be justified.

It will be remembered that the Vth Plan made industrial competitiveness the primary target for the first time and its construction was the occasion for a dispute between the CGP and the government over how much slack to leave in the economy. These factors were mirrored in the budgetary aspects of the plan. Thus, in its overall budgetary targets the plan declared that there would be an emphasis on spending which promoted industrial competitiveness, but even this did not go far enough for the tough minded officials of the Finance Ministry who were gradually asserting their authority against the social orientation of the planners. They got their opportunity after the May 1968 events, the expansionary aftermath of which prompted the government to engage in a bout

Table 6.1 Public Investment and the Plan, 1962–75: Implementation Rates and Sectoral Priorities

	Implementation rate[a]	Share of total planned public investments (%)
The IVth Plan		
Total	98	100
Agriculture	98	17
Education	92	37
Transport	110	18
PTT	103	14
The Vth Plan		
Total	85	100
Schools and Universities	83	25
Rural investments	84	12
Roads	75	20
PTT	106	15
The VIth Plan[b]		
Total	89	100
Education and training	83	16
(of which professional training)	(56)	(1.5)
Urban Development	85	15
Transport	87	12
Research	86	16
PTT	100	23

[a]Implementation rates as given by Bravo are defined as in Chapter 3 of this volume. Sub-total figures are given only for major categories.

[b]The VIth Plan contained 'low' and 'high' public investment growth forecasts. These data are with respect to the 'low' hypothesis.

Source: Bravo (1976), various tables.

of spending cuts which fell particularly hard on social expenditures. Total 'programmed' spending was only 85 per cent of the planned level, and the implementation rates varied from 54.1 to 105.8 per cent. As Bravo (1976) comments, the 'orientations traced by the plan were not respected' (p. 22).

The VIth Plan took a different approach from its predecessors. The overall objective of the plan, the 'impératif industriel', meant an official commitment to slower growth of public spending, which had risen as a fraction of GDP during the 1960s but was now supposed to stabilize. In keeping with the increased technical sophistication of the VIth Plan at a time of decreasing real relevance, the plan undertook to forecast not merely public investment but all public spending, by category. However, these figures were simply forecasts, and had no status as targets at all. The 1973 oil shock led to cutbacks, even from the relatively low public sector growth rate implied by the plan. The explanation of this given to us by one CGP official was that the government was trying to prevent the share of GDP going to the state from rising as private spending fell with the recession. In fact, despite the complete absence of any real linkage between the impressive plan forecasts of government expenditure and the actual budgets, the overall completion rates for the VIth Plan expenditure forecasts were better than for the Vth. As Table 6.1 shows, the implementation rates were reasonably good, if rather patchy and less impressive than for the IVth Plan. Perhaps the most striking implementation rate concerns expenditure on professional education, which was only 55 per cent of the forecast level. The area was declared to be a major priority in the plan, in order to increase the flexibility of the market economy, yet little serious action was actually taken.[2]

The very limited impact of the planners on public sector decisions in this period was mitigated, however, by one procedural innovation. The VIth Plan contained six 'programmes finalisés': small public expenditure programmes which were actually worked out at an operational level and constituted formal expenditure commitments. In fact, despite their contractual format, even these ultimately depended on the annual budget for funds but in practice they could not be so easily ignored as the vague overall budgetary envelopes that were all the plan contained to guide the remainder of the public sector. Table 6.2 describes these programmes and their outcomes. The programmes were not fully implemented, with financial fulfillment rates ranging from 69 to 96 per cent. The innovation became the centrepiece of planning for the public sector in the VIIth Plan.

By the VIIth Plan, the authorities had dropped all pretence of programming overall public expenditure, though predictions of the

Table 6.2 The Programmes Finalisés of the VIth Plan

Programme	Planned outlay (m. 1970 Fr.)	% Implementation Rate[a]
1 New towns	3,340	71
2 Road safety[b]	2,349	70
3 Reduction of infant mortality[b]	258	85
4 Improved functioning of the labour market[c]	805	96
5 Domiciliary care for elderly	1,128	—[d]
6 Safeguarding Mediterranean forests	492	75

[a]Actual spending as percentage of plan.

[b]These programmes had quantitative targets of numbers of deaths to be reduced, a link with the work on social indicators.

[c]This programme mainly concerned the state employment exchanges, but also dealt with aid to employment for the handicapped.

[d]No figure given.

Source: Loi des Finances (1976), *Rapport d'Exécution du VIe Plan.*

distribution by heading of the 1980 budget were made. The government announced that experience had shown it was impossible to plan public spending as a whole, so instead they restricted the planners' activities to a fraction of the overall budget in the spirit of the 'programmes finalisés', with money set aside to finance 'Programmes d'Action Prioritaire' (PAPs). These were a series of expenditure programmes, costing around 15 per cent of total state spending, that were to constitute a hard core of the budget immune from future cuts. One planner referred to them as 'fixed points' for government expenditure in the medium term. They were intended to be the most cherished and vital priorities put forward by the various spending ministries, although they were not subsumed under the normal general expenditure headings because, in principle, they were inter-ministerial projects rather than the programmes of particular ministries. The objectives of these expenditure programmes were defined in quantitative rather than only cost terms.

In fact, there is little evidence that the PAPs fulfilled their potentially useful role during the VIIth Plan. For instance, there is some reason to believe that the spending ministries did not take the innovation very seriously. Bravo (1976) notes that the credits initially requested when the various departments were invited to state their priorities far exceeded the final total allocated. The government had to whittle these down to the twenty-five programmes in the plan by a procedure which is far from clear. Similarly, Green (1980) argues that the ministries did not put forward top priorities at all and we encountered some feeling within the CGP that ministries had treated the whole PAP exercise casually. Yet there was no obvious prior reason for such attitudes. Although the final twenty-five programmes only accounted for 15 per cent of state expenditure, this is a significant amount given that so much is already pre-committed from past decisions. The problem is that it is hard to see the twenty-five programmes listed in Table 6.3 as representing the nation's real choice of priorities after the oil crisis. Table 6.3 also shows implementation rates for the twenty-five programmes. Half the total outlay, it will be noted, was allocated to posts and telecommunications, which had anyway been an increasing priority of the government over the years. The other programmes look like a fairly random selection of worthy but not dramatic projects that include 'facilitating access to justice', 'improving road safety', and 'encouraging the care of old people at home'. They were distinguished by the fact that they were supposed to contain quantitative non-financial objectives and a set of specified instruments for realizing them, as well as the required fixed sum of constant-price francs.

The one programme that stands out as a classic prestige public relations project was the Rhône–Rhine Canal, which was promised in the plan despite scepticism about the feasibility. In fact, this project was quietly scaled down in the 'adaptation' of the VIIth Plan, but otherwise Table 6.3 suggests that the remaining schemes were implemented rather better than the VIth Plan's Programmes Finalisés. However it must be remembered that the objectives of the projects were rather modest. For example, although Programme No. 8 was to reduce the dependence on imported energy and gave a quantitative figure of 25 per cent of energy production to come from nuclear power by 1985, the funding actually provided via the PAP was a tiny fraction of what was actually going to be spent on the nuclear programme. In fact, the important decisions were made outside the framework of the CGP[3] so the plan procedure did not provide an occasion to evaluate the nuclear commitment. Nor for that matter did the existence of a plan prevent conflict between Electricité de France and the nuclear industry over choice of reactors (see Pavitt, 1981).

Thus, although the PAPs in the VIIth Plan were not the immutable medium-term projects at the top of the list of public sector priorities that they had been intended to be, the relatively modest and sensible schemes were approximately carried out. Perhaps it is surprising that the government should have treated them in such a

Table 6.3 The PAPs of the VIIth Plan and Their Implementation Rates

Programme	Planned total expenditure in b. 1975 Fr.	% Implementation rate in 1980
1 Strengthening food and agriculture industries	3.4	90
2 Promoting industrialized building	0.1	86
3 Promoting small and medium firms	1.5	114
4 Development of telephone system (PTT)	104.4	91
5 Improvement of transport for West, South-West and Massif Central	5.8	99
6 Rhône–Rhine Link	0.8[a]	78
7 Development of overseas territories	1.3	95
8 Reducing dependence on imported energy and raw materials	1.5	96
9 Export promotion	3.8	90
10 Improving the public employment service	3.1	89
11 Vocational training for the young	5.9	117
12 Upgrading manual work conditions	6.2	76
– of which in PTT	(3.3)	(99)
13 Promoting equal opportunity in schools	20.6	107
14 Family policy	1.0	72
15 Domiciliary care for elderly	0.5	82
16 Preventative health care	4.0	109
17 Easier access to justice	0.8	115
18 Consumer protection	1.9	95
19 Improvement of accommodation and nursing standards in hospitals	3.7	72
20 Road safety	0.9	91
21 Improvement of urban life	12.9	76
22 Conservation of architectural heritage	1.0	104
23 Rural development	2.9	105
24 Environmental protection	2.2	78
25 Research and development	10.5	91
Total	200.7	93
– of which PTT	(107.7)	(92)

[a]The original figure was 1.6b. Fr., which was reduced in the 'adaptation' of the VIIth Plan.
Source: VIIth Plan, *Loi des Finances* (1980); Green (1980).

relatively privileged manner, given the general decline in the plan, but one suspects that the projects may have been important to other sections of the administration. Whatever the reason, the VIIIth Plan announced that it would also contain PAPs. This may have been to make that otherwise rather vague document look like a plan, but the PAPs probably also survived M. Barre's axe because they were actually more of a device for monitoring public expenditure than for articulating priorities. The next section considers the extent to which the public sector is planned at all, let alone by the CGP. In fact, French budgeting policy appears to have made virtually no use of partial planning or programming techniques (Milleron *et al*., 1979; Ullmo, 1978), which may make the socialist promise to plan more seem credible despite the difficulties. One could hardly plan less.

Planning and Programming Techniques in the Public Sector: The Micro-Economic Side

We have seen that, apart from the attempt to bring the two together in the IVth Plan, there was no effective link between the plan's macro-economic projections for the public sector and the annual budget. In this section we will consider the micro-economics of budgeting policy, that is, the choice of priorities and the evaluation of alternatives in the state sector. The methods seem to have been almost entirely administrative until around 1970 when the techniques of budgetary management and cost–benefit analysis brought by Mr R. McNamara to the Pentagon were taken up enthusiastically in France under the label RCB ('Rationalization des Choix Budgetaires'). At that time, attempts were made to recast departmental budgets as programme budgets, with expenditure categorized by objective, rather than administrative or financial function, and individual items of spending scrutinized by the RCB method. Progress was slow, to such an extent that in 1977 Prime Minister Barre set up a Committee of Enquiry to find out what was causing the delays, the report of which is published as Milleron *et al*. (1979).

Discount Rates and Investment

The general area of discounting within the public sector is not well documented, but it would appear that the activity is far from widespread. In his letter of instruction to the Committee of Enquiry on these issues, M. Barre was clearly irritated by the idea that, although the Vth Plan had decided on a common test discount rate for the public sector, 'In practice economic calculation is only used for a small fraction of public or publicly aided investments' Milleron *et al*., 1979, p. 61). As far as we can see, the rate that is calculated by the CGP is employed whenever discounted returns are used as a basis for public investment decisions. It is certainly curious that, in France, the state has not sought to use a device such as the 10 per cent real discount rate employed in the UK to control public spending. This is all the more surprising when we discover that the planners' discount rate appears to be calculated by rather elegant means which pay no attention at all to political criteria. The planners use what is known as the 'inverse optimum' method. Roughly speaking, they estimate a production function for the economy and work out what the marginal product of capital in the private sector would have to be to generate the planned growth rate over the period, which is taken to be the social opportunity cost of capital.

Calcul Economique et Planification (CGP, 1973) is a semi-technical official text enunciating the principles of general equilibrium and capital theory on which the planners' calculations are based. The text emphasises that the discount rate emerging from these calculations should equal the rate of return on the marginal investment, rather than being an expression of public preference for income in the present as against the future. The method of calculation is indirect inference through a macro-economic growth model rather than directly estimating the return on the marginal private investment. This method produced a 10 per cent real rate for the VIth Plan and a 9 per cent rate for the VIIth (see Bernard, 1978), but, as far as we can discern, these were not widely used in major public sector expenditure decisions. It seems likely that the planners were permitted to dominate in the area of test discount rates by the rest of the administration precisely because such criteria were not generally employed, and one suspects that M. Barre would not have used the planners to spearhead a wider dissemination of such methods.

RCB and Expenditure

Once the discount rate has been set, it is supposed to go into RCB studies of overall programmes and individual projects. In the early 1970s, it was hoped that those new methods of budgetary management would enable better monitoring and control of public spending. The Finance Ministry instructed spending ministries to draw up their accounts in two different ways: traditionally, with global budgets broken down under such headings as labour materials, capital spending, etc.; and as a 'programme budget' giving details of the allocation of funds between the various objectives of the department.

At first this was done on a somewhat experimental basis, with an attempt in 1975 to get all departments to produce three-year projections of their spending by programmes. However, Ullmo (1978) remarks that such budgetary devices do not in any way enter into the process of budgetary planning, merely serving to provide additional information, while Green (1980) considers the impact of the new procedures to have been 'negligible' (p. 107). They do permit a more detailed analysis of spending programmes and one CGP official concerned with controlling public spending was very keen on the new procedures during an interview with us in 1979. But programme budgeting is simply an accounting innovation, and not an improvement in decision-making. Ullmo (1978) observes that the programme budgets and the three-year programme projections do not seem even to have been used at all during the VIIth Plan.

The Plan, RCB, and Cost–Benefit Analysis

There does appear to have been slightly more headway made in the application of RCB and cost–benefit methods to certain projects and decisions within the public sector, and in their report, Milleron *et al*. praise certain departments highly. Indeed, the traditions of cost–benefit analysis in French budgetary policy engineering goes back to Dupuit (1844). An attempt was made in the late 1960s to institute RCB methods to those parts of the administration that did not use them, but this extension of the system in general failed. It had been hoped that the RCB system could be used to evaluate competing programmes, rather than merely calculate the least-cost way of achieving a given objective. This is a similar notion to that underlying the idea of PAPs, and it had been hoped that the plan, using such methods, might be able to articulate such choices. In fact, this type of overall evaluation failed to materialize. Thus, although a large number of RCB studies were undertaken during the 1970s and some departments did use cost–benefit methods to appraise public investments, the RCB approach had a far more limited impact than its proponents had wished.

An example of this is the relationship between RCB and the public expenditure commitment in the VIth and VIIth Plans. The six 'programmes finalisés' of the VIth Plan were conceived quite independently of the RCB exercises being instituted, though as it happened RCB studies had been done for programmes on Road Safety and Perinatal Policy. Moreover, the PAPs selected for the VIIth Plan were not chosen according to RCB criteria (see Carassus, 1978. p. 61), nor were they integrated into ministries' programme budgets. Carassus claims that, despite the limited impact of RCB in spending ministries and on the plan itself, the format of the PAPs is a gesture in the direction of programming in a manner consistent with economic principles. However, this seems to be a rather optimistic inference from the format of the accounts and the innovation of attempting to measure non-financial benefits by social indicators.

General Problems of the Public Sector

We have seen how limited the impact of programme budgeting

was on the overall choice of priorities and how patchy was the use of RCB methods within the administration. Ullmo (1978, p. 67) notes that 'the link between Planning and RCB poses problems that are institutional and political rather than methodological'. We have remarked in the previous chapter that there is an extensive literature on French planning and public policy that sees no haphazardness in the choice of priorities but a systematic programme of support for the status quo and the requirements of big business. It is not our intention to deny the generally conservative pro-business policies which certainly dominated the period 1965–81. However, we feel the evidence of Milleron *et al.* and others (Green, 1980; Ullmo, 1978; and Carassus, 1978) strongly supports the view that these policies were carried out in a genuinely unco-ordinated way and were affected by the administrative structures through which they were applied. It is worth examining the three reasons for this given by Milleron *et al.* (1979, p. 16): first, oversimplified and overambitious expectations gave rise to disappointment and rejection; secondly, traditional budgetary procedures did not permit medium-term programming; thirdly, the institutional structure and position of analytical divisions were unsatisfactory.

The first point is a familiar one elsewhere. The movement to apply cost–benefit criteria in the USA and the UK in the late 1960s also offered a tantalizing vision of unique technocratic solutions to problems, which in reality posed unsolved and sometimes insoluble technical and political problems.[4] Milleron *et al.* remark that it was frequently engineers working in the tradition of Dupuit who tried to demonstrate the universality of simple economic calculations, leading to wholesale dismissal of their ideas as a result of, for example, naive attempts to use financial valuations of human life.[5] Meanwhile in the Agriculture Ministry, trying to put the whole of agricultural policy on a 'rational' basis around 1965 risked upsetting the delicate balance of political forces that existed and led to the complete discrediting of economic modelling in this area, which on a more modest scale would have been valuable.

The traditional French budgetary procedures did not permit any role for medium-term programming; rarely were any calculations made of the budgetary implications for future years of current decisions. No more notice was taken of RCB calculations in the individual spending ministries than in the Finance Ministry. Milleron *et al.* report a total lack of communication between the 'services d'études' and the budgetary decision makers, who were governed by political considerations to a very large extent. The institutional setting of the analytical services was no help to their useful functioning, either. At a purely practical level, it proved hard to strike a balance between over-centralized research in a ministry and fragmentary work related to each separate problem. Moreover, the bureaucratic environment was unreceptive to the analysts. Milleron *et al*. (1979, p. 18) quote from instructions to candidates for the ENA[6] examinations, which imply a generalist rather than a specialist orientation, advising the would-be administrator to have research carried out rather than to undertake it, and to 'read' rather than 'write' calculations. This may come as a surprise to people who see the French Civil Service as embodying hard professionalism in contrast to the amateurism for which the British Civil Service is often criticised. Anne Stevens (1980) reports on the way rivalries between civil service groups affect the way decisions are made within and between departments.

Thus, French public spending tended to be governed more by political than technocratic considerations. However, whatever the politicians' motives, the apparent lack of concern for social priorities has not led to a low share of public expenditure in GDP. EEC data for 1979 (see EEC, 1981) put France around the European norm in this respect, though because of a particularly high share of social security transfers; the share of direct goods and services was low. The French social security levy, at 36 per cent of wages, was the highest in Europe in 1979, and its reduction was one of the major concerns of the VIIIth Plan. The VIIth Plan discussions highlighted the anti-redistributive character of the social security system, despite its scale (see *Rapport de la Commission Inégalités Sociales* (GCP, 1975d, p. 39) and Greffe, 1975), because the link between earnings and benefits was closer than between earnings and contributions. The Committee on Incomes and Transfers (CGP, 1976f) examined the possibilities for major redistribution but stressed the difficulties as well as the urgency of the need. The VIIth Plan did at least generate data and discussion of the issue, prompted by Giscard's temporary interest in redistribution on taking office and perhaps also by the OECD report (see Sawyer, 1976) which gave France the lowest income equality rating of any country for which it had data. However, the momentum for reform ultimately faltered in the face of lack of interest from Giscard and Barre. It is not clear what the Socialists will do about all this. We have noted the preference of Mitterand's adviser, J. Attali, for more public and less private goods (see Attali, 1978). Premier Mauroy, in his speech to the National Assembly presenting the government's programme, promised a public debate about the future of the social security system (see *Le Monde*, July 10, 1981). He noted that higher benefits for the needy would mean higher contributions and that the choices would be 'difficult, painful even', but he also reminded his audience that voters had opted

for a just society in electing Mitterand. The government programme did not specifically promise that the planning system would
be the forum for the promised debate, but our previous discussions
(see Chapter 2) suggest that it would be an ideal vehicle for
legitimating such costly decisions as are taken. The stated aim of
greater decentralization of the state would also generate a need for
consultative and 'contractual' planning (see Fuchs, 1977).

The Nationalized Industries

Whether or not the new government decides to use the plan as a
way of articulating public expenditure programmes, the Left has
always wanted to co-ordinate the nationalized industries through
the plan.[7] We commence our discussion of the state sector with a
brief summary of the government's holdings before 1981. This
leads to a consideration of why, despite the rhetoric of planning
and a penchant for intervention, there has been little serious
attempt to incorporate the public sector of industry into an overall
strategy, of that of the national plan or any other, which indicates
some of the problems the new regime may face.

Vessillier (1977)[8] contains a valuable summary of the relevant
data. Neither the total share of employment in the economy in
nationalized industries nor the share of output were particularly
high by European standards, at 7.5 and 11.5 per cent in 1973 as
against 8.3 and 11.0 per cent in Germany. What distinguished
France from other European countries with the exception of Italy
was the diversity of the state's industrial holdings, which included
aero-engines, oil (Elf), chemicals (various firms), cars and machine
tools (Renault), shipping (Compagnie Générale Maritime), the
main radio and TV stations (including shares in commercial stations), as well as the traditional areas of energy (coal, gas, electricity), public transport (SNCF and RATP), and telecommunications
(PTT), the last of which was a major destination for public investment in the 1970s. It may be relevant to the role of the state in a
consumer society that the state has traditionally had a major stake
in the tobacco sector (SEITA, set up as a state monopoly.) The
government has also had major holdings in the financial sector
since the war. The biggest banking institutions were all in state
hands – the BNP, Crédit Lyonnais, Société Generale, Crédit
National – to name but a few. In addition, the state controls a large
part of the insurance market, 27.5 per cent in 1974, in the form of
a variety of life and general insurance companies, which, as it
happens also invest a higher proportion of their assets in company
shares and a lower fraction in government stock than is the case for

the private insurance companies. All this, together with the state's own financial institutions such as the FDES and the Caisse des Dépôts et des Consignations, gives the state a high degree of *potential* control of capital formation in the country, greater than would be suggested by the 15 per cent of gross fixed capital formation carried out by the non-financial public enterprises in 1973.

It would appear that little or no attempt was made to use this power for the purposes of planning from the late 1960s onward. CGP officials we spoke to were quite emphatic that nationalized industry investment plans were in no way under their control or influence. Except in its earliest years, the plan never gave specific obligations to individual firms and it does not seem to have distinguished in this respect between private and public firms. Cohen (1969) and Shonfield (1965) report that in the 1950s the planners sometimes had less difficulty influencing private firms to follow their suggestions than large commercial state firms such as Renault. (It will be remembered that any operational advice from the CGP would have had to go far beyond the rather general targets in the plans themselves.)

In the 1960s, the incoherence of policy toward nationalized industries led to the proposals of the Nora Report (Nora, 1967) for greater day-to-day and financial autonomy for state firms, but strategic coordination via 'contrats de programmes' (planning agreements) to be signed with the government. Only two such agreements were signed for the VIth Plan, however, and the idea was shelved.[9] Bonnaud (1976) states that the planners never attained their goal of a 'public enterprise policy that was not simply the sum of sectoral policies' (p. 100) and Bauchet (1969) observes that, 'In France, planning does not, as such, ensure coherence in the behaviour of public enterprises' (p. 470). In fact, the government instead adopted an apparent commitment to 'liberalization' of capital markets in the late 1960s, encouraging state enterprises to borrow and lend commercially in the real and the financial sector. But the government actually did intervene widely in the management of the state sector throughout the 1960s and 1970s, on a very ad hoc basis. Often the motives were directly political, and use was made of price controls for electoral purposes here as elsewhere in the economy, most strikingly in the holding down of Paris Metro fares.

However, the state's financial holdings adhered to the policy of liberalization in the sense of not acting in concert with the plan, and the banks do not seem to have had any overall guidance on credit strategy.[10] Financial institutions that were under the direct management of the state, such as the FDES and the Caisse des Dépôts et des Consignations, certainly implemented state policy, but there is no evidence in their accounts that this was part of an overall strategy to influence the pattern of investment in the private or public sectors. This point can be illustrated by considering the role of the FDES, a body which appears to have incorporated plan-related criteria into loan decision more than any other. Thus, certain FDES disbursements are officially attributed to particular programmes, though these are identified by name, such as the 'Plan Calcul', etc., rather than as part of the national plan. It is appropriate to review the work of the FDES here rather than in the next chapter because, although concerned with industrial policy, its principal borrowers were the nationalized industries.[11] These took 46 per cent of its disbursements in 1977, some 28 per cent of their borrowing requirements. A further 20 per cent of the FDES disbursements were for various non-industrial purposes (such as ports or tourism), which left around 34 per cent of the total for use in industry. Overall, the FDES did not make a major contribution to industrial policy; in 1977 it lent around 3b. Fr. (around 1b. to private industry) compared with the 50b. Fr. being spent on the PAPs in the same year, itself under 16 per cent of the state budget.

The VIth Plan gave 'priority' to development in the mechanical engineering, electronics, and chemicals sectors, which one might hope would have been given particular attention in the FDES's disbursements. The tables describing the breakdown of FDES funds for 1974–76 (between 1.4 and 1.9b. Fr.) separately identify 'plans' for mechanical engineering, steel, and computers. But the 100m. Fr. in total for 'mécanique' was spread out so thinly that it was getting less than 10 per cent of FDES loans in all three years. Only one loan was made under this heading in 1975, and none in 1976. Money for electronics outside the 'Plan Calcul' was not separately identified but there was little room for serious contributions from the general headings it could have come under, while 'glass, chemicals and rubber' taken together received a negligible fraction of total loans. In practice, the lion's share of FDES loans were absorbed by steel and cars in 1974 and 1975, and in 1976 most of the industry money came under the general heading 'plan de soutien à l'économie'. Even the funding allocated through the inter-ministerial committee, CIASI,[12] amounted to less than 10 per cent of the FDES total. Data on the size of loans show that 74 per cent of the disbursements in 1976 was absorbed by the five largest of the 162 loans, while 98 of them were under 1m. Fr. (£125,000). The FDES is clearly a long way from being what it was in Monnet's day (see the Hacketts, 1963). Moreover, though operationally defined 'plans' can be programmed, at least in accounting terms, there is little evidence of a link between the national plan and this category of spending despite the continued presence of the Planning Commissaire on the FDES Council.

If it is hard to see the connection between the loan policy of the FDES and the plan, it is almost impossible to find any further evidence from the activities of other state financial institutions. One body that has been identified with the plan is the Caisse des Dépôts et des Consignations, which Hayward (1973) described as 'the investment bank of the Plan' (p. 163). When we visited the Caisse in 1979, a spokesman was very surprised that this label had been applied to it, and suggested that an examination of its balance sheet would show that this could not be the case. The official purpose of the Caisse is to act as a banker to France's network of savings banks and to re-deposit their funds. It makes loans to local authorities to finance projects that have been approved by the government and in this sense can be said to be financing public expenditure during the course of the plan, but it would not appear to have any executive role in deciding how the funds are used. The Caisse also holds a portfolio of shares in major companies, for example, 5 per cent of Péchiney-Ugine-Kuhlman. Other major state banks also hold shares in private firms, for example, the BNP and Crédit Lyonnais with 15 per cent of Thompson. Vessillier (1977, p. 154) observes that these state shareholdings were very rarely used to influence the strategy of the firms in question.

Despite the espousal of economic liberalism, and the absence of any co-ordinated public sector or industrial strategy made through the plan and implemented by direct or indirect manipulation of capital market, the government increasingly used its credit institutions to finance nationalized industry losses. Vessillier (1977) notes that the deficits of state firms began to rise in the late 1960s and le Pors and Prunet (1975) establish in their study of government aids to industry that financial flows to the state's own firms outweighed aids to the private sector (see Chapter 7 for more details of this study). This state of affairs was exacerbated by the de-facto government takeover of the loss-making steel industry in 1978.[13] All these points appear to lend credence to the Marxist theory of 'State Monopoly Capitalism' (which is closely related to the radical critiques of planning discussed in Chapter 4). From this perspective, the state is seen as taking over firms to 'socialize losses' rather than to run them in the national interest, which explains the lack of any co-ordination in the public sector. Private firms who find they are losing their monopolistic power to exploit consumers and workers ask the state to take over their industry and use the tax system to extract the necessary funds. The private capitalists move into some other lucrative line of business, asking the state sector to provide it with any services it cannot produce profitably itself (see Herzog, 1971, for a full account of this view).

Therefore, the state did not successfully rationalize its own activities, nor use the potential for co-ordination embodied in its diverse industrial and financial holdings in the 1960s and 1970s. The nationalized industries were largely autonomous and unplanned, despite their heavy reliance on public sector funds, and even those parts of the state's financial holdings most closely associated with planning in the past, such as the FDES, did not implement plan priorities. It would appear that in the absence of any real contribution from the planners, no other body was bringing coherence to the range of the state's industrial and financial activities, though the French Left saw a conscious strategy to aid private business. An alternative interpretation is offered in the next section.

The Political Economy of the State Sector

It seems difficult to explain the absence of co-ordination in the state sector during the 1970s. The commitment to liberalism may appear important, but in fact the government *was* willing to intervene widely in the state sector; it merely kept such activities discretionary and ad hoc. Of course, the CGP was too unpopular within the administration to be allowed any real say in this side of policy, any more than toward the private sector, but this does not explain why systematic co-ordination was not attempted through other agencies.

We have seen that the Left constructed an explanation, which cannot be directly refuted since we are not in a position to offer a convincing account of French politicians' motives. However, whether or not the politicians were deliberately ignoring any social considerations other than the appeals of private business, we have already discussed at length other factors that would have made it very difficult to organize co-ordinated activities. The problems arising from administrative rivalries within the public sector have been discussed in Chapter 4. Of a more serious nature are a host of organizational problems that make it very difficult to implement a systematic medium-term strategy, even with the best will in the world. The informational imperfections discussed in the first part of this book make it impossible for a single decision maker or administrative body to grasp the details of what amounts to a holding company encompassing more than 10 per cent of national production (see Lindblom, 1977, and Chapter 2 particularly on this point). McArthur and Scott (1969) remark that the corporate structures and managerial attitudes of the French private sector in the 1960s made it peculiarly difficult to achieve integrated strategies across what was often a maze of interlinked subsidiaries. According to Malézieux (1980), the steel industry still had this form in 1978. Precisely the same problems of co-ordination were among the factors cited in explaining the difficulties faced by American and British corporate mergers in the late 1960s and early 1970s (see Meeks, 1977).[14]

This is not to deny that there are great gains to be had from analysing and exploiting corporate interdependences in either the public or private sector, but informational imperfections limit what one can hope to achieve. A perception of these difficulties may have been one of the factors which led the earlier French regimes not to attempt co-ordination of the public sector. If so, they may have been unduly pessimistic; a loose 'strategic' plan for the state could highlight inconsistencies and broaden opportunity sets. But the consequences of the new Socialist government's declared intention to plan the state's activities will depend on precisely what they intend to do. Some of the socialist literature envisages a medium-term programme of fixed pre-commitments for the state sector, which faces the same dangers as the IVth and Vth Plans, and may founder on unforeseen events like the latter plan. In a complex and open economy such as France in the 1980s, the Socialists cannot rely on repeating the success of the IVth Plan.

The Socialists also propose to significantly increase the size of the public sector through nationalization, which brings the prospects for successful co-ordination even more sharply into focus. However, an enlarged state sector could favourably influence the operation of a planning exercise in three respects; macro-economic, co-ordinational, and social. It is an appealing idea to use public sector productive investment as a way of stimulating the economy (see Holmes, 1980), though only new investments can be used in this way. It is only sensible to take over existing assets in pursuance of this goal if this provides access to profitable opportunities otherwise not available to the state. However, it is not clear how control of existing firms will actually provide an entrée into the 'industries of the future' that both past and current administrations want to foster (see Chapter 7). In fact, the Socialists have never intended to concentrate expansion in any particular segment of the economy, such as the nationalized industries, and Prime Minister Mauroy stated that private investment would be the motor to restimulate the economy (see *Le Monde*, July 10, 1981).

Similarly, nationalizations could make a contribution to public sector co-ordination if the firms in question had external linkages to each other and the rest of the state sector, but in practice this does not seem to have been a major criterion. The proposed extensions to the state sector seem likely to exacerbate co-ordination problems without giving the planners anything approaching responsibility for the entire economy. Finally, the new government has declared its intention of using the state sector as the vanguard of new social objectives for industry. The enlargement of the state sector is to be reconciled with the desire to decentralize through 'autogestion', or workers' self-management,[15] to be implemented initially in the state sector. Another avowed objective of the Socialist Party and the CFDT (which was stressed to us by Hubert Prévot) was to shift the balance of political power in favour of the state and against the capitalist class, and in particular against the multinationals. But it seems unlikely that the absorption of a further 5 per cent of GDP into the state sector, leaving the total below 20 per cent of national output, could be an effective spearhead for these fundamental social changes.

There is no doubt of the government's intention to use its additional industrial muscle, but the acts of nationalization will probably not generate in themselves solutions to the problems of how the state sector can be co-ordinated. It will be necessary to process and use enormous amounts of information to produce a plan that even considered, let alone achieved, the co-ordination of the different elements of the state and their interface with the private sector. The prospects of continued administrative rivalries, and the arguments of Chapter 2, lead to suspicions about the likely impact of the Socialists' more grandiose proposals for planning the public sector.

Notes

1 Prate (1978, p. 147) reports that although de Gaulle wanted the IVth Plan to be compulsory, he also initiated the Stabilization Plan.
2 In 1977, planning officials complained that the establishment of a system of public employment exchanges for the first time was being frustrated by the refusal of state firms to use them.
3 By the 'Commission PEON'; see Chapter 7.
4 Self (1975) and Hall (1980) offer critiques of this technocratic approach which include examples of the problems.
5 Mishan (1971) offers a discussion of the numerous problems in this area.
6 See Chapter 4 on the ENA, which was a major training ground for public sector officials.
7 See, for example, the special issue of *Nouvel Observateur* on the Socialist Party's industrial policy (April 1977).
8 All data from Vessillier (1977) unless otherwise specified.
9 Mariano (1973, p. 266) reports sharp personal hostility between Finance Minister Giscard d'Estaing and Simon Nora; with J. Delors, Nora was a per-

sonal adviser to Prime Minister Chaban-Delmas. Mariano also documents Chaban-Delmas's quarrels with Giscard.

10   See McArthur and Scott (1969) for evidence on this from the 1960s.

11   All data from the FDES Annual Report for 1977, published as an appendix to the 1978 *Loi des Finances*.

12   Comité Inter-Ministeriel sur l'Aménagement des Structures Industrielles; see Chapter 7.

13   Green and Cerny (1980) give the details. Under the 1978 arrangements, the state did not exploit the potential for control implicit in the financial support given. Berry (1981) surveys the literature in this field.

14   Even General Motors is not immune from problems of organizational coherence, if an account attributed to De Lorean is to be believed; see Wright (1980).

15   Delors told us that he saw 'autogestion' as a general notion to be used against centralization. He did not wish to copy any particular system, such as the Yugoslav (see Estrin, 1982, on the Yugoslav model of self-management, and its consequences).

7 Planning and Industrial Policy

Introduction

This chapter considers the links between French planning and industrial policy. It is not an attempt to discuss the success or otherwise of French industrial policy, let alone evaluate the performance of French industry. Instead, we will investigate the specific and additional contribution that planning was able to make to the conduct of industrial policy.[1]

The CGP had two significant roles in the early years of planning. It genuinely sought to discover key intersectoral priorities and press for them to be respected, and, perhaps even more importantly, it had a catalytic influence on decisions concerning external finance that passed through state channels. Even so, McArthur and Scott (1969) suggest that the CGP were actually offering views on the individual merits of each project rather than their conformity with the plan. It will be remembered that all real decision-making rested with the Finance Ministry until the mid-1970s. The planners were also engaged in informational and 'educative' activities,[2] and the documents of the period reveal a willingness to become involved in the minutiae of some industrial sectors. For example, a Report on Sectoral Activities in Metropolitan France (1949) devotes 196 pages to enumerating every single investment carried out in sixteen industrial sectors, including details of location, completion date, and capacity, and the same meticulous attention to detail continued until the IVth Plan.[3]

The experience of the 1960s is given detailed attention in the following section because it was both a determinant of later developments and a potential blueprint for the future activities of the new Socialist administration on the industrial front. The planners moved away from attempting to select priorities toward trying to co-ordinate the full range of government policies to ensure that every sector grew as quickly as possible. In so doing, they paid no attention to criteria that could be used to establish the relative priorities of various sectors, while no alternative centre for industrial planning emerged within the administration. The third section considers the VIth Plan, in which certain priorities were identified although the general strategy remained to make every branch competitive on world markets. Even before the oil crisis of 1973,

177

the authorities did not act to implement the planned priorities. The planners effectively lost any say in the running of industrial policy for the VIIth Plan, considered in the fourth section, either in terms of overall strategy or detailed mechanisms, as the responsibility had been formally shifted to the Industry Ministry. The last years of Giscard saw the gradual emergence of a new philosophy for industrial policy oriented toward international demand, with planning as little more than forecasting for international specialization. The chapter concludes with a discussion of the likely trends under the Socialists.

The IVth and Vth Plans

The 1960s saw a change in the relationship between planning and industrial policy (see Chapters 3 and 4). The IVth Plan did not choose and focus attention on a few priority sectors, but provided targets for the whole of industry and made grandiose claims that government policies would be co-ordinated for implementation. The Vth Plan was somewhat less ambitious, with the emergence of a general objective to merely create a favourable climate for competitive industrial growth. In this whole period, the plans came to define a set of guidelines which, had serious efforts been made to render them more operational, could have permitted the construction of an overall industrial strategy and component industrial policies. However, the planners were unable to carry out their promises, and there is little evidence of genuine planning in the industrial sphere during the 1960s, either in terms of determining an operational strategy apart from rapid growth in every sector or in the co-ordination of industrial policies.

The IVth Plan broke precedent on the industrial front with ambitious proposals for implementing a long-term industrial policy and an attempt to cover the industrial sector exhaustively for the first time (see Estrin and Holmes, 1980).[4] This was the era of Commissaire Massé's 'indicative planning' (see Chapter 1), based on supposedly internally consistent and self-fulfilling sectoral forecasts. The IVth Plan claimed (p. 36) that it was likely to succeed because, on the one hand, it identified a 'general equilibrium of goods and services at the outcome of the plan' and, on the other, because there was a formal commitment to the use of the full panoply of government policy in the interests of implementation. These included 'quasi-contracts' (planning agreements), procurement policies, and the state's extensive control over the sources of external finance, and the CGP itself was to be closely involved in the implementation process though final decisions, as always, rested with the Finance Ministry. The plan stated that only 100 per cent self-financed projects would escape the planners' attention.[5] Every single externally financed project was therefore meant to be scrutinized for conformity with the targets, and if projects passed this test the Commission would see that sufficient tax and credit incentives would be made available.

Despite the numerical accuracy of the IVth Plan (see Estrin and Holmes, 1980), in so far as one can tell the planners never actually managed to direct the full coercive powers of the state in the manner envisaged. For example, McArthur and Scott (1969) concluded that 'the national planning process had little influence on the selective measures and programmes used by the state to control industries and companies' (p. 26). There are a number of reasons for this failure. As was mentioned in Chapter 4, one would have expected the planners to have less influence over the formation of long-term policies once there was a stable and active central government, and the Finance Ministry responded against their efforts to appropriate real power. Moreover, the extended scope of the plan probably further reduced the ability of the small number of planners to judge whether particular enterprise actions actually conformed with plan objectives. Firms' previous experience had probably led them to regard the plan figures as purely suggestive and, with their increased independence and self-confidence, themselves partly the consequence of earlier plans, some businessmen may have chosen to call the planners' bluff.

In fact, the nature of the plan itself had changed, containing overall objectives of faster growth across the board without the operational strategy around which to co-ordinate industrial policy. This can be seen from the gradually evolving status of the industrial forecasts during the 1960s. In the earlier plans, the sectoral targets were the only ones with any type of operational significance. It was the overall rate of GDP growth that was actually the target of the IVth and Vth Plans. Certain basic industry figures were also targets for the IVth Plan, but for the Vth Plan, industrial forecasts were only released as information to help firms to take action that would contribute to the overall growth figure; they were described as proxy targets that needed to be realized if the overall ones were to be attained. Thus, though the overall targets were the objective of the state, which, on paper, committed itself to attaining them, no specific undertakings were made by anyone at the industrial level. The industrial forecasts would appear to have been conditional *predictions* based on the overall industrial production *objective* derived from the state's overall growth *target*.[6] There were never enterprise-level details so the plan had to be implemented on the basis of the branch targets alone, and these were not formally the objectives of anyone in particular. The plans may have contained a general framework for a strategy, but they had limited operational significance for industrial policy since it was difficult to determine precisely what conformity with the plan might mean at a disaggregated level.

The Vth Plan documents reflect a subtle change of emphasis and make a cooler appraisal of the possibilities for coercive industrial policy in a planned national framework (Vth Plan, pp. 72–5). While the IVth Plan had stressed that the role of the state is to ensure that firms conform to the directives of the plan, the Vth Plan asserts that the 'primary responsibility for industrial development belongs to industrial managers' (p. 72). For the first time, a plan document proposed to base industrial development on the primacy of the market, with the state left merely to create a favourable climate for private initiative and to discover the policies that would best support the strategies devised by private industry. An important example of the new thinking was the promotion of industrial concentration to improve international competitive-ness,[7] a general policy for industry as a whole. The plan sounds a note of warning about the possibility of implementing a coherent industrial strategy through the general range of incentives: 'the reinforcement of co-operation between the state and industry undoubtedly requires certain new procedures. Too great a disper-sion of administrative centres of decisions in particular constitutes an obstacle to rapid decisions which are often called for by the situation to be remedied. Arrangements will soon be made to increase the centralisation and efficiency of administrative inter-ventions through an Industrial Development Committee' (Vth Plan, p. 74). This suggests that a lesson had been learnt from the IVth Plan; from as early as 1965 the CGP itself was not regarded as capable of co-ordinating government actions on industrial inter-ventions. Indeed Massé, in his Foreword to McArthur and Scott (1969), recognizes that the planners had more indirect than direct influences on policy-making, even in this period.

It is interesting to see what was actually happening to French industrial policy during the 1960s, to establish that there were no successful attempts to co-ordination outside the CGP, and to set the stage for developments in the 1970s. McArthur and Scott (1969) consistently observe the incoherent character of French industrial policy, and the same picture is drawn in Bonnaud (1970). He summarizes his conclusions about financial incentives for industry.

It may be interesting to observe that, except for achieving the goal of industrial localisation, they are relatively non-selective, and are distinctly tending to be granted on a virtually automatic basis and according to a number of posted criteria; contractual agreements by branch are being sought for. Government frequently makes a point of using individually applied measures as an opening for discussions with firms, enabling them to be informed about the exact implications of the rather vague instructions embodied in the plan. (p. 555)

This makes clear that the vagueness was intentional, making it possible for a firm or government agency to claim conformity with plan objectives. He notes, concerning non-regional incentives, 'that the discretionary character may present a danger for the execution of the plan: the imprecision of the criteria for selection contained in the Plan, and the too loose administrative co-ordination of interventions may in fact weaken or prevent the effects of those interventions' (p. 595). The separate divisions of the Finance Ministry, Regional Planning bodies such as DATAR, and the state's financial institutions were operating somewhat independently of each other.

The critique of government practice in this area was most eloquently expressed in Lionel Stoléru's *L'Impératif Industriel* (1969). He condemned previous industrial policies for their lack of coherence, and stresses the unworkability of the maze of criteria for government interventions which, he notes, did not include the concept of competitiveness. He sums up the experience of industrial policy as follows, 'From the moment one sees that *intrasectoral* action lacks the most elementary co-ordination, one should not expect, a fortiori, to find coherence in the *inter-sectoral* strategy of the state; so one would have difficulty to say which sector the state gave priority or, even without going this far, to describe how a group of sectors were "mobilised" for a particular objective' (p. 150). Stoléru saw the only answer to be taking competitiveness in international markets as the prime goal, and his views were very influential on the organization of the VIth Plan.

The only example of a concerted industrial strategy in the 1960s was the attempt to concentrate French industry in order to produce 'National Champions'.[8] Legal and tax rules were changed in 1965 to promote mergers, the number of which rose from 482 in 1960–64 to 576 in 1965–69. These figures understate the impact of the policy because the average value of each merger also increased; from 703m. Fr. of capital changing hands in 1964 to 5556m. Fr. in 1969 (in current prices; the price level rose around 20 per cent over the period; Gorge and Tande, 1974). The objective was to have two or three dominant firms in every sector but the change in industrial concentration was not in fact marked; the average share of the top four firms in each of forty-eight sectors considered increased from 20 to 22 per cent between 1965 and 1969 (Jenny and Weber, 1974). Thus, this undisputed goal of the government, articulated through the Vth Plan and pursued single-mindedly (the French, unlike the British, did not simultaneously attempt to promote deconcentration through a Monopolies Commission) was not achieved, and it remained a strategy for the industrial sector as a whole involving no sense of priority about which sectors were most likely to succeed. We should be able to find examples of such concerted policy activity in greater numbers and with more significance if the reasons for the success of French industry in this period lie in the superior general co-ordination of industrial policy.

The thinking of the CGP on all this is revealed incidentally in its *Report on the Implications of May 1968 for Planning* (CGP, 1968). In effect, it suggests that it is virtually impossible to co-ordinate the large and growing number of government interventions. Noting the general incoherence of the authorities' actions, the report argues that 'such coherence has been obtained for certain sectors by the use of "plans professionnels", such as in steel or information technology', although there was a warning that full coherent programmes could not be drawn up for every sector, if only for fear of undermining the market-based industrial strategy. Bonnaud (1976) notes that the planners were sometimes able to use their personal skills, though not the notion of planning, to influence a few industrial decisions. He reports that the government asked the CGP to carry out work for the sectoral programmes on steel, ship-building, and chemicals among others during the Vth Plan, and to undertake studies on other industrial sectors on the same ad-hoc basis as their involvement with incomes policy. These reports were unpublished but Bonnaud suggests that they were influential and reflected a real desire by the government to have an integrated policy which was somehow linked to the plan's objectives.

The VIth Plan

The VIth Plan emphasized the promotion of an economic environment conducive to competitiveness in world markets. The Modernization Commissions of the previous plans were replaced by a single Commission for Industry, although the Agriculture and Food Processing sector was given its own Commission as well, leading to confusion as to whether its promotion was part of 'industrial' policy or not. The industrial figures were further de-emphasized with only the overall growth objective being given full normative status, reducing the operational significance of the plan still further. Even so, there was an actual attempt to give priority to certain sectors, with three or four being chosen as the key areas for future policy intervention; chemicals, mechanical engineering, telecommunications, and electronics. The latter two were frequently conflated into a single entity whose description often altered.[9] These sectors were to be the object of 'plans professionnels' of a coherent character, while the rest of industry was to be offered a favourable environment and such ad-hoc interventions as the government saw fit. Thus, the VIth Plan did contain a general framework for a strategy, and industrial policy could be said to have been coherent in the sense that the government had expressed a commitment to a certain set of priorities in the context of a planning exercise. However, it is not clear that the existence of the planning system gave the choice of the sectors a rationale and logic that otherwise would have been absent, or that the authorities actually acted to promote those sectors.

A number of reports published during the VIth Plan period provide evidence on these issues. The OECD study of French industrial policy (1974) noted that 'the multiplicity of decision-making centres within the government has not been conducive in the past to the formulation of a coherent industrial policy', but saw the VIth Plan as a step forward.[10] Other accounts however do not always support the view that a coherent strategy was ever drawn up, even for the priority sectors. For example, Bonnaud (1976) observes:

> It was also impossible to secure a multi-annual government commitment in the Plan's priority sectors, such as mechanical engineering, chemicals, agricultural and food industries, civil electronics. On the other hand, the government did enter into financial commitments in non-priority industries such as steel, and also where initial decisions were taken outside the planning process, such as the Concorde programme. Thus, in practice the notion of industrial priorities was abandoned. (p. 106)

He also notes (pp. 97 and 101) that although the Nora Report of 1967 had recommended that 'contrats de programme' (planning agreements) should be signed with all public enterprises to ensure fulfillment of the plan's objectives, this was only done for the VIth Plan with the state's electricity, railways, and the radio and TV undertakings. Even this attempt to programme public sector investment on a partial basis was later shelved.

The ambiguity about which sectors had been chosen for priority, noted above, extends to which sectors had actually benefited. Paul Dubois, who was associated with the preparation of the Industrial Commission Report for the VIIth Plan, wrote (Dubois, 1978):

> The sectoral orientations of the VIth Plan in favour of food and agriculture, chemicals, mechanical engineering and electronics–computers have not been put into effect except in the latter sector. On the other hand, important funds have been kept for major programmes in other sectors (steel, shipbuilding, aerospace). (p. 149)

However, the OECD (1974) refer specifically to food and agriculture as an instance of a sector benefiting from government assistance (12 per cent of total investment funds being provided by the state in 1970–72). Whatever actually transpired, the existence of ambiguity in the record as to whether certain sectors were given preferential treatment would make it hard for an investor, ex ante, to know what to expect when he heard that a particular industry was to be given priority.

There is fuller evidence from official sources on the implementation of planned priorities – a study carried out within the Direction de la Prévision, summarized in le Pors and Prunet (1975)[11], which tried to evaluate the entire array of financial flows between industry and the state including all aspects of taxation and subsidized loans. Obviously, one cannot attribute all general government expenditure categories in such a way as to calculate profits in the absence of the state, but the authors tried to cover as many fields as possible including the degree of transfer implicit in low interest loans. Thus, one can get a measure of the impact of industrial policy on particular sectors and an idea of the relative impact of general measures. The overall conclusion was that the bulk of transfers between government and industry went to firms owned by the government itself. In terms of the sectoral composition of the funding, it emerged that from 1970 to 1972, when industrial policy was supposed to be concentrated on the three (or four) new key areas of future industrial growth, the traditional areas were actually absorbing the bulk of subsidies, notably steel, ships, and aircraft.[12]

The researchers had some difficulty in trying to ascertain what was happening to the supposed priority sectors, not least because they could not pin down the statistical categories to which the VIth Plan was referring. Using the nearest categories they could identify, they found that although food and agriculture was indeed a leading net recipient of funds, the priority industrial sectors of the VIth Plan were actually subjected to negative net transfers after allowing for taxes. The four (or five) priority sectors taken together (including the fortunate food and agriculture sector) received about the same percentage of gross transfers to industry (6.4 per cent) as did iron and steel, shipbuilding, and armaments (5.1 per cent).

This evaluation is confirmed for the period 1970–73 in the Report of the VIIth Plan's Industry Commission (CGP, 1976d), and its conclusions are worth quoting in full.

Finally, the sectors whose development was made a priority did not achieve the ambitious targets set for them. If, taken together, these sectors did receive a degree of implicit preferential treatment for general measures (aids for development and exports), it must be noted that the state has not carried out specific policies aiming at supporting their development (except in the case of telecommunications thanks to public procurement policies). The absence of sectoral policies for chemicals and mechanical engineering is probably due to the imprecision of the overall objectives fixed which in any event proved difficult to define for such vast and heterogeneous sectors, to the absence of consideration of the methods of selective intervention, to the inappropriateness of available instruments, and due also to the structure of the sectors themselves (fragmented and lacking in motivation by enterprises) (pp. 45–8).

The next section of the report covers the post-oil crisis period 1974–75, and notes that the government did undertake a more active industrial policy (mainly via CIASI, the inter-ministerial committee on industrial restructuring), but it singles out for mention specific sectoral policies only in automobiles and information technology.

The official evaluations of the VIth Plan, published as annexes to the 1974 and 1976 Budgets (Lois des Finances), draw a rather more optimistic picture, although there is still ambiguity about which sectors were actually prioritized (the 1974 Report refers to four priority sectors and the 1976 Report to three). The authorities pat themselves on the back for actions taken, with the 1974 Report referring to decisions about mechanical engineering taken in 1971 by CIASI and IDI, and special loans from FDES, and the 1976 Report noting the 100m. Fr. special credits to the sector from FDES, although it was pointed out that problems remained for the VIIth Plan and the original objectives were over-ambitious. Whatever gloss the authorities may wish to place on their actions, it is hard to see these activities as a serious example of the implementation of nationally planned priorities for the industrial sector, and the reports permit us to put together what actually did happen.

Although mechanical engineering obtained some finance, there was agreement that objectives had not been achieved by 1975.[13] The reports have little to say about the chemical industry, although they note that its growth was impeded before 1973 by the absence of external finance for which the plan had anticipated state support. Thus, this is an implicit admission that the planners giving priority to the chemical industry meant very little to the relevant authorities. However, there was action in the 'electronics' sectors, with several distinct sectoral programmes set up under assorted auspices, including the Plan Calcul for computers, and major public spending on telecommunications. However, it is unclear whether this activity related to industrial policy or French national prestige. For example, the purchase of telephone equipment, which was a major expenditure programme in the VIIth Plan (see Chapter 6), was as much oriented to satisfy social as industrial goals.

Finally, we must consider the general strategy that international market competition should determine the pattern of industrialization outside the priority sectors, implicit in the Vth and explicit in the VIth Plan. In fact it appears to have had little impact on French industry. McArthur and Scott (1969) criticize the absence of a clear stance from the planners on the issue of specialization in international trade, the question of 'make or buy', and the issue was not resolved in the later plans. For example, the policy of encouraging industrial concentration was clearly conceived as a way of making *all* French industrial sectors more efficient, but it was apparently never envisaged that any sector was going to have to contract. The government was hoping to bail out lagging firms and industries in the hope that they would ultimately become 'competitive' as well, and the issue of relative contraction was never explicitly considered.

The problem of specialization stands out very clearly in electronics, a sector sketched in detail by J. Zysman (1975) (see also Zysman, 1977). He argues that the government attempted to promote indigenous technology across the board in computer technology, resulting in an infant industry which never grew up. He sees the policies of the late 1960s and early 1970s as promoting a widespread dependence on state aid rather than fostering genuine competitiveness. This may even have led to a weakening of firms' ultimate ability to produce in the areas where France could have expected a real comparative advantage, such as electrical domestic appliances. The promotional efforts in the electronics sector, in Zysman's view, fundamentally evaded the issue of specialization.

The experience of the 1960s showed that the planners could not coordinate policies for the industrial sector in either a highly detailed or a comprehensive way. However, like its predecessors, the VIth Plan did contain a general framework for a strategy, which could have provided an outline for a co-ordinated industrial policy. The problem was that the general orientations were never translated into operational policies. There was no alternative strategy being operated from other centres of power in the administration; a vast array of non-specific instruments had no particular objective, but ran counter to both the general international market orientation and the sectoral priorities of the VIth Plan. Having given up the attempt to co-ordinate overall industrial policies, the planners no longer had even the administrative clout to ensure that the national priority sectors were given preferential treatment.

Industrial Policy and the VIIth Plan

Such co-ordination of industrial policy as there was in the VIIth Plan was not conducted under the auspices of the CGP. Along with the other administrative changes discussed in Chapter 4, the planners' nominal co-ordinating role had been formally moved to the Industry Ministry,[14] which was then given substantial financial autonomy. Under Barre, one began to see the outlines of a new industrial strategy based on 'positive adjustment' to areas of comparative advantage. The planners provided analytic backup by forecasting international demand[15] – an open economy form of traditional indicative planning – but the CGP had no policy-making role.

There was a single Industry Commission for the VIIth Plan. The main part of its report concentrates on generalities, accepting the logic of international competitiveness but displaying the ambiguity toward the market characteristic of the Gaullist era. However, in its detailed deliberations the Commission did pinpoint a number of priorities, and urge additional support for growing industries while accepting the decline of others. One can see the outcome of an intense debate here. Despite the general theme of international competitiveness, numerous sectors are put forward as candidates for support under few headings (pp. 27–8): traditional areas of state involvement, such as steel or computers; sectors where public procurement can help, such as telecommunications; strategically

important sectors, such as machine tools; and key sectors with
limited growth prospects or in decline (no examples cited). The
review of sectoral problems provides the embryo of an industrial
policy, although not a policy itself, singling out fairly traditional
sectors as ones where additional state intervention could produce
higher employment or trade gains – chemicals, mechanical and
electrical engineering, wood and paper, and 'Industries Diverses –
Arts – création – Loisir'. The Employment Committee remarked
that 50,000 industrial jobs were to be created in the Industry
Commission's Report by 'unspecified means' (see Chapter 5), but
in fact the report gives, more than any other plan for many years, a
breakdown by sector of the hypothetical 50,000 posts, as well as
the impact on the balance of payments. It specified a total of 9b.
Fr. to be invested. However, as in the VIth Plan, there is no clear
indication of why these sectors were singled out for special attention, nor does even this degree of detail provide something that
could be implemented as it stands.

In addition to the Industry Commission, each industrial sector
had a 'Groupe Sectoriel d'Analyse et de Prévision' (GSAP),
reporting jointly to the planners and the Industry Ministry. These
elaborated quite detailed micro-economic projections related to
the main macro scenarios, but we were told that the exercise was
not taken very seriously by the participants, especially in the case
of the deliberately over-optimistic figures produced by the steel
GSAP. The VIIth Plan's Energy Commission held further meetings in 1978–79, producing a report (*Perspectives Energétiques
Françaises*) (CGP, 1979c) which queried the official cost estimates
for nuclear power but did not question the predominance of the
Commission PEON which was the government's real advisory
body on nuclear energy.

Promotion of research and development in industry was also the
responsibility of the Industry Ministry in this period, and it continued to play a positive role in this area, even after non-
intervention was in vogue. The VIIth Plan had a Research Commission (one of whose members was J. Delors), the report of
which acknowledges the state's commitment to increased funding
for scientific research and makes a detailed examination of the
priorities within each discipline and technical area. Specific proposals were made concerning the allocation of future funding
based on a government target of 3 per cent employment growth
per year during the VIIth Plan. This commitment continued to be
taken quite seriously by M. Barre. Otherwise, the CGP itself was
quite peripheral in industrial policy-making; one official remarked
to us around this time that 'we found out about industrial policy
from the newspapers'.

The Barre Era, 1976–81

The Barre government committed itself to its own form of industrial policy in the *Report on the Adaptation of the VIIth Plan* (1978, pp. 64–75). This stated that the authorities would no longer subsidize lame ducks, but would grant aid for 'well defined' objectives: 'maintenance of national independence, regional development, innovation, energy saving, development of activities of the future and export promotion' (p. 65). The government was going to make much more use of contractual agreements ('Contrats de Croissance', 'Contrats de Progrès'). Moreover, industrial price controls, selective concessions of which were once seen as a means of plan implementation (see Shonfield, 1965), were abolished.[16] The overall aim of the new policy was to support those firms and products, rather than whole sectors or branches, where France had or was expected to have its greatest international strength. Declining activity elsewhere was not to be resisted despite the short-run costs.

The planning system had to find a small new niche for itself at this time. It promoted studies of the future trends in world markets; see, for example, Berthelot and Tardy, (1978). The *VIIIth Plan: Options Report* stressed the need for more information about the world economy and, despite the general downgrading of planning, a research centre linked to the CGP was established to monitor its trends: CEPII, headed by Christian Sautter (an INSEE forecaster and expert on Japan). A number of studies were produced along the lines of *La Specialisation Internationale des Industries à l'Horizon de 1985* (CGP 1978). CEPII's work was intended to open people's minds to future possibilities rather than produce formal models of world demand. Sautter told us that CEPII's first publication made a point of not using the word 'France' until half-way through the text to highlight the need to look outside the frontiers. In his evidence to the Development Commission of the VIIIth Plan, he stressed the need to alleviate the 'myopia of the market', and supported a vision of industrial planning that has clear echoes of Massé's 'collective market research'. He had been preoccupied with the need for information about developments in the outside world in his previous jobs as head of forecasting at INSEE.[17]

The most influential text of the period was written by Christian Stoffaës of the Industry Ministry (Stoffaës, 1978). Like Stoléru a decade before, he criticizes previous policies. He sees industrial policy from 1968 to the mid-1970s as combining very general measures with grandiose projects, rather than being genuinely selective by sector (with a few exceptions) or firms, and with the objective of competitiveness actually taking second place. The Barre administration had consolidated a new phase in which the individual firm would be the focus of industrial policy, and the products to be promoted would be proposed by firms rather than the state. He urges government intervention to promote positive adjustment, reporting Industry Ministry studies categorizing sectors for promotion or decline. Aids should be strictly temporary, contractual, and conditional on performance. A Planning Commission stripped of broader pretensions should have the role of co-ordinating all government economic policy to ensure conformity with the new 'industrial imperative', of monitoring the performance of contractually agreed programmes, and be at the centre of measures to speed up information about and responses to future market developments.[18]

It does appear that French industrial policy was finally beginning to develop a certain logic in the late 1970s, though under the guiding hand of the Industry Ministry rather than the CGP. An EEC study on Industrial Policies in the Community (1981) described French policy in words that might have been written by Stoffaës: selective intervention on very strict criteria based on potential competitiveness and contractual agreements. Rendeiro (1980) found impressive ideas for the machine tool industry, a sector that had been a problem for a long time. But the progress must not be overstated; the positive adjustment approach had not displaced all other features. Although the Industry Ministry had block funding for its spending programme by 1979, figures given verbally at a conference in Sussex (1979) by M. Sauzey of the Industry Ministry suggested that the sectors which had traditionally absorbed public subsidies were continuing to get the lion's share. For example, the restructuring plan for steel involved massive state funding as well as a progressive run-down (see Green and Cerny, 1980). But Molitov (1980) saw the French approach moving closer to that of Germany, and one CGP official opined that the lack of an underlying strategy for industrial policy had actually become more marked under Barre. Green (1981), in a study for the UK government, saw some shift in the direction of positive adjustment and contractual agreements with firms in growth areas, but support for traditional sectors had by no means disappeared and the number of 'contrats' was limited.

Actual policies included general measures, highly specific growth promoting measures, assistance to the reconversion of some declining sectors, and a large dose of cash support to prop up 'canards boîteux'. What had ceased were the big prestige projects and the vague aims to be self-sufficient in various fields regardless of cost. Investment grants to industry appear to have remained at a slightly lower level in France than in the UK throughout the 1970s. Data from the EEC (1981) suggest that investment grants as a percentage of GDP fluctuated beteen 0.27 and 0.67 per cent in France from 1973 to 1977, as compared with 0.47 to 0.69 per cent in the UK.[19] The developments in France in the 1970s were not so much in the actual practice as in the theoretical rationale for industrial policy in an open economy, namely, the assistance of adjustment toward points of strength and the anticipation of external market developments.

The Socialists in Power: More Industrial Planning?

It is not clear whether the embryonic, world-market-oriented strategy will survive under socialist administration. The new government has declared its priorities to be the promotion of high technology industries of the future, but these may not be the same products as chosen by Barre and the 'market'. In an interview with *Nouvel Economiste*, Pierre Joxe (1981), Mitterand's interim Industry Minister, said[20]:

> Our prime concern is the multiplication and growth of dynamic firms. What was done by my predecessor is not, on the whole, to be criticised, in particular the emphasis on innovation, the technological irrigation of the industrial tissue, the desire to promote the industries of the future. What will change is the scale of action; the framework it is situated in: the Plan; the spirit behind it, consultation, dialogue; the priority given to employment.

The priority to be given to industries of the future was supposed to be reflected in the creation of a separate Ministry of Research and Development which shared some responsibilities for industrial planning with the Industry Ministry, the new Planning Ministry, and the CGP. The Socialists were also emphatic that the newly expanded state sector should be used as an instrument for the implementation of the plan. At the same time, the plan would have a key role controlling the investments of the nationalized industries, though one CGP official expressed scepticism at the idea that his small office might be expected to evaluate Renault's investment programme when we spoke in 1979.

Some on the French Left see 'reconquering internal markets' rather than international specialization as the prime objective of industrial policy. Multinational companies are seen as having adverse effects on economic development by suppressing inter-industry linkages because of their use of components from other countries. It is also argued that natural technological spillover effects are being eliminated; French industry will not continue to modernize if multinationals buy sophisticated inputs from their own plants abroad. Commissaire Prévot put views along these lines to us in an interview in 1977 (when he was at the CFDT). A CFDT document *Planification et Nationalisation* (1977) asserts that 'Employment depends too much on exports and imports' and that 'popular forces' will not attain their objectives unless they refuse to submit to the logic of the international capitalist market system. The CFDT see the purpose of nationalization as bringing about a structural change in society, to alter the balance of forces between the public and private sectors, and to permit the widening of 'Autogestion' (self-management).

Conclusions

In the early years planners sought to alleviate the inability of the market mechanism to spontaneously balance supplies and demands in a real economy. In the 1960s the absence of a 'make or buy' perspective in Massé's vision meant the CGP could not find a convincing rationale for industrial planning in an open economy. If it was considered at all, comparative advantage was seen as the outcome of, not a potential determinant of, industrial policy, but this idea remained implicit. The breakthrough of the 1970s in conception, if not wholly in reality, was to give Massé's indicative planning an international dimension, the ambition being to provide information not so readily available in France.

However, there are likely to be substantial changes in the organization of industrial policy and the role of the planners with the arrival of the Left in power. For example, it is hard to see a continuation of the purely indicative concept of planning in advance of the market, either domestic or international. The Socialists are likely to foster a more active industrial policy, and return to the notion that comparative advantage is merely the endogenous product of industrial policy. It is too early to make very strong predictions, but it seems very likely that the Socialists will attempt to re-establish the ambitions of the IVth Plan on the industrial as well as the macro and social fronts. The aim would be to give a more active role to the CGP in future industrial policy with a diminution of the purely indicative planning under free trade. But the socialist programme contained two somewhat contradictory strands: continuation of the priority to 'industries of the future' but also 'reconquering internal markets' with its implication of import controls. This conflict could be resolved by a return to the somewhat discredited notion of self-sufficiency in all high technology. However, the likelihood of a complete break with the previous policies is lessened by the government's wish for financial restraint and the fact that many officials from the CGP went on to senior appointments under Mitterand. In view of the great importance of the quantitative element in economic and industrial policy analysis, Mitterand's inheritance of the technical apparatus used by his predecessors also makes for continuity of thinking.

Notes

1　Thus, we propose to take it for granted that the rapid growth of the French industrial sector until 1973 constituted a 'success', though some authors are less sanguine (e.g. Stoléru, 1969), and it seems reasonable to suppose that the complex of actions covered by the term industrial policy must have played some part.

2　This aspect is particularly stressed by Shonfield (1965) and Carré *et al.* (1975); see Chapter 3.

3　The IIIrd Plan Report of the Chemical Industry (1957), for example, breaks down the overall target into forty-six product categories and lists every major investment due to later take place between 1957 and 1961.

4　In fact, the IVth Plan retained some of the earlier biases toward heavy industry at a detailed level; the figures for producer goods were 'vital targets' but the exact composition of consumer goods was to be determined by relative prices and demand (IVth Plan, p. 36).

5　This commitment is explicit, though it is added that the CGP itself would not be competent to make appraisals for a branch or firm, and other 'bureaux d'études specialisées' would be called in.

6　This complicated state of affairs may explain the apparent confusion in Massé (1965) between projections and targets.

7　This also happened in the UK at the same time, with at least as great an effect. This point is that such a policy may develop a 'favourable economic climate', but is not exactly planning.

8　The British established the Industrial Reorganisation Corporation (IRC) in this period to secure advantages from economies of scale, and it is ironic that the French counterpart body – the IDI – was modelled on this British example.

9　The Agricultural and Food Processing sector was also given priority so, depending on whether or not it is counted, there were either three, four, or five sectors to be awarded preferential treatment in industrial policy.

10　With due respect, it is possible that diplomatic niceties affected the OECD's conclusions.

11　The main author, A. le Pors, subsequently became a communist senator and minister under Mitterand.

12　Fifty-six per cent of net transfers went to shipbuilding, iron and steel, aerospace, and agriculture and food processing, plus what were categorized as 'commerce' and 'services'.

13　Indeed, one former INSEE economist remarked that nothing had been achieved for the sector by 1979. The Industry Ministry constructed a programme for machine tools during the 1980s which was to be part of the VIIIth Plan (see Rendeiro, 1980).

14　It was called the Ministry of Industry and Scientific Development. There existed a separate Delegation Générale à la Recherche Scientifique et Technique for inter-ministerial co-ordination. The Socialists have set up a separate Ministry for Research.

15   The planners also provided backup for the system of forecasting 200 industrial products associated with the PDG system (see Chapter 5). The level of disaggregation distinguishes nineteen types of building materials, for example, cement, concrete blocks, slates, etc. The industrial information from this forecasting system will be marketed through the BIPE.

16   The Socialists restored a limited price freeze after the October 1981 devaluation.

17   It is a little ironic that the French forecasters have the OECD on their doorstep, but there appears to be some rivalry between the two groups of forecasters.

18   For further reflections on industrial policy in France see Massé *et al.* (1976).

19   EEC (1981), p. 26. The figures refer to 'investment grants to non-financial corporate and quasi-corporate enterprises'. Figures for other countries are of comparable orders of magnitude.

20   Joxe was replaced by Pierre Dreyfus, former head of Renault, after the 1981 Legislative Elections. In 1982 Dreyfus resigned and J. P. Chevenement's ministry took over all responsibility for industrial policy.

8 Final Conclusions

The most important conclusion from our study can be summarized very simply: both the models and the French experience of planning suggest that a market economy and a traditional administrative system could benefit substantially from the activities of a consultative and co-ordinating agency. The Commissariat Général du Plan successfully carried out these functions after the war, but has failed to do so since about 1965, largely because of institutional and political factors which could be reversed by a government committed to the idea of planning. However, contemporary circumstances make the kind of exercise that would be relevant and feasible rather different from the ambitious procedure envisaged in much of the literature (e.g. Massé, 1965; Beckerman, 1965; Meade, 1970; Holland, 1975) and by the French planners themselves in the 1960s.

Our case rests on informational imperfections in both the public and private sectors, which would justify the existence of a planning agency, costing a few million pounds a year, whose job would be to gather and process information to help everyone carry out the activities they would wish to do if they were better informed. Conservatives are right to stress the omnipresent characteristic of uncertainty, and the impossibility of dispelling it by government intervention, however widespread and expensive, but wrong to draw the conclusion that nothing useful can be done. Radical writers tend to incorrectly underplay the consequences of uncertainty, therefore sometimes implying that planners could offer full information and the unlimited evaluation of alternatives, but at least do see a role for a planning exercise. We are proposing a form of planning which meshes with actual private and public sector decision-making procedures, co-ordinating and disseminating the imprecise information about the medium term, spotting inconsistencies or unexploited possibilities, and legitimating policy decisions. Informational imperfections limit the scope of planning in a market economy, but its potential for improving choices should not be underestimated. The greater the uncertainty in the economy, the looser the form of co-ordination will have to be and the greater will be the need for it.

The role of expectations in economic decision-making has been given considerable stress of late. For the most part, the emphasis has been on price and monetary expectations, and it is surprising that the manipulation of monetary aggregates has been the chosen policy instrument to the exclusion of all others. Yet indicative planning could help even this policy option, with the technical and consultative apparatus acting to explain the implications of aggregate targets to individual agents in the appropriate disaggregate form, avoiding the costly consequences of inconsistent micro-expectations. More generally, the procedure could be important in the formation of macro-economic expectations over real as well as monetary variables. It is not hard to see a certain element of self-fulfilling prophecy in the low levels of industrial investment that have prevailed since 1973. The degree of announced commitment by the government to real expansion, in the context of a co-ordinated exercise that included prices and incomes, could have as great an influence on real growth as its current financial stance in a time of recession. An indicative planning system in essence formalizes this effect, and can therefore be viewed, as Harrod (1973) suggests, as a substitute for the largely discredited demand management approach. Despite an aversion to fine tuning, France appears to have benefited from expectations augmentation in this way during the 1950s and early 1960s. Since the problems of more recent years can be largely attributed to political and institutional factors, they do not invalidate conclusions from the earlier period.

The decline of planning in France up to 1981 can be explained by rivalries within the administrative sector and an ideological aversion to the exercise on the part of the government. Despite the planners' lack of any real decision-making authority, their Finance Ministry colleagues systematically acted to undermine the exercise, perhaps from fear of the real power that a body capable of determining the national consensus on any issue could still accumulate. The replacement of de Gaulle by the more conventionally conservative regimes of Pompidou and Giscard also played a role. There were fundamental ideological differences between the planners, whose very existence brought into question the underlying efficiency of free markets, and the politicians. The government was wary of tying itself down to any medium-term commitments in an open and uncertain economy, and in effect used the need for flexibility as an excuse to downgrade traditional planning, pushing it to political irrelevance in the VIth Plan and giving it the kiss of death in the VIIth by seeming to embrace the process again in a way that destroyed its credibility. However, there were real flaws in the old approach to planning, the consequences of which can be seen in the declining forecasting performance after 1965. It is impossibly cumbersome to spend two years in drawing up a comprehensive schema for the next five, based on firm and unalterable projections. The planners themselves seem to have realized this, and responded to the increasing complexity of the economy and growing environmental uncertainties with numerous technical innovations. For example, the VIIIth Plan was right to search with the aid of DMS for those strategies that would pay off in all likely states of the world, and the VIIth Plan's proposal to programme the top priorities into the budget in advance, deciding what would not be altered and therefore what might be cut, was also sound. The trouble was that by then, things had gone too far, and the government never did what it promised. The budgetary commitments in the VIIth Plan did not describe the nation's most vital priorities and the search for robust policies for full employment and to reduce social inequalities was abandoned. Perhaps if the planners had responded to the emerging problems somewhat earlier, the authorities would never have had the excuse to downgrade the exercise, though one suspects that the administrative and political elements were sufficiently deep-rooted to have made the decline inevitable in Pompidou's and Giscard's France.

What does all this tell us about the new government's prospects on the planning front? The lack of even elementary attention to economic rationality and co-ordination in the 1970s was largely due to administrative rivalry and inertia which a wholly new administration of any sort may be able to sweep clean. The new regime has an ideological commitment to planning, and the presence of a former planner, Jacques Delors, at the Finance Ministry gives some hope for revival, though the creation of a Planning Ministry may yet cause new debilitating rivalries. The Socialists would be making a major contribution in simply implementing what was previously promised, but the new government wants to go further with planning than the stated aims of the past regime. The notion of 'planning agreements' signed between state agencies and outside bodies with the planners as co-ordinators is potentially fruitful, though there are dangers from excessive pre-commitment. However, to carry out large-scale nationalization, the possible introduction of some form of workers' control, the restoration of full employment while maintaining financial stability, and massive decentralization of the state within the framework of a national plan would be an ambitious task under even the most favourable economic circumstances. It will be especially fraught with difficulties in the economic climate of the 1980s.

Bibliography

Items have been divided between official and non-official sources for convenience but the division is very arbitrary because in France many academic researchers are in state employment and the official publisher, Documentation Française, publishes a large amount of commercial or academic material. It should be noted that the journal *Economie et Statistique* is actually published by INSEE; inclusion of articles from it under Non-Official Sources is simply because the material it contains is of a research nature and the authors are often the same as those who publish in other journals. In general, however, works by individually named authors published by official bodies (including the OECD) have been included under Official Sources.

Non-Official Sources

Abramowitz, M. (ed.) (1959), *The Allocation of Economic Resources* (Stanford, Calif.: Stanford University Press).

Akerlof, G. (1979), 'The Case Against Conservative Macro-Economics', *Economica*, vol. 46, pp. 219–37.

Albin, P. (1971), 'Uncertainty, Information Exchange and the Theory of Indicative Planning', *Economic Journal*, vol. 81, pp. 61–90.

Allen, R. C. (1979), 'Collective Invention', mimeo., University of British Columbia, Canada.

Andréani, E. (1978), 'Planification Sociale et Indicateurs Sociaux; les Leçons de l'Expérience Française', in C. Sautter and M. Baba (eds), *La Planification en France et au Japan*, Collections de l'INSEE, series C, No. 61, Paris.

Arrow, K. J. (1953), 'Le Rôle des Valeurs Boursières pour la Répartition Meilleure des Risques', CNRS, Paris.

Arrow, K. J. (1970), *Essays in the Theory of Risk-bearing* (Amsterdam: North-Holland).

Atreize (pseudonym) (1971) (1976, 2nd edn), *La Planification Française en Pratique* (Paris: Editions Ouvrières).

Attali, J. (1978), 'Towards Socialist Planning', in S. Holland (ed.), *Beyond Capitalist Planning* (Oxford: Blackwell).

Bank for International Settlements, *Annual Reports*.

Barrère, A. (1969), 'Internal Consistency in the Public Economy', in J. Margolis and H. Guitton (eds), *Public Economics* (London: Macmillan).

Barro, R. J. (1979), 'Second Thoughts on Keynesian Economics', *American Economic Review*, vol. 69, Papers and Proceedings, pp. 54–9.

Bauchet, P. (1969), 'The Coherence of Public Enterprises: Planning vs. Market Forces', in J. Margolis and H. Guitton (eds), *Public Economics* (London: Macmillan).

Baum, W. (1958), *The French Economy and the State* (Princeton, N. J.: Princeton University Press).

Beckerman, W. (ed.) (1965), *The British Economy in 1975* (Cambridge, England: Cambridge University Press).

Beckerman, W. (ed.) (1972), *The Labour Government's Economic Record* (London: Duckworth).

Bell, D.S. (ed.) (1980), *Labour into the Eighties* (London: Croom-Helm).

Bell, D. S. and Criddle, B. (1982), *The French Socialist Party* (Oxford: Oxford University Press) (forthcoming).

Bernard, A. (1978), 'Le Taux d'Actualisation et la Crise d'Energie', in C. Sautter and M. Baba (eds), *La Planification en France et au Japan*, Collections de l'INSEE, Series C, No. 61, Paris.

Berry, H. (1981), 'An Analysis of the Conflict between Sectoral and Regional Policies with Special Reference to the Steel Industry in GB and France', MA dissertation, University of Sussex, Brighton.

Blackaby, F. (ed.) (1978), *British Economic Policy 1960–74* (Cambridge, England: Cambridge University Press).

Bonin, J. (1976), 'On the Design of Managerial Incentive Schemes in a Decentralised Environment', *American Economic Review*, vol. 66, pp. 682–7.

Bonnaud, J. J. (1970), 'Les Instruments d'Exécution du Plan Utilisés par l'Etat à l'Égard des Entreprises', *Revue Economique*, vol. 21, pp. 554–96.

Bonnaud, J. J. (1976), 'Planning and Industry in France', in J. Hayward and M. Watson (eds), *Planning Politics and Public Policy* (Cambridge, England: Cambridge University Press).

Bornstein, M. (ed.) (1974, 3rd edn) (1979, 4th edn), *Comparative Economic Systems* (Homewood, Ill.: Irwin).

Bornstein, M. (ed.) (1975), *Economic Planning East and West* (Cambridge, Mass.: Ballinger).

Bowles, R. A. and Whynes, D. K. (1979), *Macro-Economic Planning* (London: George Allen & Unwin).

Breton, A. and Scott, A. (1978), *The Economic Constitution of Federal States* (Toronto: University of Toronto Press).

Brunhes, B. (1980), 'Planification Sociale et Modèles Econometrieques', *Revue Economique*, vol. 31, pp. 881–93.

Buchanan, J. and Flowers, M. (1979), *The Public Finances* (Homewood, Ill.: Irwin).

Buiter, W. (1980), 'The Macro-Economics of Dr. Pangloss', *Economic Journal*, vol. 90, pp. 34–50.

Buiter, W. (1981), 'The Superiority of Contingent over Fixed Rules in Models with Rational Expectations', *Economic Journal*, vol. 91, pp. 647–70.

Canadian Business, May 1980.

Carassus, J. (1978), 'The Budget and the Plan in France', in J. Hayward and O. Narkiewicz (eds), *Planning in Europe* (London: Croom-Helm).

Carré, J. J., Dubois, P. and Malinvaud, E. (1972), *La Croissance Française* (Paris: Seuil), translated as Carré *et al.* (1975), *French Economic Growth* (Oxford: Oxford University Press).

Cave, M. E. (1981), 'Macro-Economic Projections and the French Plan', mimeo., Brunel University, London.

Cave, M. E. and Hare, P. G. (1981), *Alternative Approaches to Economic Planning* (London: Macmillan).

Cerny, P. and Schain, M. (1980), *French Politics and Public Policy* (London: Methuen).

Charpin, J. *et al.* (1979), 'Une Projection de l'Économie Français à l'Horizon de 1983', *Economie et Statistique*, no. 115, pp. 3–21.

Charpin, J. M., Vallet, D. and Vignon, J. (1979), *Pour Mieux Comprendre DMS* (Paris: CGP/INSEE).

Chow, G. C. (1976), 'Control Methods for Macro-Economic Policy Analysis', *American Economic Review*, vol. 66, Papers and Proceedings, pp. 340–5.

Cipolla, C. (ed.), *Economic History of Europe*, Vol. 5 (London: Fontana).

CLARE Group (1981), 'Macro-Economic Policy in the UK: Is there an Alternative?', *Midland Bank Review*, Autumn/Winter, 1981.

Coase, R. A. (1960), 'The Problem of Social Cost', *Journal of Law and Economics*, vol. 3, pp. 1–44.

Cohen, S. S. (1969) (1977a, 2nd edn), *Modern Capitalist Planning, The French Model* (Berkeley, Calif.: University of California Press).

Collins, C. and Turner, R. K. (1977), *Economics of Planning* (London: Macmillan).

Confédération Française Démocratique du Travail (1977), 'Planification et Nationalisation', mimeo., Paris.

Courbis, R. (1972), 'The FIFI Model Used in the Preparation of the French Plan', *Economics of Planning*, vol. 12, pp. 37–78.

Courbis, R. (1973), 'La Théorie des Economies Concurrencées Fondement du Modèle FIFI', *Revue Economique*, vol. 24, pp. 905–22.

Courbis, R. (1975), *Competitivité et Croissance en Economie Concurrencées* (Paris: Dunod).

Courbis, R. (1977), 'Un Processus Collectif de Choix: l'Exemple de la Planification Française', *Revue d'Economie Politique*, vol. 87, pp. 389–414.

Courbis, R. (1978), 'La Planification Régionale en France et l'Elaboration d'un Modèle Intégré Régional-National', in C. Sautter and M. Baba (eds), *La Planification en France et au Japan*, Collections de l'INSEE, series C, No. 61, Paris.

Courbis, R. *et al.* (1981), 'L'Economie Française en 1981–2', *Le Monde*, June 30, 1981.

Dasgupta, P. and Heal, G. M. (1979), *Economic Theory and Exhaustible Resources* (Cambridge, England: Cambridge University Press).

Debreu, G. (1959), *The Theory of Value* (New York: Wiley).

Deleau, M., Guesnerie, R. and Malgrange, P. (1972a), 'Planification Incertitude et Politique Economique: l'Opération Optimix', Parts 1 and 2, *Revue Economique*, vol. 24, pp. 801–36 and 1072–103.

Deleau, M., Guesnerie, R., and Malgrange, P. (1972b), 'Planning, Uncertainty and Economic Policy; The Optimix Study', *Economics of Planning*, vol. 12, pp. 79–115.

Deleau, M. and Malgrange, P. (1977), 'Recent Trends in French

Planning', in M. Intrilligator (ed.), *Frontiers of Quantitative Economics*, Vol. III B (Amsterdam: North-Holland).

Delors, J. (1971), *Les Indicateurs Sociaux* (Paris: SEDEIS).

Delors, J. (1978), 'The Decline of French Planning', in S. Holland (ed.), *Beyond Capitalist Planning* (Oxford: Blackwell).

Drèze, J. (1964), 'Some Post-War Contributions of French Economists to Economic Theory and Public Policy', *American Economic Review*, vol. 54, *Suppl.*, pp. 1–64.

Dubois, P. (1978), 'La Planification Industrielle en France', in C. Sautter and M. Baba (eds), *La Planification en France et au Japan*, Collections de l'INSEE, Series C, No. 61, Paris.

Dupuit, J. (1844), 'Public Works and the Consumer', in D. Munby (ed.) *Transport* (London: Penguin, 1978).

Ensemble (1965), *Le Contre-Plan* (Paris: Seuil).

Estrin, S. (1982), *Self-Management: Economic Theory and Yugoslav Practice* (Cambridge, England: Cambridge University Press) (forthcoming).

Estrin, S. and Holmes, P. M. (1980), 'The Performance of French Planning 1952–1978', *Economics of Planning*, vol. 16, pp. 1–20.

Estrin, S. and Holmes, P. M. (1982), 'The Models Used in French Planning', mimeo.

Federal Reserve Bank of St. Louis, *International Economic Conditions, Annual Data 1961–1981*.

Flouzat, D. (1975), *Analyse Economique et Comptabilité Nationale* (Paris: Masson).

Fuchs, G. (1977), 'Autogestion, Plan et Marché', *Cahiers Français*, no. 181, pp. 13–15.

Galbraith, J. K. (1967), *The New Industrial State* (Boston: Houghton Mifflin).

Gauron, A. and Maurice, J. (1980), 'Des Politiques Economiques pour le VIIIe Plan', *Revue Economique*, vol. 31, pp. 894–929.

Giscard d'Estaing, V. (1977), *Towards a New Democracy* (London: Collins).

Gordon, R. J. (1978), 'What can Stabilisation Policy Achieve?', *American Economic Review*, vol. 68, Papers and Proceedings, pp. 335–41.

Gorge, J. P. and Tande, A. (1974), 'La Concentration des Entreprises', *Economie et Statistique*, no. 58, pp. 45–61.

Granick, D. (1962), *The European Executive* (Garden City, New York: Doubleday).

Gravier, J. (1947), *Paris et le Désert Français* (Paris: Flammarion).

Green, D. (1978), 'The Seventh Plan – the Demise of French Planning?', *Western European Politics*, vol. 1, pp. 60–76.

Green, D. (1980), 'The Budget and the Plan', in P. Cerny and M. Schain (eds), *French Politics and Public Policy* (London: Methuen).

Green, D. (1981), 'French Policies to Promote Industrial Adjustment', Department of Industry, mimeo.

Green, D. and Cerny, P. (1980), 'Economic Policy and the Governing Coalition', in P. Cerny and M. Schain (eds), *French Politics and Public Policy* (London: Methuen).

Greffe, X. (1975), *La Politique Sociale* (Paris: Presses Universitaires de France).

Grémion, P. and Worms, J. P. (1976), 'The French Regional Planning Experience', in J. Hayward and M. Watson (eds), *Planning Politics and Public Policy* (Cambridge: Cambridge University Press).

Grossman, S. J. and Stiglitz, J. E. (1976), 'Information and Competitive Price Systems', *American Economic Review*, vol. 66, Papers and Proceedings, pp. 246–53.

Grossman, S. J. and Stiglitz, J. E. (1980), 'The Impossibility of Informationally Perfect Markets', *American Economic Review*, vol. 70, pp. 393–408.

Groupe d'Analyse Macro-économique Appliqué (1981) or GAMA (1981), 'Premières Estimations sur les Nouvelles Perspectives de l'Economie Française en 1981–2', Note no. 348; and 'Scenarios pour l'économie Française en 1981–2', Note no. 351, University of Paris–Nanterre, mimeo.

Groves, T. and Loeb, M. (1975), 'Incentives in Public Inputs', *Journal of Public Economics*, vol. 4, pp. 211–26.

Guardian, October 8, 1981.

Guesnerie, R. and Malgrange, P. (1972), 'La Formalisation des Objectifs à Moyen Terme. Application au VIème Plan', *Revue Economieque*, vol. 23, pp. 442–92.

Hafer, R. W. and Resler, D. H. (1980), 'The Rationality of Survey Based Inflation Forecasts', *FRB St. Louis Monthly Review*, vol. 62, No. 9, pp. 3–11.

Hackett, J. and Hackett, A-M. (1963), *Economic Planning in France* (London: George Allen & Unwin).

Hahn, F. (1963), 'On the Disequilibrium Behaviour of a Multisectoral Growth Model', *Economic Journal*, vol. 73, pp. 442–57.

Hahn, F. (1966), 'Equilibrium Dynamics with Heterogeneous Capital Goods', *Quarterly Journal of Economics*, vol. 80, pp. 633–46.

Hahn, F. (1980), 'Monetarism and Economic Theory', *Economica*, vol. 47, pp. 1–17.

Hahn, F. and Matthews, R. C. O. (1964), 'The Theory of Economic Growth', *Economic Journal*, vol. 74, pp. 779–902.

Hall, P. (1980), *Great Planning Disasters* (London: Penguin).

Harrod, R. F. (1939), 'An Essay in Dynamic Theory', *Economic Journal*, vol. 49, pp. 14–33.

Harrod, R. F. (1973), *Economic Dynamics* (London: Macmillan).

Hart, O. D. (1975), 'On the Optimality of Equilibrium When the Market Structure is Incomplete', *Journal of Economic Theory*, vol. 11, pp. 418–43.

Hayward, J. (1973), *The One and Indivisible French Republic* (London: Methuen).

Hayward, J. and Watson, M. (eds) (1976), *Planning Politics and Public Policy* (Cambridge: Cambridge University Press).

Hayward, J. and Narkiewicz, O. (eds) (1978), *Planning in Europe* (London: Croom Helm).

Heal, G. M. (1973), *The Theory of Economic Planning* (Amsterdam: North-Holland).

Helliwell, J. (1965), 'Taxation and Investment: Capital Expenditure Decisions in Large Corporations', *Study No. 3 for Royal Commission on Taxation*, Ottawa, Canada.

Helliwell, J. (1968), *Public Policies and Private Investment* (London: Oxford University Press).

Henderson, J. M. and Quandt, R. E. (1958), *Micro-Economic Theory* (New York: McGraw-Hill).

Herzog, P. (1971), *Politique Economique et Planification en Régime Capitaliste* (Paris: Editions Sociales).

Hirschman, A. (1958), *Strategy of Economic Development* (New Haven, Conn.: Yale University Press).

Hirshleifer, J. and Riley, J. G. (1979), 'The Analytics of Uncertainty and Information', *Journal of Economic Literature*, vol. 17, pp. 1375–421.

Hodge, M. and Wallace, W. (eds) (1981), *Economic Divergence in the European Community* (London: George Allen & Unwin).

Holland, S. (1975), *The Socialist Challenge* (London: Quartet).

Holland, S. (ed.) (1978), *Beyond Capitalist Planning* (Oxford: Blackwell).

Holmes, P. M. (1978), *Industrial Pricing Behaviour and Devaluation* (London: Macmillan).

Holmes, P. M. (1980), 'Growth and Unemployment', in D. S. Bell (ed.), *Labour into the Eighties* (London: Croom-Helm).

Holmes, P. M. and Estrin, S. (1976), 'French Planning Today', University of Sussex Discussion Paper No. 76/14, Brighton.

Houthakker, H. (1959), 'The Scope and Limits of Futures Trading', in M. Abramowitz (ed.), *The Allocation of Economic Resources* (Stanford, Calif.: Stanford University Press).

Hudson Institute Europe (1973), *L'Envol de la France* (New York: Hudson Institute).

Jenny, F. and Weber, A. P. (1974), 'L'Évolution de la Concentration Industrielle en France 1961–69', *Economie et Statistique*, no. 60, pp. 45–53.

Jenny, F. and Weber, A. P. (1975), 'Concentration Économique et Fonctionnement des Marchés, *Economie et Statistique*, no. 65, pp. 17–29.

Jobert, B. (1978), 'Aspects of Social Planning in France', in J. Hayward and O. Narkiewicz (eds), *Planning in Europe* (London: Croom-Helm).

Johansen, L. (1978), *Lectures on Macro-Economic Planning*, vol. 2, (Amsterdam: North-Holland).

Jones, D. T. (1981), 'The Role of Industrial Policy', in M. Hodge and W. Wallace (eds), *Economic Divergence in the European Community* (London: George Allen & Unwin).

Jones, H. G. (1975), *An Introduction to Modern Theories of Economic Growth* (London: Nelson).

Joxe, P. (1981), 'The Prime Role of the Plan', interview in *Nouvel Economiste*, June 15, 1981.

Keynes, J. M. (1931), *Essays in Persuasion* (London: Macmillan).

Keynes, J. M. (1936), *General Theory of Employment Interest and Money* (London: Macmillan).

Kindleberger, C. P. (1967), 'French Planning', in M. F. Millikan (ed.),

National Economic Planning, National Bureau of Economic Research (New York: Columbia University Press).

King, M. A. (1977), *Public Policy and the Corporation* (New York: Chapman and Hall).

King, M. A. and Matthews, R. C. O. (1977), 'The British Economy: Problems and Policies in the late 1970s,' *Midland Bank Review*, February.

Kirzner, I. (1979), *Perception Opportunity and Profit* (Chicago, Ill.: University of Chicago Press).

Kuisel, R. F. (1981), *Capitalism and the State in Modern France* (Cambridge: Cambridge University Press).

Laidler, D. (1981), 'Monetarism', *Economic Journal*, vol. 91, pp. 1–28.

Le Pors, A. and Prunet, J. (1975), 'Les "Transferts" entre l'Etat et l'Industrie', *Economie et Statistique*, no. 66, pp. 23–9.

Leruez, J. (1978), 'Macro-Economic Planning in Mixed Economies', in J. Hayward and O. Narkiewicz (eds), *Planning in Europe* (London: Croom-Helm).

Liggins, D. (1975), *National Economic Planning in France* (Farnborough, England: Saxon House).

Lindblom, C. (1959), 'The Science of Muddling Through', *Public Administration Review*, vol. 19, pp. 79–88.

Lindblom, C. (1975), 'The Sociology of Planning', in M. Bornstein (ed.), *Economic Planning East and West* (Cambridge, Mass.: Ballinger).

Lindblom, C. (1977), *Politics and Markets* (New York: Basic Books).

Lindblom, C. and Hirschman, A. (1962), 'Economic Development, R. and D, and Policy-Making, some Convergent Views', *Behavioral Science*, vol. 7, pp. 211–22.

Lipsey, R. G. (1970), 'The Relationship between Unemployment and the Rate of Change of Money Wages in the UK', *Economica*, vol. 27, pp. 1–31.

Lund, P. J., Martin, W. E. and Bennett, A. G. G. (1980), 'Price Expectations and Their Role in Investment Intentions', *Journal of Industrial Economics*, vol. 28, pp. 225–40.

Lutz, V. (1969), *Central Planning for the Market Economy* (London: Longman).

Maarek, G. (1980), 'Modèles Macro-économiques et Programmation Linéaire', *Revue Economique*, vol. 31, pp. 982–98.

McArthur, J. B. and Scott, B. R. (1969), *Industrial Planning in France* (Cambridge, Mass.: Harvard University Press).

MacLennan, M. (1963), 'French Planning: Some Lessons for Britain', *Planning*, PEP, vol. 29, no. 475.

Maddison, A. (1976), 'Economic Policy and Performance', in C. Cipolla (ed.), *Economic History of Europe*, vol. 5 (London: Fontana).

Malézieux, J. (1980), 'Crise et Restructuration de la Sidérurgie Française', *Espace Géographique*, vol. 9, pp. 183–97.

Malinvaud, E. (1977), *The Theory of Unemployment Reconsidered* (Oxford: Blackwell).

Malinvaud, E. (1980), *Profitability and Unemployment* (Cambridge: Cambridge University Press).

Margolis, J. and Guitton, H. (eds) (1969), *Public Economics* (London: Macmillan).

Mariano, A. P. (1973), *La Metamorphose de l'Economie Française 1963–73* (Paris: Arthaud).

Massé, P. (1959), *Le Choix des Investissements* (Paris: Dunod).

Massé, P. (1962), 'French Methods of Planning', *Journal of Industrial Economics*, vol. XI, No. 1, 1962, pp. 1–17.

Massé, P. (1965), 'French Planning and Economic Theory', *Econometrica*, vol. 33, pp. 265–76.

Massé, P. *et al.* (1976), *Politique Industrielle et Stratégie d'Entreprise* (Paris: Masson).

Matthews, R. C. O. (1968), 'Why have we had Full Employment since the War?', *Economic Journal*, vol. 78, pp. 555–69.

Meade, J. E. (1936), *Economic Policy and Analysis* (London: Oxford University Press).

Meade, J. E. (1970), *The Theory of Indicative Planning* (Manchester: Manchester University Press).

Meade, J. E. (1971), *The Controlled Economy* (London: George Allen & Unwin).

Meeks, G. (1977), *Disappointing Marriages* (Cambridge: Cambridge University Press).

Mériaux, B. (1975), 'L'Emploi dans les Travaux Préparatoires à l'Orientation Préliminaire due VIIème Plan', *Economie et Statistique*, no. 69, pp. 45–51.

Mignot, G. and Voisset, M. (1977), 'L'Exécution d'un Plan', *Cahiers Français*, no. 181, pp. 36–43.

Miller, J. B. (1979), 'Meade on Indicative Planning', *Journal of Comparative Economics*, vol. 3, pp. 27–40.

Miller, J. B. (1980), 'A Method for Determining the Appropriateness of National Planning in a Market Economy', *Quarterly Journal of Economics*, vol. 95, pp. 261–76.

Millikan, M. F. (ed.) (1967), *National Economic Planning*, National Bureau of Economic Research (New York: Columbia University Press).

Mishan, E. J. (1971), 'The Evaluation of Life and Limb', *Journal of Political Economy*, vol. 79, pp. 687–705.

Molitor, B. (1980), 'Politique Industrielle et Planification en France', *Revue Economique*, vol. 31, no. 5, September 1980, pp. 837–52.

Le Monde, June 14, 1980, July 17, 1980, July 10, 1981, June 30, 1981, June 26, 1981, September 23, 1980, September 9, 1981, July 8, 1981, September 15, 1981, September 17, 1981, October 22 and 25, 1981.

Nizard, L. (1976), 'Planning as the Regulatory Reproduction of the Status Quo', in J. Hayward and M. Watson (eds), *Planning Politics and Public Policy* (Cambridge: Cambridge University Press).

Nizard, L. (1979), 'Les Rapports des Pouvoirs Entre l'INSEE, la D.P., et la CGP', *Revue Française d'Administration Publique*, no. 10, pp. 125–40.

Nouvel Observateur (1977), Special Issue on the Socialist Party's Industrial Policy, April.

Opie, R. (1972), 'Economic Planning and Growth', in W. Beckerman (ed.), *The Labour Government's Economic Record* (London: Duckworth).

Pagé, J. P. (ed.) (1975), *Profil Economique de la France* (Paris: Documentation Française).

Pascallon, P. (1974), *La Planification de l'Economie Française* (Paris: Masson).

Pavitt, K. (1981), Review of P. Papon, *Le Pouvoir et la Science en France*, in *Minerva*, vol. 19.

Phelps, E. S. (ed.) (1971), *The Micro-Economic Foundations of Employment and Inflation Theory* (London: Macmillan).

Posner, M. V. (ed.) (1978), *Demand Management* (London: Heineman).

Postan, M. (1977), *Economic History of Europe 1945–64* (London: Methuen).

Prate, A. (1978), *Les Batailles Economiques du Général de Gaulle* (Paris: Plon).

Radner, R. (1968), 'Competitive Equilibrium under Uncertainty', *Econometrica*, vol. 36, pp. 31–58.

Radner, R. (1975), 'Economic Planning under Uncertainty', in M. Bornstein (ed.), *Economic Planning East and West* (Cambridge, Mass.: Ballinger).

Rendeiro, J. (1980), 'The French Machine-Tool Industry', University of Sussex, SERC, 1979, mimeo., Brighton.

Richardson, G. B. (1971), 'Planning vs. Competition', *Soviet Studies*, vol. 22, pp. 433–47.

Rossignol, P. (1975), 'La Nouvelle Donnée Économique Mondiale et le Modèle FIFI', *Economie et Statistique*, no. 64, pp. 5–19.

Rothschild, M. (1973), 'Models of Markets with Imperfect Information', *Journal of Political Economy*, vol. 81, pp. 1283–308.

Roux-Vaillard, P. (1976), 'Les Projections à Moyen Terme et l'Incertitude Economique', *Economie et Statistique*, no. 84, pp. 9–17.

St. Geours, J. (1969), *La Politique Economique des Principaux Pays de l'Occident* (Paris: Sirey).

Samuelson, P. A. (1957), 'Intertemporal Equilibrium: Prologue to a Theory of Speculation', *Weltwirtschaftliches Archiv*, vol. 79, pp. 181–219.

Samuelson, P. A. (1976), *Economics* (10th edn) (New York: McGraw-Hill).

Sautter, C. (1975), 'L'Efficacité et la Rentabilité de l'Économie Française 1954–74', *Economie et Statistique*, no. 68, pp. 5–23.

Sautter, C. and Baba, M. (eds) (1978), *La Planification en France et au Japan*, Collections de l'INSEE, series C, No. 61, Paris.

Schollhamer, H. (1969), 'National Economic Planning and Business Decision-Making, the French Experience', *California Management Review*, reprinted in M. Bornstein (ed.), *Comparative Economic Systems* (Homewood, Ill.: Irwin).

Seibel, C. (1975), 'Planning in France', in M. Bornstein (ed.), *Economic Planning East and West* (Cambridge, Mass.: Ballinger).

Self, P. (1975), *Econocrats and the Policy Process, the Philosophy of Cost-Benefit Analysis* (London: Macmillan).

Sen, A. K. (ed.) (1970), *Growth Economics* (London: Penguin).

Sheahan, J. (1963), *Promotion and Control of Industry in Post-War France* (Cambridge, Mass.: Harvard University Press).

Shell, K. and Stiglitz, J. E. (1967), 'The Allocation of Investment in a Dynamic Economy', *Quarterly Journal of Economics*, vol. 81, pp. 592–609.

Shonfield, A. (1965), *Modern Capitalism* (London: Oxford University Press).

Simon, H. A. (1957), *Models of Man* (New York: Wiley).

Simon, H. A. (1978), 'On How to Decide What to Do', *Bell Journal of Economics*, vol. 9, pp. 494–507.

Smyth, D. J. and Briscoe, G. (1969), 'Investment Plans and Realisations in UK Manufacturing', *Economica*, vol. 36, pp. 277–94.

Stevens, A. (1980), 'The Higher Civil Service and Economic Policy Making', in P. Cerny and M. Schain (eds), *French Politics and Public Policy* (London: Methuen).

Stoffaës, C. (1978), *La Grande Menace Industrielle* (Paris: Calmann Levy).

Stoléru, L. (1969), *L'Impératif Industriel* (Paris: Seuil).

Tideman, T. N. and Tullock, G. (1976), 'A New and Superior Process for Making Social Choices', *Journal of Political Economy*, vol. 84, pp. 1145–59.

Tinbergen, J. (1964), *Central Planning* (Amsterdam: North-Holland).

Ullmo, Y. (1978), 'Les Méthodes de la Planification Économique en France', in C. Sautter and M. Baba (eds), *La Planification en France et au Japan*, Collections de l'INSEE, series C, No. 61, Paris.

Vasconcellos, A. and Kiker, B. (1969), 'An Evaluation of French National Planning 1949–64', *Journal of Common Market Studies*, vol. 8, pp. 216–35.

Vessillier, E. (1977), *L'Economie Publique* (Paris: Masson).

Wasserman, M. and Wiles, P. J. (1969), review of V. Lutz, *Central Planning for the Market Economy*, *Economica*, vol. 36, pp. 444–9.

Weitzman, M. (1976), 'The New Soviet Incentive Model', *Bell Journal of Economics*, vol. 7, pp. 251–7.

Wickham, S. (1963), 'French Planning; Retrospect and Prospect', *Review of Economics and Statistics*, vol. 45, pp. 335–47.

Wilson, R. (1975), 'Informational Economies of Scale', *Bell Journal of Economics*, vol. 6, pp. 184–95.

Winter, S. G. (1964), 'Economic "Natural Selection" and the Theory of the Firm', *Yale Economic Essays*, vol. 4, pp. 225–72.

Wright, J. P. (1980), *On a Clear Day You Can See General Motors* (Caroline House: Aurora, Ill.).

Zysman, J. (1975), 'Between the Market and the State: Dilemmas for the French Electronics Industry', *Research Policy*, vol. 3, pp. 312–37.

Zysman, J. (1977), *Political Strategies for Industrial Order* (Berkeley, Calif.: University of California Press).

Official Sources

French

In many cases the distinction between a published document and one that has been merely circulated in the CGP is not easy to establish. Titles followed by 'DF' have been issued by the official publisher Documentation Française. In other cases documents were made available to us directly, in nearly all cases by the CGP or INSEE.

Planning Documents Pre-1970
CGP, Ist, IInd, IIIrd, IVth, Vth and VIth Plans. DF.
CGP (1949), *Rapport sur les Actions Sectorielles en France Metro-politaine.*
CGP (1968), *Rapport sur les Problèmes Posés par l'Adaptation du Ve Plan.* DF.

Texts Associated with the VIIth Plan
INSEE (1975), 'Deux Projections pour 1980', mimeo.
CGP (1975a), *Rapport de la Commission: Croissance, Emploi, Financement.* DF.
CGP (1975b), *Rapport de la Commission: Relations Economiques et Financières avec l'Extérieur.* DF.
CGP (1975c), *Rapport: Consultation des Régions.* DF.
CGP (1975d), *Rapport de la Commission Inégalités Sociales.* DF.
CGP (1975e), *Rapport sur l'Orientation Préliminaire du VIIème Plan.*DF.
CGP (1975f), *Rapport de la Commission Aménagement du Territoire.* DF.
CGP (1976a), *Rapport de la Commission Développement.* DF.
CGP (1976b), *Rapport de la Commission Aménagement du Territoire.* DF.
CGP (1976c), *Rapport de la Commission Recherche.* DF.
CGP (1976d), *Rapport de la Commission Industrie.* DF.
CGP (1976e), *Rapport du Comité: Emploi et Travail.* DF.
CGP (1976f), *Rapport du Comité: Revenus et Transferts.* DF.
CGP (1976g), *Rapport du GSAP Sidérurgie.* DF.
CGP (1976h), *VIIth Plan: Dossier Quantitatif.* DF.
    (1976), *VIIe Plan de Développement Economique et Social.* DF.
CGP (1976i), *Les Indicateurs Economiques et Sociaux.* DF.
CGP (1977), 'Enseignements Tirés des deux Premières Années d'Execution du VIIème Plan', mimeo.
Barre government (1978), *Rapport sur l'Adaptation du VIIème Plan.* DF.

Texts Associated with the VIIIth Plan
CGP (1979a), Commission de Développement: *Rapport: Phase des Options,* mimeo.
Barre government (1979), *Rapport sur les Options Principales du VIIIème Plan.* DF.
INSEE (1979), 'Un Jeu de Projection de référence à l'horizon de 1983', mimeo.
CGP, 'Présentation et commentaire des projections économiques effectués par l'INSEE, mimeo.

CGP (1979b), 'Dossier sur l'Emploi', mimeo.

CGP (1980a), *Rapport du Comité Economie Internationale et Echanges Extérieurs*. DF.

CGP (1980b), *Rapport de la Commission Emploi et Relations de Travail*. DF.

VIIIe Plan de Développement Economique et Social. DF.

Miscellaneous Texts Associated with the Planning Process

CGP (undated), Résumés of Ist to VIIth Plans, mimeo.

CGP (1973), *Calcul Economique et Planification*. DF.

CGP (1979c), *Perspectives Energétiques Françaises*. DF.

CGP (1979d), Un outil pour la planification d'entreprise: 'Les PGD: Liste des Indicateurs', mimeo.

INSEE, *Tendances de la Conjoncture*.

Albert, M. and de Marcillac, M. (1978), 'Le VIIème Plan: un Nouveau Tournant de la Planification Française', in C. Sautter and M. Baba (eds), *La Planification en France et au Japon*, Collections de l'INSEE, series C, No. 61, Paris.

Barre, R. (1979), Speech to Economic and Social Council on occasion of Debate on Options Report for VIIIth Plan; text supplied by CGP.

Berthelot, Y. and Tardy, S. (1978), *Le Défi Economique du Tiers Monde*, CGP/DF.

Bertin, P. (1975), *L'Industrie Française face aux Multinationales*, CGP/DF.

Bravo, J. (1976). 'Les Administrations dans la Preparation et l'Execution du Plan en Matière de Finances Publiques', mimeo., CGP; also in *Cahiers Français*, no. 182 (1977).

Cavallier, C. (1977), 'La Planification Régionale et Locale', *Cahiers Français*; no. 182.

Charpin, J. *et al.* (1979), *Pour Mieux Comprendre DMS*, CGP/INSEE/DF.

Courcier, M. and Malsot, J. (eds) (1978), *La Spécialisation Internationale des Industries à l'Horizon de 1985*, CGP/DF (a study commissioned by the CGP jointly from CEPII and BIPE).

Fouquet, D., Charpin, J. M., Guillaume, H., Muet, P. A. and Vallet, D. (1979), 'DMS: French Medium Term Forecasting Model', mimeo., INSEE, paper presented to the European Meeting of the Econometric Society in Helsinki.

Milleron, J. C., Guesnerie, R. and Crémieux, M. (1979), *Calcul Economique et Décisions Publiques*, CGP/DF.

Mignot, G. and Voisset, M. (1977), 'L'Exécution d'un Plan', *Cahiers Français*, no. 181.

Nora, S. (1967), *Rapport Sur les Entreprises Publiques*, DF.

Olive, G. (1970), 'L'Exécution du Plan et la Confrontation des Prévisions à Court et à Moyen-Terme', Ministry of Finance, mimeo.; paper presented to the World Econometric Society Conference, Cambridge, England, 1970.

Ripert, J. (1976), 'French Planning and the VIIth Plan', paper presented to a conference at the London School of Economics, October 1976.

Roux-Vaillard, P. and Vignon, J. (1976), 'Medium Term Projections and Economic Uncertainty', paper presented to a Conference on Medium Term Assessment, Paris, 1976; CGP mimeo.

SOFRES (1979a), 'L'Image du Plan auprès des Chefs d'Entreprise', mimeo., CGP.

SOFRES (1979b), 'L'Image du Plan: Les Syndicalistes', mimeo., CGP.

Vignon, J. (1979), 'Les PGD, un Pont Entre la Macro-Économie et les Entreprises', CGP, mimeo.

Other Official Publications from French Sources
Assemblée Nationale (1976), *Rapport de la Commission des Finances sur le projet de Loi des Finances pour 1977, Annexe 39.*

Loi des Finances (1974), (1975), (1976), (1978), (1980), *Annexes, Rapport d'Exécution du Plan.*

FDES Annual Report 1977, Appendix to 1978 *Loi des Finances.*

Ministère de l'Industrie (1976), *Rapports des Groupes Sectoriels d'Analyse et de Prévision.*

Cahiers Français (1977), Special Issues on Planning, Nos. 181 & 182. DF.

Official Sources: Non-French
OECD (1974), *The Industrial Policy of France.*

OECD (1977), *Towards Full Employment and Price Stability* ('McCracken Report').

OECD (1978), *The case for Positive Adjustment.*

M. Sawyer (1976), *Income Distribution in OECD Countries*, OECD Occasional Study.

G. E. Llewellyn and L. W. Samuelson (1981), 'Forecasting Experience at the OECD', OECD mimeo.

OECD (1976), *France* (Country Surveys).

OECD, *Main Economic Indicators.*

OECD, *Quarterly National Accounts.*

Report of the Committee on Finance and Industry ('Macmillan Report') (London: HMSO), (1931).

House of Commons (1973), *Report of the Select Committee on Nationalised Industries (1973/4): Capital Investment Procedures.* (London: HMSO).

EEC (1981), *Report of the Study Group on Industrial Policies in the Community: State Intervention and Structural Adjustment.*

S. S. Cohen (1977b), 'Recent Developments in French Planning', Study for the Sub-committee on Economic Stabilisation and growth of the Joint Economic Committee. US Congress.

Index